Integration or Disintegration?

Towards a
Non-racist Society

Integration or Disintegration?

Towards a Non-racist Society

Ray Honeyford

The Claridge Press
London and Lexington

First published 1988

by The Claridge Press
43 Queen's Gardens London W2 3AA
and Box 420 Lexington Georgia 30648

© Ray Honeyford 1988

ISBN 1–870626–80–X (clothbound)
ISBN 1–870626–85–0 (paperback)

Honeyford, Ray
        Integration or Disintegration?
        1. Education   2. Sociology

Typeset by
The Word Shop, Rossendale, Lancs
and printed by
Short Run Press Exeter, Devon

Contents

Personal Declaration ix

Introduction 1

1 The Nature of a Multi-ethnic Society 5

2 What Kind of Multi-ethnic Society? 25

3 Special Needs versus Human Capital 53

4 Multi-ethnic Education 73

5 The Anti-racist Lobby 107

6 The Swann Enterprise: A Critical Commentary 163

7 The Language Issue 211

8 Multi-ethnic Education and the Schools: A Case Study 241

Postscript to Chapter 8 283

Epilogue: Reflections on Britain's Multi-ethnic Society 299

Index 303

To Angela with love

Personal Declaration

Racism is an evil thing, and those who practise it damage not only the victims but themselves. Individuals, groups and regimes that preach the doctrine of racial discrimination cannot be defended. They pollute the moral climate, and create discord and conflict where there should be understanding and harmony. That any person should be judged by the colour of his or her skin is an outrage, and any society that permits this stands condemned by all those with any claim to decent, moral instincts.

At the same time I am convinced that the proper moral indignation caused by racism is being exploited for political purposes by those in our society who preach and practise the theories of 'anti-racism'. By projecting the moral issue as a simple choice between being a racist or anti-racist, the anti-racists not only deliberately oversimplify, they also deny the possibility of a third choice – that of the non-racist. This is the position I occupy. Rightly or wrongly, I believe that this is the position of the great majority of my fellow-countrymen.

It is to illustrate and defend the non-racist position that I have written this book.

Ray Honeyford

Autumn 1987

Introduction

My intention in writing this book was twofold: to clarify my own position and to stimulate public debate about the nature of Britain's multi-ethnic society. The book is not a contribution to 'theory' or an academic treatise, nor does it claim to represent any views but my own. It is very much a personal attempt to come to grips with an issue which is of crucial importance to the character and future of Britain.

The book really began the day I became the headmaster of a multi-ethnic school in Bradford. I had been teaching children from the ethnic minorities for a number of years, and had concluded that the necessity to integrate them into British society as quickly as possible was self-evident. After all, Asian and black children are British citizens. Their parents came to Britain in order to enjoy the benefits arising from being a British citizen and they seek to confer those benefits on their children. Moreover, an increasing number of ethnic-minority children are British born: they are not immigrants and they are emphatically not foreigners. Britain's established immigrant communities – for example, those from central Europe, including the Jews – have always pursued a policy of integration with the indigenous host community, and they have clearly flourished as a result.

I arrived in Bradford assuming that one of the functions of my school would be to enable the pupils to realise that they were fully British and very much part of, and able to contribute to, established British life. This purpose was entirely compatible with the school's respecting the parents' philosophical convictions and religious sensibilities, and it in no way clashed with the desirable probablity that they would maintain a flourishing Asian culture privately and in the wider community. By working together, home and school could

1

help to sustain that bi-cultural identity which the parents' decision to come to Britain had conferred on their children. This recognition of the cultural partnership between home and school was well expressed by one of my Asian fathers: 'You look after my child's English education, Mr Honeyford, and I shall take care of his Asian culture.'

However, I quickly discovered that the local council appeared not to share, let alone endorse, this understanding. The politicians, officials and advisers who comprised the local education authority did not support my view that integration was the underlying objective. They had created the notion of multicultural education, of which 'anti-racism' was a pervasive component (see Chapter 5). These notions appeared to be based on the assumption that, far from integrating the Asian child and perceiving him or her as essentially British, the school was to regard the child as a special case, whose presence must involve the school in radical reform of both curriculum and ethos. This purpose was to be effected by the imposition on the schools of a series of mandatory documents drawn up by officials and advisers, ratified and, to some extent, inspired by local politicians.

These documents did not seem to me to be educationally convincing. They provided no criteria for selection of specific curriculum items and no convincing rationale for the proposed radical shift in the school's established purposes. Moreover, I was very disturbed by the advocacy of 'anti-racist' censorship. This was based on unsupported assumptions about the character of existing teaching materials, implied that teachers were insensitive to their pupils' cultural sensitivities and set a dangerous precedent for the continued challenging of the teacher's academic freedom. Moreover, the concept of a 'multiculture' based not on those natural human processes of integration and enrichment which occur when people from different cultures and traditions live and work together but on the cogitations of bureaucrats, 'experts' and politicians did not seem to me either feasible or sensible. The people responsible did not appear to understand that culture in the deepest sense is a matter for society, not for the state and its agents. I was also worried about the manifestly tendentious view of British history, institutions and traditions that the mandatory documents contained. Perhaps most telling of all, my objection was to the constant suggestion that all white people, and only white people, are 'racist', and could only expiate their guilt by supporting the multicultural/anti-racist bandwaggon. I could not see how the transmission of this manifestly questionable, not to say offensive, allegation to children could possibly augur well for future race relations.

Moreover, the proposed changes had no connection with public opinion. In no way did they reflect the wishes of parents. In 16 years of meeting and talking to black, Asian and majority parents I had never been asked about 'multicultural education' or 'anti-racism'. Ethnic-minority parents have a practical, instrumental view of the function of schools. They expect them to equip their children with the understanding and knowledge necessary to enable them to progress in a meritocratic society which, increasingly, demands high levels of educational achievement. This view is shared by the great majority of British white parents. I am one of those people who believe that development in the education of children should follow what parents say they want. The developments I complained of clearly ignored this principle. They were entirely a function of that political and bureaucratic power structure which effectively controls the state education service.

One of the dangers of imposing a 'multicultural curriculum' on the schools is that one can so easily convince the white, English parents – who comprise just over 95 per cent of the population – that *their* culture is being undermined. This development reduces public confidence, and is scarcely conducive to better race relations. As I write, 26 white parents are refusing to send their children to a multiracial school in Dewsbury, Yorkshire. Their motives are, no doubt, mixed. However, one factor is likely to be the local council's commitment to 'multicultural education' and 'anti-racism', without benefit of public support.

In short, I found myself in conflict with the local authority that employed me. In facing and coming to terms with the crisis in my professional life this caused I came to understand that this was not an exclusively educational issue. Education functions in a distinctive historical, institutional and ideological context. If I were to understand better the education aspect, I had to consider larger issues. For instance, what precisely was 'anti-racism', and what was its structure and ideological nature? What were the antecedents of 'multiculturalism' and what is the purpose? What are the options for a multi-ethnic society such as contemporary Britain? Who are the gurus of 'multiculturalism' and 'anti-racism', and what are their assumptions, methods and purposes? What is the role of the state in race relations? I have given some thought to each of these issues, since they provide the background to the specifically educational questions.

A subsidiary purpose has been to introduce the work of Thomas Sowell to a British readership. Sowell, an American scholar, is an authority on the history and development of multi-ethnic communities. Much of the comparative and historical data I use are taken from this source – particularly Sowell's great work, *The Economics and Politics of Race*.

CHAPTER 1

The Nature of a Multi-ethnic Society

It is not possible to pursue the questions raised in this book without examining certain key issues first. This is necessary both to dispel possible misunderstanding and to provide an appropriate context. There are few issues where clear thinking is more important, and even fewer which are likely to raise temperatures so quickly or which can create misunderstanding, resentment and even conflict.

What is ethnicity?

Defining ethnicity is difficult but necessary. Much of the confusion surrounding the debate about a multi-ethnic society arises from the failure of the protagonists to define their terms. This is an understandable fault; dictionaries often claim that the term 'ethnic' is a synonym for 'race', 'caste', 'nationality' or even 'culture'. To confuse the issue further, there is a contemporary tendency to attach the word to a distinctive group distinguished by a physical characteristic (for example, 'ethnic hairstyle' or 'ethnic vote').

However, there appears to be a useful consensus amongst social scientists: 'ethnic' should be used only when we refer to a group sharing a common culture and defined largely by descent. This is a much broader definition then the term 'race' could encompass. 'Race' refers more specifically to common descent and perhaps physical similarity. 'Ethnic' partakes, as it were, of elements of both race and culture. A West Indian, for instance, is likely to be of the negro race, but references to his ethnicity would have to include such notions as language, religion, social customs, cultural artefacts and characteristic ways of doing things.

To simplify, a multi-ethnic society is one in which different ethnic

5

groups live together. On this basis, Britain is now clearly a multi-ethnic nation. It has an ethnic majority which comprises about 96 per cent of the population and an ethnic minority of about 3 million, or about 4 per cent. (There is no agreement about precise figures.) Within the immigrants, two broad groups can be discerned: Asians (from the Indian subcontinent) and Caribbeans. We need to be careful, though, to distinguish Asian, in this sense, from Chinese and Vietnamese, both of which form ethnic groups in Britain, and both, of course, in a more general sense are Asian. We need also to be aware that race as indicated by physical characteristics is not always a good indicator of ethnicity: Britain now has a significant number of Africans whose culture is very different from that of the West Indies. Indeed, 'West Indian' is a term which is by no means ethnically consistent. The 'Island Question' is of great concern to people from the Caribbean – there are significant cultural variations according to the island of origin. A Jamaican would not thank us for confusing him with someone raised in Trinidad.

Simply naming the major ethnic groups makes clear the diversity of peoples and cultures now in Britain. There are great variations in language, religion, dress and diet as well as differences in concepts of family relationships, child-rearing, the roles of the sexes and political behaviour. If we add to this ethnic variety the fact that Britain has a considerable national diversity (for example, Polish, Ukranian, Hungarian, Greek, Italian and Cypriot, not to mention the historic and very influential Jewish groups) we clearly see a picture of great complexity.

Ethnic Variations

Britain is by no means unique in this. A degree of ethnic complexity is to be found in virtually every part of the world. As Thomas Sowell has pointed out, hybrid populations are the norm. If we think of race, for instance, in purely biological terms then it could apply only to very small groups living in isolated conditions. In Europe, Asia and the Americas we find considerable evidence of inter-racial marriage over the centuries and groups of considerable genetic complexity. In the USA, for instance, it is generally agreed that more than three-quarters of the black population have at least one white ancestor, while millions of whites have at least one black forebear. If we think in broader, ethnic terms, then again the principle of complexity holds good. Smith[1] has identified the following countries as being multi-ethnic to a significant extent: Canada, the USA, Mexico, Brazil, Peru, Trinidad, Bolivia, Romania, Czechoslovakia, the USSR, Cyprus, Israel, Jordan, Syria, Lebanon, Saudi Arabia, Egypt, Turkey, Iran, Pakistan, Afghanistan, India, Burma, Sri Lanka, China, Malaysia, Indonesia, Vietnam, Laos, the Philippines, Australia, New Zealand, Morocco, Algeria, the Sudan, Ethiopia, Kenya, Uganda, Tanzania, Zambia, Zimbabwe, South Africa, Namibia, Angola, the Congo, the Cameroons, Nigeria, Ghana, the Ivory Coast, Sierra Leone and Senegal.

Moreover, various developments appear to be hastening this movement towards multi-ethnicity and the breakdown of more homogeneous populations. Increases in the speed of transport, refugees in large numbers, instant electronic transmission of cultural items across frontiers, the universalising process of advanced capitalist marketing, the end of Empire and the attraction of the former 'mother-country' are all features of contemporary life tending to accelerate the movement towards multi-ethnic populations.

The British Experience

However, it is important not to press this principle too far when considering Britain. There is a pronounced tendency in the literature produced by the British race relations lobby to assert that Britain has always been multi-ethnic, and that the large influxes of Asian and Caribbean in post-war years was part of a continuing historical process. This is a very doubtful proposition. It is truer to say that, until about 1950, Britain was a relatively homogeneous nation in terms of ethnicity. A brief historical excursion should make this clear.

Although many different groups from abroad have settled in Britain over the centuries, major immigration ceased with the Norman Conquest. Moreover, the relationship of the immigrant groups to the existing society, and their motives, were very different from those of Britain's post-war immigrants. Up to and including the Conquest the pattern was clearly defined – conflict followed by conquest. The Celts, Romans, Angles, Saxons, Vikings, Danes and Normans had a single objective – to defeat the indigenous population and establish hegemony over it. Once this process had, in varying degrees, been carried out, a *modus vivendi* (which might be described as despotism gradually giving way to a more settled way of life) was established. Clearly, this phase of immigration into Britain can have no connection with post-war patterns.

More recent history continued the process of settlement from abroad, but numbers were always relatively small. Motives, too, differed from those of Britain's post-war immigrants from Asia and the West Indies. Trade, royal marriages, flight from religious persecution and the effects of revolution and war in the homeland have all been the basic causes in the past. The Jews came to England originally because the Norman kings needed their money and business acumen – and were expelled for four centuries when their usefulness was deemed to have been exhausted. The foreign craftsmen of the Middle Ages, such as the Flemings and the Dutch, came to offer much-needed craft skills. Small groups of foreigners came as a result of the English court's close link with European royal houses and the dynastic marriages by which political ambitions were fulfilled and international quarrels settled. In the Middle Ages, too, foreign merchants from all over Europe came to England, attracted by lucrative markets and royal protection. By the fifteenth century there were small settlements of foreign traders in most large English cities and towns. The Reformation and Counter-Reformation, and the religious ferment and conflict they generated, created demands for sanctuary in England. In the late seventeenth century the Huguenots arrived to escape the persecution of Louis XIV. A significant number of Jews were re-established in the eighteenth century; while the slave trade led to an increase in the small population of black people who had originated as servants to merchants and the aristocracy in the middle of the sixteenth century. The French Revolution produced about 80,000 emigrés; flight from hunger saw the establishment of a sizeable Irish community in the 1800s; and the Jewish community was swelled by the pogroms of Tsarist Russia in the 1880s. In the twentieth century Britain has had the settlements of East Europeans: Polish refugees, Hungarians after the 1956 uprising and Czechs escaping from Russian invaders.

Moreover, previous immigrant groups have had little political power, but the gradual extending of the franchise in the nineteenth century and votes for women in the twentieth means that any ethnic group of significant size can now have unfortunate electoral consequences if it votes in consistent ways. The growing sense of ethnic awareness can be gauged from the fact that, according to the official handbook *Britain 1986*, in Britain there are now some 70 newspapers and magazines produced by ethnic minorities, over 40 of which are printed in Asian languages.[2] Although up-to-date information is hard to come by, there is fairly general agreement that the Labour Party obtains as much as 70 per cent of the ethnic vote, although there is also evidence of an 'ethnic floating vote' in areas of high ethnic concentrations whose direction is associated with the major parties' current policy on immigration and race relations. There is also evidence of a middle-class Asian vote for the Conservative Party. The important point, and one which is unique in British history, is that if the ethnic vote is ever used to reflect specific ethnic concerns, then the political results would be significant. The emergence of a Black Section in the Labour Party suggests that the first signs of this can be seen.

So, although we can say that Britain is no stranger to the process of immigration, we can also note that in terms of numbers and motives there are no historical precedents since 1066 for what we now call Britain's multi-ethnic society. Immigration had been a gradual process of relatively small numbers of people who have been integrated into the general population by a process of natural absorption.

The uniqueness in the history of Britain's present multi-ethnic population can be appreciated by pointing to certain simple facts:

(1) There are an increasing number of inner-city schools in which the ethnic minority consists of white children. There are certain districts in which the majority population is of Asian origin.

(2) There have been, post-war, unprecedented religious developments. Britain now has significant numbers of Hindus, Sikhs and Moslems, and there are more Moslems than there are practising Anglicans, most of them non-European.

(3) About 160 community languages are now spoken in Britain.[3] There are immense cultural distances involved. Attitudes to women, for instance, vary, from the orthodox Moslem family,

which believes in virtual seclusion of females, to the liberated couple with a planned family, where the wife functions as a full-time professional worker.

Any one of these facts would be sufficient to indicate that post-war immigration, and the society it has produced, are fundamentally different from anything that has gone before. Taken together, they present an image of Britain unique in its history.

Ethnicity and Identity

A significant factor in considering any multi-ethnic society is the phenomenon of ethnicity as a rallying cry. Both individual identity and group solidarity are now tending to be expressed in ethnic terms. Nationality, family, class, religion—all powerful emblems of self and group—appear to be losing ground to ethnic images, beliefs and aspirations. We do not know, in any scientific sense, why this is so, but several commentators have produced interesting speculations, notably Nathan Glazer.[4] It may be that both individuals and groups experience many aspects of modern life as de-humanising. Urbanisation, mass education, a popular egalitarian culture which tends to eliminate local features and the mass media, with their deadening and all-pervasive electronic imaging, may all be creating a new sense of personal and social alienation; and this, in turn, produces new ways of seeking and maintaining feelings of personal and collective worth. Revealed religion has lost ground to science and determinism; consumerism is an inadequate vehicle for carrying the burdens of identity and aspirations for power; the family is in decline; the state is suspect, being associated with conflict, war and chauvinism. Perhaps ethnicity provides a satisfying substitute. There is certainly good evidence of ethnic revivals in Africa, the USA and Europe. For instance, certain tribes translated to life in cities and towns in Africa are forming new ethnic groups along tribal lines (for example, the Hausa, Ibo and Yoruba). In the USA, European immigrants—Poles, Italians and Slovaks—have formed influential ethnic identities, and they are now closely followed by Latinos and Japanese. Irish Americans, of course, have always been a distinctive group. The 'Black Power' movement can also be seen in this way. In Europe there are the Basque, Italian,

Scottish and Welsh separatist movements. Sri Lanka is currently enveloped in ethnic conflict over the future of the Tamils. Latterly in Britain there are influential organisations and political aspirations clustered around the term 'Asian' and 'West Indian'. Again, the movement pressing for separate Black Sections in the British Labour Party may well be a manifestation of the growing influence of ethnicity as an organising principle. This may have implications for Britain's sense of national identity, political institutions and social stability.

The International Dimension

When a country becomes significantly multi-ethnic, i.e. when large ethnic minorities come to live and settle within its borders, both government and public need to take account of the fact that decisions affecting minorities have to be justified to a worldwide audience. This is particularly so for a country like Britain, with its legacy of Empire and history of active diplomacy. British membership of the Commonwealth, the UN and the EEC means that it is unable to care about only parochial opinion. Moreover, ethnicity plays a major part in the view of the world projected by the media—notably television. The persecution of Soviet Jews, communal conflicts in India, the Tamil campaign for independence in Sri Lanka and the campaign against Apartheid in South Africa all help to underline the universal nature of issues and problems connected with ethnicity.

A further international aspect is emphasised by the personal links between Britain and the country of origin of its ethnic-minority citizens. Many West Indians, Pakistani and Indian citizens, for instance, have dual nationality, and make regular visits to their homelands. They inevitably take and convey a distinctive view of contemporary multi-ethnic Britain.

A key factor in the perception of a society by a member of an ethnic minority will be the level of hostility or discrimination he meets. Although cultural, rather than specifically racial, differences may play the largest part in determining inter-ethnic relations, there is a sense in which race *does* play a significant part. Variations in skin colour are likely to make integration into existing populations and institutions more difficult. Strangers are always treated with reserve, particularly if they arrive in significant numbers, but they are more readily accepted if the hosts can identify with them. Poles, Hungarians and Jews, for instance, have been assisted in their quest for acceptance in Britain by not standing out in a crowd. However, this cannot be so easily achieved by immigrant Asians and West Indians and their descendants. These have the great disadvantage of carrying their sense of separateness around with them. Previous immigrants who began as foreigners would sometimes change their names to Anglicised forms to assist in the process of integration, but this cannot apply to racial minorities. It is more likely, too, that prejudice, which is common to all races, will be translated into discrimination when faces proclaim ancestral foreign origins.

This is not a simple or inevitable process. It is by no means the case that discrimination *has* to cross racial boundaries. Hostilities *within* the same racial groups can reach horrifying proportions. Intra-group violence has always been, and continues to be, a general predictable feature of the world we live in. As I write, there are black people in South Africa who are placing tyres round the necks of their own kind, pouring petrol on them and setting them alight. The Bulgarian authorities are currently systematically depriving their Turkish, Moslem subjects of their historic identity by cruel and inhuman methods—and there is very little physical difference between the groups involved. During the Jewish Holocaust the victims were so similar to their persecutors that insignia, tattoos or official papers had to be used to distinguish victims from murderers. In Northern Ireland people with identical accents and physical features, and who occupy houses yards from one another, are in daily fear for their lives and properties. The Vietnamese 'boat people' met often tragic ends at the hands of people biologically identical to them.

Nevertheless, since differences in skin colour are readily discernible, it does seem more likely that irrational responses in the majority population will be evoked. One distinguished anthropologist, commenting on the 1950s and 1960s in Britain, put the matter this way: 'With a massive immigration of West Indians, and later of Asians, after the war and an increasing proportion of "colonial" people, the issue of racial awareness and racial friction came to the surface more openly.'[5]

The Effects of Multi-ethnicity

The consequences of allowing a society to become significantly multi-ethnic are the subject of continuing debate. Broadly speaking, we tend to find two rival claims. There are those who claim that the admixture of languages, religions, nationalities and cultures will prove an enriching experience. The advocates of 'multicultural education' take this view, as does the whole of the race relations lobby. Various local education authorities (LEAs), particularly those with large, ethnic populations, are actively seeking to promote this perception among teachers, parents, pupils and governing bodies. The new ethnic languages are presented as a 'national asset', while it is claimed that new religions, such as Islam, may well produce a fresh spiritual awareness in a nation virtually bereft of religious vitality. A new spirit and energy may also be injected into British cultural life. The poetry of the Caribbean, the dancing of India and the great architectural traditions of Islam may all signal a new renaissance. Economic life may also benefit from the entrepreneurial energy brought by certain immigrant groups.

However, this enrichment thesis is not shared by all. Others point to the potential for conflict inherent in a society where groups have very different (and possibly conflicting) ideas about culture, politics and personal behaviour. Islam, for instance, a growing presence in Britain, will tend to be perceived not in terms of a beneficial spiritual presence but rather as the spearhead of a holy war, whose influence in Iraq, Iran, Libya and Lebanon has been counterproductive. Realists will point to the repressions of Khomeini, or indeed the authoritarianism of Zia's Pakistan. The Caribbean influence may be understood not as a creative cultural injection but as the underlying cause of the appalling inner-city riots Britain has experienced in recent years.

In this latter perspective, defenders of multiculturalism will tend to be perceived as a disruptive force undermining feelings of national coherence, continuity and solidarity; what to the ethnic minority leadership will be seen as legitimate demands will be interpreted as cries for privileged treatment. Any criticism of Britain's history, institutions or goodwill will be resented. While the supporters of enrichment will perceive attempts to control immigration as 'racism', the realists will continue to demand an end to, or very strict control of, ethnic influx as a pragmatic response to a steadily worsening situation.

These conflicting perspectives are exacerbated by political and class differences. The enrichers—or, at least, the politically aware among them—will tend to espouse liberal or left-wing positions and read, for example, the *Guardian*; although this will not apply to the masses who vote Labour—they will tend towards pessimism, and look to the *Mirror* to reflect that. The realists, broadly speaking, will be located on the political right and read the *Daily Telegraph*—and there is less likelihood here of the kind of social class divisions found within the Lib/Lab spectrum. At the extremes, the ideological influence will create distinctive and very positive forms of belief and action. The extreme Right will tend to exploit the presence of racial minorities in Britain to prosecute their odious notions of white superiority and racial purity; the extreme Left will do all it can to exploit real or imaginary minority grievances to create the social conflict which prefigures the revolutionary solutions Marxists long for—for them, a new, untried and exploitable proletariat is a godsend.

Whose Fault is It?

A recurring theme in the debate about Britain's multi-ethnic population is responsibility. How are the ethnic minorities faring, and if they are doing less well than the majority, where does the responsibility lie? Here a curious contradiction occurs. Whereas the race lobby, like those who support it, takes an optimistic cultural view of the minorities, it consistently has a pessimistic one of their life chances. The materials produced by the Commission for Racial Equality (CRE), the various Community Relations Councils (CRCs), the Runnymede Trust, the Institute for Race Relations—as well as the myriad voluntary bodies and pressure groups operating in this area—all stress the concept of responsibility in relation to the socio-economic welfare and progress of the ethnic minorities. They all take refuge in the notion that the minorities are, comparatively speaking, failing, and that the responsibility for this is a malign system of discrimination operating at both the institutional and personal levels. Here, for instance is a typical opinion expressed by the Runnymede Trust: 'There are the policies and practices of institutions and organisations which continue to "disadvantage" black people because they frequently fail to take account of the "cultural differences" between groups with different ethnic origins.'[6] Here, in typically unequivocal style, is Mr Ambalvaner Sivanandan, Director of the Institute for Race Relations: 'Ethnic minorities do not suffer disabilities because of ethnic differences, but because such differences are given differential weighting in a system of racial hierarchy.'[7] The question of how far the ethnic minorities *are* failing, or doing less well than they might reasonably be expected after such a comparatively short settlement, I intend to look at later. What I should like to do here is examine the question of responsibility, so as to bring out how a key issue involving ethnicity can be far more complex than received opinion might suppose. In order to do so I enlist the views of two academics—one British (Ceri Peach[8]), and one American (Thomas Sowell[9]).

Peach has considered a basic issue involving the allocation of responsibility—segregation in housing. The race relations lobby, and those academics on which it depends to supply supporting evidence, have always argued that the ethnic minorities' tendency to congregate in inner-city areas is the result of various kinds of discrimination, racial and economic. Lack of money and rejection by the majority have combined to compel immigrants and their desendants to occupy substandard housing in the least attractive parts of towns and cities. This 'constraint' school of thought asserts that West Indians and Asians have been compelled by force of hostile circumstances to go for those multi-occupied rooming houses which lie at the very bottom of the housing market—the Marxist theory of capitalist exploitation supplies the necessary explanation of how this occurs. Segregated housing is taken as the symbol of degradation imposed by majority compulsion.

However, detailed empirical investigations have created what Peach calls a 'choice' school of thought. While the constraining effect of low incomes, access to different housing markets and prejudice are undoubtedly influential in determining housing outcomes, variations in aspirations and differentiations within the minorities also play important roles.

For instance, single male Pakistanis might well choose multi-occupied dwelling places not from lack of choice but as the *desired* solution to communal needs. Similarly, West Indians' perception of housing needs might arise from the fact that they re-united families much earlier than the Asians, rather than from compulsion. Moreover, the tendency to segregate operates along selected ethnic lines rather than as a result of any crude black-versus-white conflict. Thus in 1971 research showed that Cypriots, whose colour was not particularly germane, were the most segregated group in London. Moreover, Indians were segregated from West Indians and Pakistanis from Bangladeshis to almost the same extent as each group was separated from the white community. Work in Blackburn showed that among Asian Moslems an important segregating factor was religion, with access to the local mosque being a key factor in housing choices. In Leicester, housing choice has been found to depend crucially on the wish to establish large, extended families, as in the homeland. Similar *cultural* preferences have been noted in the area of Asian business enterprise, while analysis of the urban riots of 1980 and 1981 showed, that, while conditions in the inner cities were bad, there was no consistent relationship between urban deprivation, unemployment and rioting; blacks, Asians and whites facing similar conditions were very differently involved.

Thomas Sowell, a black American economist and an authority on race and ethnicity, has placed the concept of responsibility in an international context. Crucially, he has demonstrated the key role of cultural values and personal choice in determining the socio-economic and political progress and status of ethnic minorities. Sowell makes the important point that attempts to ignore group culture and to highlight prejudice in determining economic performance is understandable: 'Against the historical background of bias, bigotry, and sweeping stereotypes on groups and national differences, this agnosticism or cultural relativism is understandable and perhaps laudable in intent.' However, this humanitarian concern for minorities ought not to prevent recognition of real culture-bound differences between groups. Failure to take this into account, however worthy the intention, is bound to render analysis and prescription superficial. If we assume that cultures are ways of getting things done, then group differences in efficiency can be shown to be vital determinants of failure; and certain groups *are* more effective than others: 'It is not simply a matter of how one chooses to look at it.' These group differences are not, of course, fixed. Relative powers and efficiencies have varied throughout history. Israel and Egypt no longer enjoy the superiority of the Pharaoh period and China has declined considerably *vis-à-vis* Europe in terms of its former immense technical and political superiority. A group or nation's position on the scale of success is not permanent, but it is real and influential in the here and now.

Sowell impressively documents his case, giving wide-ranging instances of cultural determinism. German immigrant farmers, for instance, always did better in the mountain valleys of the eastern United States than the Scotch–Irish groups with whom they competed. Although these groups existed under the same climatic, geographical, legal and political conditions (and indeed the Scotch–Irish tended to have the better lands, since they pioneered in advance of the Germans) it was always the case that the Germans outshone their rivals, and the key factor was variation in work habits. The same phenomenon can be demonstrated in South-east Asia. The Chinese immigrants there have invariably achieved more than the indigenous populations, as have various Indian groups. In Brazil and Argentina the original Spanish and Portuguese settlers failed to tap the vast natural resources there, but when the later German, Italian and Japanese immigrants arrived, new agriculture and whole new industries were created to an astonishing extent; and the Jews have tended to flourish throughout, despite consistent and, at times, murderous discrimination. Interestingly, these kinds of variations in outcome are now being found in Britain. Asians are consistently out-performing West Indians in both the socio-economic and educational fields, yet both groups exist under identical geographical, legal and political conditions, and there is no evidence that West Indians suffer more from racial prejudice.

Sowell is refreshingly frank about this. Not only does he assert the importance of cultural values, as opposed to discrimination, he also emphasises the role of personal and group choice in determining outcomes:

> Much contemporary social philosophy proceeds as if different patterns of group 'representation' in various occupations, institutions, activities or income levels must reflect discrimination decisions by others—that is, as if there were no substantive cultural or other differences among the various groups themselves. Yet this key assumption is nowhere demonstrated and is in many ways falsified. Even in activities in which no discrimination is possible, people are not proportionately represented. Activities solely within the discretion of the individual —choices among television programmes to watch or card games to play, the age of marriage, or the naming of children—show widely differing patterns between different racial, ethnic and national groups.

Although Sowell is here speaking of the American situation, there is little doubt that similar ethnic variations occur in Britain.

The question 'Whose fault is it?' then, requires analysis in its implicit assumption of inevitable ethnic failure and in terms of applying all the relevant variables to explain variations in socio-economic outcomes. This is not simply an academic matter. The work of people such as Peach and Sowell matters as much for its emotional as for its intellectual value. They provide, as it were, the basis of hope. By stressing the power of the group to overcome discrimination, and showing the influence of self-direction and choice, they underline the possibility of ethnic-minority progress. The consistently pessimistic attitudes of the race relations lobby is shown to be both inadequate and unhelpful. They may, indeed, be positively destructive. If as a black youngster, you are brought up to perceive yourself as the victim of malign and insuperable forces of hostility, you are likely to do one of two things; sink into a life of passive welfare dependency or attach yourself to anti-social groups or political extremists who preach direct action and rioting as the solution. If, on the other hand, you are provided with instances of the successful overcoming of disadvantage, you are more likely to make a concerted effort to progress.

Some recent observations on this question of responsibility bring out the importance of hope and optimism in determining the fate of minorities. The Church of England's Commission on Urban Priority Areas Report, *Faith in the City* (1985), took the view that the ethnic minorities were the victims of economic and political forces over which they had no control. This tendency to despair was given impetus by a report collated in 1986 by the Reverend Kenneth Leach, the Church of England's race relations field officer. This document, based on a conference convened by the Race, Pluralism and Community Group of the General Synod's Board for Social Responsibility, argues direct action as the solution to 'racism'. Conventional methods of protest are condemned, ' . . . more dramatic, symbolic actions of protest and defiance and the serious study of alternative methods of action to those currently used' are called for: 'The Church needs to lose its respectable image and espouse unrespectable causes . . . Essentially it means getting out of the committee rooms and onto the streets.'

It is not difficult to imagine the effect of that kind of rhetoric, on those anti-racist groups already committed to violence on the streets, and on any lively black youngster in the inner cities seeking excitement. Moreover, those who challenge this approach are to be shown the error of their ways. An index of all Anglicans in positions of power who are not sympathetic ought, we are informed, to be established: 'Those members would be regularly and systematically challenged to examine their actions in the light of their Christian commitment.'· This intimidatory and authoritarian disposition is probably inevitable when ethnic minorities are viewed either as the victims of history—as portrayed by the determinist sociologists whose influence is paramount in *"Faith in the City"*—or as groups hostile to the system and needing to be roused into street politics, as perceived by the rather excitable Reverend Leach.

However, a more constructive approach becomes possible if we shift the angle of perception from despair to hope. Just before *Faith in the City* was issued, Rabbi Jonathan Sachs published a paper called *Wealth and Poverty*, a Jewish analysis. Instead of castigating 'the system' and denigrating the rich and powerful, or idealising the poor, Sachs pragmatically suggests that the best way forward is to find ways of helping the poor to become less so: 'The best charity is that which helps the poor dispense with charity.' Echoing Sowell, he insists on the importance of clear thinking: 'Compassion, the sub-strata of judgement, must not distort judgement . . . the rule is that moral passion must yield to moral rationality if it is to achieve its end.' Confusing moral denunciation with notions of causation is a perennial error in the literature of race relations. The way forward is through neighbourly compassion and self-help. A similar optimism and honesty is found in *From Doom to Hope* (1986), by the Chief Lord Rabbi, Lord Jacobvits, a response to *Faith in the City*. He insists that minority groups have the character resources to overcome majority hostility and disadvantage. Those qualities of energy, creativity and intelligence that all groups possess can be harnessed to values which can ensure progress:

How did we [i.e. the Jews] break out of our ghettoes and enter the mainstream of society and its privileges? Certainly not by riots and demonstrations. Above all, we worked on ourselves, not on others. We gave a better education to our children than anybody else. We hallowed our home life. We channelled the ambition of our youngsters to academic excellence, not flashy cars. We gave better education to our children than anybody else. We rooted out crime and indolence from our midst by making every Jew responsible for all Jews. We made ourselves highly acceptable and indispensable by our industrial, intellectual and moral contribution to society.

Determining the locus of responsibility for the fate of minorities is not a simple matter. There is not the slightest doubt that, throughout history, minorities in every part of the world have suffered injustice and oppression, sometimes to a murderous extent, but it is equally true that there are innumerable instances of such groups overcoming disadvantage without the assistance of either inflammatory rhetoric or social insurrection. Hope and a determined effort to succeed have formed the basis of success. Despair, and the tendency to blame others or 'the system', can have serious consequences. As Sowell has said:[10]

> In various countries around the world, the rise of extremism, racial or ethnic political movements has progressively undermined and co-opted moderates, and swamped all other political issues under over-riding group antagonisms . . . The use of extremism in one group has led to counter-extremism in politics, in civil disorders, or even outright civil war.

It is perhaps interesting to note that the writers whose work I have quoted, and who insist upon the importance of hope and self-help, are members of the two ethnic minority groups which have suffered most from hostility—the Jews and the blacks.

Racism

Of all the issues connected with multi-ethnic societies and their nature, 'racism' is perhaps the most emotive. Not surprisingly, it is also the one which evokes the greatest confusion. It is no exaggeration to say that 'racism' is currently one of the most abused words in the language. Failure to define what it actually means lies at the root of much unnecessary conflict. To some it is a biological or genetic concept. To others it is a political rallying cry; the ascribing of it to an individual or institution can be sufficient, without any evidence, to ensure condemnation. Yet others use it to explain variations in the job market, housing and education. Often the various meanings are used interchangeably, even in the same speech or piece of writing. Reason is the victim, inevitably. How ever, a reading of the literature suggests that two broad definitions are possible:

(1) The belief in the genetic superiority of one group of people and the genetic inferiority of others.
(2) The process by which an individual or group is disadvantaged due solely to skin colour.

It is essential for these meanings to be kept separate: one does not necessarily imply the other. Human beings do not need theories — scientific or otherwise—to justify the ill-treatment of others. The horrors of slavery existed for hundreds, perhaps thousands, of years before the emergence in the late nineteenth century of theories of racial, genetic variations. It is not a question of saying that one definition is right and the other wrong. What matters is for the particular meaning ascribed to the term to be made clear.

There are two specific uses of the word 'racism' that cause confusion. First, the tendency of anti-racism as a movement—and the 'official' wing, including bodies such as the CRE and the various CRCs, is as responsible here as the political extremists who engage in street politics—the tendency to use 'racism' as an insult to be attached to those, who, while owing no allegiance to racial genetic theories and deploring discrimination, are nevertheless condemned as 'racist' because they disapprove of the anti-racist movement. The determination to politicise the issue is now very marked among anti-racists. One is either for or against the cause. Inevitably, this mentality tends to employ words not to create understanding but to defeat the enemy and rally the faithful.

Second, 'racism' is often used to conflate two distinct concepts; prejudice and discrimination. Prejudice, or the tendency to pre-judge, without the necessary experience and information to form an informed and balanced judgement, is in the nature of a mental attribute, which may or may not be translated into actual behaviour. Discrimination, on the other hand, refers to an act. Someone acts in such a way that another person is somehow disadvantaged. Now a person may be both prejudiced and discriminatory in his behaviour, but—and this is the crux of the issue—he may *not* be. It is perfectly possible for someone in the majority population to be ignorant of the history and culture of another in a minority population, and to hold certain stereotyped beliefs as a result. However, that same person may not allow his beliefs to determine his behaviour. Social psychologists have repeatedly warned against a too-simple relating of attitudes to behaviour; the relationship, in reality, is often complex; using 'racism' to include both prejudice and discrimination violates this principle. The prejudiced non-discriminator is a common phenomenon.

A report from the Policy Studies Institute[11] is relevant here. The researchers established from written essays that recruits to the Metropolitan Police displayed prejudiced attitudes towards ethnic minorities, but they also found that these attitudes were very rarely translated into actual behaviour. On the contrary, the relationship between the police and black and Asian people was often relaxed and friendly. The assumption that most interactions are marked by hostility was found not to be the case: 'Standards of conduct are probably higher than in many other police forces in developed countries, and probably higher than they were, say, 50 years ago in London.' Lord Scarman in his report in 1981 on the Brixton riots formed a similar judgement.

This is not simply a semantic quibble. The careless or deliberately malign use of the word 'racism' can have very serious consequences for the individual. For instance, the Bristol schoolteacher, Jonathan Savery, made it clear in a published article that he disapproved of the anti-racist mentality and movement. It was therefore assumed that he must be a racist. He was arraigned before a quasi-judicial tribunal involving bureaucrats, politicians, lawyers and trade unionists, and underwent a 'trial'. Although he was acquitted, the virulence of the attack on him by local 'anti-racists' '—which continued even after his acquittal—meant that he had to seek sanctuary in another school. His career may well have been ruined. If we misuse words, we may misuse people—'racism' is a case in point.

Conclusion

Understanding the nature of Britain's multi-ethnic society is far from easy. Even perceiving it accurately raises difficulties. There are few phenomena so likely to be influenced by bias, bigotry and ideology. There is a need for honest thinking, respect for words and humane concern for the underdogs of our society. In determining the key issue of responsibility we need to learn from history. Our attitudes towards the innate capacity of minority groups to overcome disadvantage will play a crucial role in determining policy decisions. Above all, we need to resist the tendency to foreclose the discussion and give way to those with an axe to grind.

References

1. A. Smith, *The Ethnic Revival*, Cambridge University Press, Cambridge (1981)
2. *Britain 1986: An Official Handbook*, HMSO, London, pp. 197–9
3. *Linguistic Minorities in England*, Linguistic Minorities Project, University of London Institute of Education (1983)
4. N. Glazer, 'The Universalisation of Ethnicity', *Encounter*, February (1975)
5. R. Firth, *Human Types*, Abacus Press, Tunbridge Wells (1975)
6. 'Race and Immigration', *Runnymede Trust Bulletin*, No. 169, July (1984)
7. A. Sivanandan, *How Racism Came to Britain*, Institute of Race Relations, London (1985)
8. C. Peach, 'Stranded in the Inner City', *The Times Educational Supplement*, 22 February 1985
9. T. Sowell, *The Economics and Politics of Race*, William Morrow, New York (1983)
10. *Ibid.*
11. D. Smith and J. Gray, *Police and People in London,* Policy Studies Institute, London (1983)

CHAPTER 2

What Kind of Multi-ethnic Society?

Britain has always been a multi-ethnic society. Over four centuries of Empire and Commonwealth it has become a multiracial society. This process is irreversible—a legacy of British history.

This is a comment made to, and quoted approvingly by, the Swann Committee (p. 7) (see Chapter 6). It reflects a view that is shared by the whole of the race relations/anti-racist lobby which has developed in Britain over the past 20 years or so. However, it suffers from a number of weaknesses. Its assertion that Britian has been a multiracial society for four centuries is dubious: until about 1950 the country was, in racial terms, a relatively homogeneous society. The number of non-white groups who came and settled permanently before this date was very small indeed. Perhaps the only distinctive community of non-whites of any size was the 'Liverpool Blacks'. This is a mixed group of African, mixed African and English and Liverpool–Irish descent, with some Asian elements. Its origins are due mainly to the settlement in Liverpool of a number of African seamen towards the end of the nineteenth century. According to the Swann Committee, estimates of the present size of the ethnic minority proportion in Liverpool vary from 20,000 to 45,000, and the Merseyside Community Relations Council considered that only half of this estimate refers to the historic Liverpool Blacks. Moreover, this group has been traditionally confined to just one district —Liverpool 8—and in cultural terms they have been indistinguishable from white Liverpudlians for decades. They speak precisely the same 'scouse' as their white neighbours, and many, in fact, have white blood relations. They scarcely constitute evidence that Britain has been multiracial for four centuries.

Second, the quotation implies inevitability—the development of

Britain as a multi-ethnic society is assumed to have been the result of irresistible historical forces. Although there is an element of truth in this (we have already indicated that multi-ethnic populations are increasingly common in the contemporary world), the size of Britain's ethnic population and the distinctive ways its multi-ethnic society has developed were by no means prefigured. In strictly objective terms the multi-ethnic society in Britain dates from the British Nationality Act 1948, which confirmed that the openness of Britain to the people of the former colonies would continue after their independence. It was this specific legislation which led to the first large influx of blacks and Asians in British history and the founding of the multi-ethnic society as we know it.

Third, the quotation is complacent. Its facile historical assumptions suggest that the adaptations involved in Britain's conversion to a multi-ethnic society can be best managed by persuading an unenlightened majority that nothing unusual has occurred. It is simply a matter of allowing an inevitable historical process to unfold. The history of Britain's multi-ethnic society in recent years suggests that this is an inadequate and inappropriate response. We have only to consider the serious inner-city riots in places such as Brixton, Toxteth, Handsworth and the Broadwater Farm Estate in Tottenham, and the horrifying treatment of such groups as the Bangladeshis of Tower Hamlets to realise that very serious and threatening developments can grow out of Britain's multi-ethnic character. The *kind* of multi-ethnic society we want is a question rarely discussed, but it is of great importance to our future as a coherent and stable society. We cannot simply allow things to happen. Choices have to be made, and they need to be based on informed debate and public opinion. The striking aspect about post-war Britain has been the absence of any kind of appeal to the public about the kind of multi-ethnic society they prefer to live in. Developments in this field have come entirely from a tiny unrepresentative group of race relations professionals, politicians and civil servants. The alternatives of assimilation, integration and 'multiculturalism' or 'cultural pluralism', (which we see in the Swann Report, for instance) are discussed without reference to any kind of public opinion survey.

I intend, therefore, to look at the choices available when a society becomes significantly multi-ethnic in its population. The literature suggests four possibilities: assimilation, multiculturalism, separatism and integration.

Assimilation

This term suffers from careless usage, and it is frequently used as a synonym for 'integration'. Provided that this is made clear, no harm results, but mixing up the two words can lead to misunderstanding. I wish to be precise about how I am using it here. By 'assimilation' I mean the process which occurs when ethnic minorities are more or less compelled to abandon their original cultures and to assume the culture of the country to which they or their forefathers have emigrated. It can also apply to those minority cultures that are indigenous. In this scenario, original languages, religions, social customs and versions of history are assumed to be alien. The intention of the majority state is to eliminate them, so as to compel attachment of minorities to the dominant culture. Where this attachment process has not been thought possible, actual expulsion, or elimination of minorities, has been attempted. The rationale behind this policy is that ethnic differences represent a threat to national unity and social and political stability—and the entirely false and malign doctrine of racial purity has often functioned as a justification.

Examples abound. Towards the end of the nineteenth century the Russian government attempted to compel Jews to assimilate: they were forced to remove their beards, dress as Russians, teach Russian in their schools and send their young people for military training, which involved Russian non-Jewish food and religious practices. The Chinese in Indonesia have been resented for generations for their separate values, life styles and economic success. In recent post-war years they have faced discriminatory laws and policies. Chinese newspapers and magazines have been banned, the numbers of Chinese schools reduced and businesses confiscated. Anti-Chinese riots have occurred as recently as 1980. In 1920 Breton-speaking French children were punished for speaking their mother-language in school, 'le symbol' (a wooden clog) being hung round the neck of offenders which could only be removed when the victim discovered a fellow pupil committing the same 'offence'.

In all the tangled and complex history of multi-ethnic societies one conclusion stands out, quite apart from the obvious moral objections. Assimilation as used here very rarely works. Indeed, the very attempt to compel cultural conformity often has the reverse of the desired effect. Minorities become more determined to hold onto their unique cultural identities, the more the authorities insist they lose them. Paradoxically, the absence of compulsion tends, over time, to encourage a process of absorption by natural, human intercourse, particularly by the economic activities encouraged by free markets. For instance, the growth of Siamese nationalism in the twentieth century saw vigorous attempts by the authorities in Siam (now Thailand) to suppress Chinese culture. Chinese schools were subject to restrictive regulations, certain Chinese books were banned, Chinese newspapers were proscribed, there was discriminatory legislation and taxation and occupations were increasingly reserved for the Siamese. However, the Chinese, beleaguered and oppressed, found strength in adversity and continued to prosper, while retaining an ever-fiercer attachment to their origins. A similar Chinese policy, together with Chinese prosperity, can be discovered in the history of the Philippines. Also, the Jews—a people who have traditionally combined economic success and cultural uniqueness—have suffered attempts to assimilate them throughout their history.

Quite apart from ethical and historical objections to assimilation there are solid, pragmatic reasons why it should be rejected as a device for coping with ethnically diverse societies. A recent study of minorities[1] has posited two objections to assimilation—at least within those open societies committed to humanitarian principles and exposed to world opinion. First, any state that seeks to deprive a minority of its original culture and identity risks insurrection from within. This would involve more than organised resistance from the minorities themselves. There are in all free, liberal societies large groups of people with a developed, humane concern for the underdog, and they would tend to resist the inevitably totalitarian nature of an assimilation policy. Second, we live in a 'global village'. This awful cliché represents a reality, in the sense that, thanks to international telecommunications, what happens in open societies is instantly known throughout the world. International pressure and —with smaller, weaker nations—the possibility of actual interventions is a powerful deterrent. The difficulties currently being experienced by the South African regime are in large measure due to the international exposure of its Apartheid policies; although the appalling Chinese suppression of traditional Tibetan society should serve as a warning about what can happen when a relatively remote and weak nation is subjected to coercive absorption by another, untroubled by world opinion and unrestrained by Western notions about the rights of minorities.

Assimilation, then, and for a variety of reasons, is not an acceptable or realistic option for Britain. It has never been the policy of any British government. The flourishing of Jewish, East European, Asian and Caribbean cultures in various parts of Britain and the continued popularity of Britain for immigration attest to the ability of the country to permit the flourishing of foreign cultures. Many of the criticisms made of Britain's attitude to immigrant cultures arise not from an honest observation of the facts but from confusing assimilation with integration.

Multiculturalism

By multiculturalism I mean not the the natural living together of different cultures in the same country but that developed and publicly funded movement and ideology which maintains that the state is obliged to reflect the multicultural nature of the population in all its institutions—not least in its educational system. Society *has* to become conscious of ethnic diversity. School curricula *have* to be 'permeated' with a multi-ethnic perspective. Minority cultures *are* to be funded out of central and local taxation. The established consensus regarding society's view of its self *must* undergo profound change, and a new, officially sponsored version of national culture and identity created. Ethnic minorities are given special legal status and protection. Race relations is elevated from its status as an unselfconscious aspect of human relations both to a subject of academic enquiry and to legal and administrative action. These radical developments require for their rationale and implementation the creation of an intelligentsia which supplies the theoretical justifications for policy-making and a bureaucracy to ensure implementation of decisions. A dialectic between theory and practice is thereby established, and a new class of people emerges whose role is to define what it means to a successful citizen in Britain's newly created multi-ethnic society. Private definitions, values and cultural norms give way to officially approved prescriptions.

This active, interventionist concept was successfully canvassed in both the USA and Australia in the post-war years.[2] It is now being vigorously urged in Britain by an increasing number of local authorities, the CRE, CRCs, the Runnymede Trust and a myriad 'anti-racist' organisations. It appears to be broadly supported by both the

Labour and Liberal–Alliance Parties. Its promise of a reconstructed society with radical institutional change makes an irresistible appeal to various small but influential (particularly at the local level) Marxist–Leninist groups, many of whom now march under the Labour Party banner. This version of the multi-ethnic society was, broadly speaking, endorsed by the Swann Committee[3] (see Chapter 6):

> We consider that a multiracial society such as ours would in fact function most effectively and harmoniously on the basis of pluralism which enables, expects and encourages all ethnic groups, both minority and majority, to participate fully in shaping society as a whole within a framework of commonly accepted values, practices and procedures, whilst allowing and, where necessary, assisting the ethnic minority communities in maintaining their distinct ethnic identities within this common framework.

(This remarkable passage, not untypical of the language of the Swann Report, cries out for detached, critical analysis. I point here simply to the unwillingness of the author to equate 'pluralism' with state intervention, and the hovering, tenuously attached participles 'shaping', 'allowing', 'assisting'. The passage is a grammatical and semantic mess.)

Provenance

The origins of this approach have not yet been systematically investigated. I simply offer an intuitive description. In general, the move towards political and administrative intervention into ethnic matters can be seen as a specific expression of a dominant, general belief that all social issues require bureaucratic handling. Parkinson's Law is not an amusing, ironic commentary on contemporary life in developed societies. It is a precise description of an all-pervasive attitude. There has been an enormous growth in both national and local government since the Second World War. Government departments and quangos dealing with virtually every aspect of the individual's and the community's life have sprung up in recent years. Britain is an increasingly regulated society. Laws and government edicts have reached gigantic proportions (starting a small business, for instance, is now a complex administrative exercise). The citizen is assailed with official forms. Today the notion that the state knows best is a major theme in the rhetoric of all British governments. The basic necessities of life, such as health and education, are assumed to be best handled by state officials.

The issues raised by Britain's conversion into a more complex, multi-ethnic nation provided this bureaucratic mentality with considerable opportunities. The creation of a race relations bureaucracy was probably inevitable in the present climate. Whether bureaucracy and professional self-interest can solve the human problems of something as complex and sensitive as race relations is another matter. Thomas Sowell has a pertinent comment on the American equivalent of the CRE:[4]

> There are powerful incentives to continue the political crusades of the past, even after the beneficial effects. Part of the reason is inertia. A large civil rights establishment inside and outside government has to find work to do.

In addition to the bureaucratic obsession there is a powerful intellectual force at work here—cultural relativism. This concept, which has been dominant in Britain's educational system for decades, has its origins in the work of anthropologists such as Malinowski, Westermack and Radcliffe-Brown. Essentially, what it says is that cultures are systems sufficient unto themselves; they cannot be understood except in terms of concepts that they themselves generate. They cannot be evaluated by any general, independent principles, since all perceptions and explanatory systems are culture-bound. The notion of cross-cultural judgement is, therefore, very dubious. Since this is the case, any attempt to assume ethnocentric attitudes is deplored, as is the idea of cultural absorption, since this would imply the superiority of major to minority cultures—however they are defined. A whole movement has been founded on this basis. The Red Indians of North America, the Aboriginal peoples of Australia and the Maoris of New Zealand are only the most obvious instances of how ethnic groups have gathered round themselves publicly funded bureaucracies founded on the notion of cultural relativism. The 'Black Studies' mentality takes much of its force from it. I am not concerned here with evaluating this notion. Suffice it to say only that (1) cultural relativism has been subjected to severe and cogent criticism, and (2) the belief that ethnic minorities created as the result of freely under-taken immigration, without any compulsion on the part of the host country, are in the same position as indigenous minorities (for example, the Maoris) is at least questionable.

A version of this kind of cultural relativism has been generated by experts working within the state education service. They have argued that unless the culture of ethnic minority pupils or, in-creasingly, that of their forebears (an increasing proportion of such children are British-born) is reflected in the schools, two things will happen: the child's self-concept will be damaged and academic performance will be depressed. The notion of the multicultural curriculum has been fashioned to prevent this. The important point is to stress here that this development has very little to do with the wishes of the parents concerned, either minority or majority; nor is there any convincing psychological or sociological evidence to support it. It is almost entirely the work of professional, academic and political interest groups who correctly perceive ethnic matters as a growth area. The fact that vested interests march under the banner of concern for the underdog does not relieve them of the need to demonstrate the validity of the beliefs involved—although, in the present climate, it is very difficult to challenge the orthodoxies of the multicultural lobby precisely because it claims to occupy the moral high ground. (Multi-ethnic education is examined in Chapter 4.)

However, perhaps the most powerful source of the multicultural thesis is the concept of imperial reparation. The fact that Britain once had colonies and controlled subject-peoples takes on the qual-ity of an accusation in the literature of multiculturalism. The expres-sion of this attitude takes three forms: (1) Britain has an obligation to provide aid to the 'Third World', whether or not there are ethical and diplomatic reasons for doing so; (2) citizens of former British colonies should have unrestricted right of entry into Britain forever; and (3) the maintenance of immigrant cultures is the responsibility of the British state. The justification for all this lies in the economic and political benefits that Britain's long-lost Empire once enjoyed. In this scenario the British were not motivated by 'the white man's burden' but by the desire to exploit; greed, arrogance and political hegemony being the motivating sources of Empire.

This notion has a long history. It is a crucial part of the traditional Marxist doctrine of exploitation of the underclass, and links with some version of classical liberalism. Perhaps its most influential exponent, in this context, has been the black French intellectual, Franz Fanon. The following is a typical Fanon observation:[5]

Europe has stuffed herself inordinately with the gold and raw materials of the colonial countries . . . Europe is literally the creation of the Third World . . . We will not acquiesce in the help for underdeveloped countries being a programme of 'Sisters of Charity'. This help should be a ratification of a double realisation by the colonial powers *that it is their due,* and the realisation by the capitalist powers that in fact *they must pay* (original emphasis).

This thesis, which combines past sores and contemporary guilt as an essential way of understanding the British Empire, has received great publicity in Britain in recent years. This deep, unrelenting and unforgiving bitterness, which can only be relieved by successive generations of British people engaging in expiation and reparation, is a dominant theme in the material generated by certain elements in the media—particularly the BBC. The most obvious recent example is the series *The Africans,* created by the Kenyan academic Ali Mazrui. In this the whole of Africa's travail is laid at the door of a rapacious West. The British Empire is portrayed as a force for evil, destroying native cultures, wrecking indigenous economies and stealing everything which could possibly benefit the colonial power. Africa, before the colonial intervention was, in this interpretation, a veritable Garden of Eden, peopled by peace-loving inhabitants living blameless and productive lives within a well-ordered tribal landscape. Mazrui states: 'Before slave days we were back in one huge African village called Africa.' Although there was some criticism in Britain of this version of colonial history and it was excoriated in the American press, its theme has deep and abiding roots in the British liberal psyche, and it was, of course, a godsend to the anti-racist movement and those left-wing radicals who inhabit it in large numbers.

A series on Channel 4 somewhat later conveyed a similar message. Basil Davidson created a set of programmes which attempted to show that an ancient and distinguished Africa, with a developed civilisation, had been destroyed by Western imperialism. The process of domination and conquest practised by the colonial powers had annihilated a successful continent. Again, this version of imperialism is manifestly one-sided. Songhai, Mali, Ghana, long-

departed African glories, were themselves the product of the imperial impulse, and attempts to revive them, as in Nkrumah's
Ghana, have proved disastrous.

The dangers of basing ethnic policy on this kind of guilt-evoking
approach have been demonstrated by Thomas Sowell after he had
made detailed observations of multi-ethnic societies:[6]

> Rewarding those who are adept at evoking guilt promises few benefits
> to any one other than themselves—whether they be Third World or
> domestic opportunists. To the extent that such rewards encourage
> further politicisation of race, they are encouraging a process that has
> ended in tragedy many times.

The history of officially approved multiculturalism in Britain is a
very short one. It is therefore difficult to perceive clearly or to assess
its chance of ultimate success. What is beyond doubt is the success
of those who advocate it in official circles, particularly in the major
official channel of cultural transmission to the young—the state
education service. It is the major theme of the whole race relations
establishment and its vigorous anti-racist offshoots. Whether the
combination of the modish belief in bureaucracy, cultural relativism, the exploitation of liberal guilt regarding colonialism and the
opportunism of the political left can provide a sound basis for the
management of Britain's multi-ethnic society, particularly in the
absence of any kind of public approval, is somewhat doubtful.

Separatism

This approach to ethnic variation within the one society is based on
the view that the differences between groups are so deep-rooted
that the only prospect for peaceful co-existence is the development
of separate areas or institutions based on ethnicity, where this is
possible. Linguistic, religious, social and historical (not to mention
racial) distinctions create such different and often conflicting aspirations and views of the world that ethnic separation is the only viable
solution. The maintenance of the group's identity, and the demands
of justice and self-determination, require a distinctive mono-ethnic
environment. The presence of different cultures living in close proximity can only lead, at best, to the creation of a mosaic of cultures

without any sustaining coherence or, at worst, to actual conflict. The rationale may be based on biological or cultural criteria, the first stressing alleged racial differences, the second, the implacable and irreversible lessons of history.

This view can point to a wide and lengthy provenance. It can, for instance, be discerned in the racial separation which ran right through the southern states of the USA before the civil rights legislation of the 1960s and the coming of Martin Luther King; in the movement for Quebec's secession before Trudeau; in the radical attempts to protect Aboriginal identity and culture in Australia; in the Red Indian rehabilitation phenomenon in the USA; and in the 'Back to Africa' migrations of those black Americans who founded Liberia. There are many current instances. As I write, the Tamil minority's movement for independence in Sri Lanka has led to the terrorist murder of 150 people in Colombo.

Separatism crosses political frontiers—both left and right, radicals and conservatives can be found urging its adoption. The radical lobbies currently urging separate and unique provision for Canadian Indians and Inuits;[7] the French Communist Party successfully campaigning for the repatriation of North Africans; concerned British Conservatives predicting social conflict and institutional breakdown if ethnic immigration continues; and British black activists campaigning for separate political sections in the Labour Party are all united in their belief in the notion of ethnic separation. All believe that the development of a multi-ethnic society spells danger for both minority and majority populations—although rather different arguments are employed to sustain policy decisions.

It is a mistake, although a popular one, to assume that ethnic segregation is always of a coercive nature, typically a dominant group imposing its will on a minority. In fact, history provides many examples of voluntary separation. Nineteenth-century indigenous Americans practised total separation from European immigrants. To this day, Russian emigrés to the USA create separate enclaves —those from Moscow, Leningrad and Odessa form segregated communities; Italian immigrants, likewise, avoid Italian Americans; and the overseas Chinese in South-east Asia have always created Fukkienese, Hainanese and other groups which go their separate ways. These, and many other instances, illustrate not only that separatism may be of a voluntary nature but that it can function along narrow culture lines within the same national groups. This suggests that, for whatever reasons, the desire to associate with those whom one recognises as one's own kind is very deep-rooted and persistent.

However, some of the most striking, even brutal, examples of moves to create ethnic separatism *have* been enforced. Many of the tribal conflicts of black Africa, for instance, have taken this form. Perhaps the most horrifying example in recent times was the massacre of all literate Hutu—some 100,000 people—by the rival Watutsi of Burundi in 1972. However, the most obvious (perhaps because the most exposed to public opinion) instance of separatism as a solution to ethnic problems is the Apartheid system of South Africa. This is a radical and sustained attempt to separate peoples on a racial basis. Although Afrikaner nationalism began as a struggle to defeat the English element in South African life, it also aimed to erect colour barriers against all non-whites. Most people would probably perceive this as an attempt at domination by a powerful élite of a less powerful and deprived majority—as, indeed, it is. However, as Geoffrey Partington[8] has pointed out, the rationale for separate development by South African whites sounds surprisingly like that of present-day radicals urging governments to respect the right of minorities to go their separate ways in order to maintain their historic identities. In 1953, for instance, Dr H.R. Verwoerd, then Minister of Native Affairs, asserted that the aim of the Bantu Education Act was 'the formulation of the principles and aims of education for natives as an independent race, in which their past and present, their inherent racial qualities, their distinctive characteristics and aptitudes, and their needs under ever-changing social conditions are taken into account'. The very large political and ideological differences which separate radical supporters of native cultures from the right-wing advocates of Apartheid—both of whom urge ethnic separation—should caution anyone from making categorical utterances about the best way to cope with multi-ethnic issues. That such different people can arrive at the same solution indicates just how complex are the problems involved.

However, an official policy of ethnic separation is not a viable alternative for Britain. The objections are too obvious: high-density urban populations, shortage of development land and the existing integrated economic, social legal and political structures all attest to the futility of separation. That is not to say, of course, that elements of ethnic separation do not or should not occur. Prevailing housing patterns, religious affiliation, leisure facilities and educational aspirations all suggest that self-chosen ethnic separateness does occur in Britain, but *within* the existing social order, not outside it. Crucially, public opinion is against the idea of formal segregation. The outcry against the attempts to use the British Labour Party as the basis for a separate racial platform is evidence of this.

Integration

This approach presupposes minimum state intervention in race relations. The preservation and transmission of ethnic minority cultures is assumed to be the responsibility of the groups concerned. All groups—majority and minority—are expected to support existing free institutions, and the schools reflect the concept of a unified, coherent society. Loyalty to a national ideal is the duty of all citizens. Such a society is characterised by unselfconscious acceptance of racial differences; since all assent to the same basic social order, no one experiences ethnic variation as a threat. Prejudice is assumed to be a purely private matter, common to all individuals and groups, while discrimination entails retribution only if it violates the law—a law based on the rights of the individual rather than those of named groups, since the concept of separate group rights tends to create inter-group jealousy and friction. In such a society thoughtful people will condemn both racial prejudice and discrimination, while taking care to distinguish between majority prejudice and legitimate opinion based on observed behaviour. The marketplace—both social and commercial—will regulate human contacts, rather than the state, and will tend to determine outcomes. The gradual coming together of major and minor cultures to create fresh understandings and forms will be assumed to be a natural, time-governed process, although those who pursue the principle of cultural preservation in such matters as religion, language, dress and diet will be entirely free to do so. This is, if you like, a non-interventionist view of a multi-ethnic society.

For instance, in the last two decades of the nineteenth century in the northern states of the USA there was a widespread sense of social and political unity. All citizens supported the American bourgeois, democratic ideal, and ethnic differences were no barrier to successful and profitable interaction. Discrimination, in voting, housing, public institutions, was in decline. A *modus vivendi* based on support for public principles and respect for private differences was emerging. The following is a summary of some of the salient features:[9]

> In nineteenth century Detroit, black physicians and dentists had predominantly white patients. The leading caterers in Philadelphia were black—and their clientèle was white. In Chicago, as well, there were black businesses whose customers were mostly white. In Michigan and Ohio, black politicians were elected by predominantly white voters. Throughout the North, there seemed to be a basis for optimism about the future of race relations.

This idyll started to collapse not because the integrating principle which underpinned it proved inadequate but for a purely demographic and unavoidable reason: the massive influx of Southern blacks which destroyed the social and political equilibrium, a development as fiercely resented by black as by white citizens.

Canada, Australia and New Zealand are also all examples of how multifarious states have successfully functioned on the basis of integration. This was not achieved without costs. Indigenous peoples undoubtedly suffered, as did their cultures. The impact of modern technology and developed economic and political ideas on Stone Age customs and outlooks inevitably caused internal conflict. The Aborigines of Australia, the Indians of Canada and the Maoris of New Zealand found that the Western notion of restless, dynamic development conflicted with the native concept of cultural stability and timeless devotion to established patterns of behaviour and beliefs. There have also been fierce conflicts *within* the European immigrant communities. The French separatist movement and the Quebec issue have threatened Canada with fragmentation. That such societies have overcome internal differences and continued in the pursuit of national ideals is a tribute to the principle of integration. Cultural and historical differences have been subordinated to more general and binding political and constitutional principles. This *modus vivendi* is currently threatened not by defects in agreed integration arrangements but rather by the rhetoric and activities of professional multiculturalists, whose notions about cultural isolation for minority groups are not dissimilar, as I have said, to the policies of Apartheid South Africa. The Canadian experience is well caught in this comment by the sociologist Howard Brotz:[10]

Thus, as far as the French and the English are concerned, there is now complete agreement, whether one likes it or deplores it, about the way of life they want to lead. And the dishonest side of 'resentment' of so-called Marxists, both French-speaking and English-speaking, is the refusal to admit that French society in Quebec had not been maintained but had maintained itself as a kind of pre-bourgeois reservation. De Toqueville saw this over a hundred years ago. But this is now finished.

Brotz goes on to say that this general assent to a unifying ideal does not mean complete uniformity in all things. Religion, linguistic and social customs of the group are all guaranteed by the existence of free institutions and civil liberties. In short, minority groups and the individuals which comprise them can successfully integrate commitment to public principles and private behaviour, an arrangement that threatens neither national solidarity nor individual freedom. The liberal–democratic insistence on the separation of state and society provides the guiding principle.

However, perhaps the most useful instance of the success of integration lies on Britain's own doorstep. As I have indicated above, Britain has been host to successive waves of immigrants many times in its history, before the creation of what we now call the 'multi-ethnic society', and a process of natural absorption had taken place. This created a society in which the immigrants and their descendants, while maintaining their original culture on a private basis, assented to certain overriding principles common to all citizens. Again, this was not achieved painlessly. The history of the Irish in Britain is a good example of how what began in circumstances of rivalry, intra-group conflict, deprivation and prejudice ended with successful integration. In the middle and late nineteenth century the Irish in Britain lived in conditions of great squalor. They were notorious for drunkenness and violence—often between men from different Irish counties. They congregated in decaying districts of towns and cities. Respectable citizens never entered Irish districts, and the police always went in large numbers. Fears about wage-cutting caused fighting between Irish and English workers competing for the same jobs. Irishmen were beaten, their huts burned and their womenfolk terrorised. Employers often had to separate workers by nationality. Riots were not uncommon. Yet a *modus vivendi* was established. The natural, human process of social interaction and economic exchange produced, over time, a settled pattern of life for the Irish who became accepted as British citizens. However, the original Irish culture did not disappear—the melting pot operated, as it were, only at the public level. They built their Catholic churches, published their own newspapers and maintained their traditions of dance and music, which were passed on to successive generations in such places as church halls. Irishmen fought alongside Britons in the Crimea and South Africa, as they did in the two world wars.

The story of the Irish in Britain is one of a people emerging from squalor, overcoming prejudice and finding a stake in the community. By 1950 more than 20 per cent of the Irish in Britain were in skilled occupations; more than 30 Labour MPs were Irish; and complete and harmonious integration was the norm. This was achieved not by the kind of pleas for special treatment that the professional race relations lobby currently makes for contemporary minorities but by the exercise of the human and cultural resources the Irish had brought with them, functioning in a free society. Much the same story could be told of the Jews who came to Britain at the end of the nineteenth century, as well as of the central European immigrants who arrived after the Second World War and following the Soviet invasion of Hungary in 1956 and Czechoslovakia in 1968.

Comment

Broadly speaking, then, in determining what kind of multi-ethnic society we want to live in we are faced with four alternatives: assimilation, separatism, multiculturalism and integration.

Assimilation

Assimilation can be ruled out since it implies a compulsion that can only obtain in closed, totalitarian states. In open and free societies, committed to the freedom and dignity of the individual, assimilation is not possible—both ethical and pragmatic considerations forbid it. Moreover, since it suppresses contrasting world views, customs and cultural forms, the success of assimilation can deprive the dominant society of a means of enriching itself. It does not, then, even make sense. In any case, in a world in which different cultures can be presented to one another instantaneously via telecommunications, the mentality that seeks to preserve an existing way of life in cultural aspic cannot be regarded as an adequate response to the real world. However, that is not the same as saying that patriotism as proper and seemly respect and love for the history and traditions of the original nation is dead. Indeed, perhaps a key question for us is, how far can Britain's ethnic arrangements allow us to respect, preserve and transmit that natural and abiding love of country that all people experience?

Separatism

In its official sense separatism means the attempt by the state to prevent that natural, human coming together of different groups which tends, over time, to overcome initial suspicion and hostility. Conservatives support it on the grounds of the supposed threat of ethnic mixing to individual identity and national unity and stability. Radicals speak of the natural man, and the infamy of dominant cultures in seeking to compromise or absorb minority ways of life. Conservatives are sustained by hard-headed references to the history of ethnic conflict; radicals by reference to the notion of live and let live and the need to defend the weak against the strong. Conservatives (the obvious case being South Africa) and radicals (as in Australia and New Zealand) may each compromise their case by creating self-serving, state-founded bureaucracies to implement separatism.

However, although there are many examples of self-chosen, ethnic segregation at the social level in Britain, and some instances of separatism due to poverty and prejudice, there appears to be little evidence of a demand for official separation. Moreover, separation would carry obvious risks. There would be a definite tendency for ethnic demands to flow along political channels—the politics of colour would become a real possibility. Ethnic differences would be emphasised and animosities underscored. The cross-fertilisation of cultures would be less likely. Social interaction across racial lines would be reduced, with all that that implies for the creation and maintenance of stereotypes based on ignorance. Demands for territorial integrity, as in Northern Ireland, Lebanon and Sri Lanka, would become a possibility. Moreover, official separation would destroy existing, open access to the single, national Welfare State currently available to everyone; and this would necessarily involve schools. The one way in which the state has acted to encourage separation so far, albeit it unwittingly, is the decision by the CRE to insist upon the end of educational dispersal, i.e. bussing. This has meant that the function of schools in creating cross-racial friendship in childhood has been severely reduced—inner-city schools now simply reflect ethnically segregated housing patterns. The long-term effect of this could well be to undermine society's commitment to official integration. The free market in goods and labour and the inevitable cross-racial interactions it encourages also undermines the case for separatism.

However, there is one continuing process which does emphasise ethnic differences and tends to delay integration—the practice of continued immigration and the frequent visits made to the ancestral homelands by our ethnic-minority citizens. The evidence shows that this constant reinforcement of the minority culture and identity helps to maintain a separatist mentality. Establishing in the minds of ethnic-minority children that they are, indeed, British is difficult when the contacts with the homeland and its cultures are constant, daily occurrences. I once asked a group of about 500 British/Asian children how many were Asian. Everyone said they were. I then asked how many were British and 90 per cent thought they were not. Integration would undoubtedly be assisted if immigration stopped—at least for a period.

Multiculturalism

The essential differences between multiculturalism and what I have called 'integration' lies in the role of the state. Multiculturalists believe that forms of culture drawing on existing minority traditions need to be fostered and financed by the authorities. In addition to the right of all groups to maintain and transmit their own distinctive world view (a right guaranteed by the existence of free institutions) it is argued there has to be positive intervention by the state. There is now a very active and influential race relations/anti-racist lobby advocating this in Britain. It was endorsed by the Swann Committee, as I have indicated. Second, this state-sponsored version of culture is a totalist concept—it has to 'permeate' all institutions, not least the schools. Third, this revised version must carry with it certain additional rights for ethnic minorities; a good example of this is the acceptance by the Inner London Education Authority (ILEA) that minority parents have the right to have their children educated in the community language.

There are several objections to all this. A basic unresolved problem is the elusive nature of culture itself. There is no consensus about what the term actually means. Originally it implied a contrast with civilisation. Whereas civilisation was thought of as a constructed, artificial thing, culture belonged to the people. Civilisation was urban and cosmopolitan, whereas culture was earth-bound and had traditional, natural ways of doing things. Culture was authentic, solid, continuous; civilisation, the product of wealth creation, issuing in the production of impressive, fabricated artefacts and increasingly complex technology. Culture implied on oral tradition which bound people with moral and religious ties. Civilisation challenged established ways of life and thought, and created a literary transmission system and diverse philosophies. In the eighteenth century culture was thought of as being superior to civilisation, and the myth of Rousseau's Noble Savage was born. However, the rise of anthropology at the end of the nineteenth century and the considerable increase in the study of exotic peoples caused a shift in the definition of 'culture'.

Culture came to mean virtually any belief, act or artefact associated with a distinctive group of people, and the culture –civilisation distinction was virtually lost as a result. The term became surrounded with controversy. The poet Hanns Johst once said 'Whenever I hear the word "culture" . . . I release the safety-catch on my pistol.' The Fontana Dictionary of Modern Thought describes it as 'this elusive and emotive word.'

If culture is difficult to pin down, how much more difficult will be the notion of a multiculture to define? None of this intellectual argument matters, of course, where culture is an essentially private concern. However, where the state sees fit to establish a fabricated version of the nation's culture then a complex and difficult intellectual exercise has to be gone through. How else will the schools know what to transmit? And how is the political problem of persuading public opinion (i.e. the approximately 95 per cent majority) that the new version is necessary?

For instance, if the concept is to work there would need to be some understanding of which items of ethnic minority culture should enter into the new version. Indeed, there would have to be agreement about which minority cultures would form the basis of cultural selections. Would *all* the foreign cultures which now flourish privately in Britain have the right to be included in the school curriculum and reflected in other public institutions? We can assume a measure of agreement about certain things, of course. No group would want, presumably, to question the importance of, say, teaching the three Rs in the schools or of inculcating moral awareness. However, what about those views and practices which would be likely to evoke controversy? Would the public, for instance, approve of ritually slaughtered halal meat in school dinners, as Moslem citizens insist? There is good evidence that public opinion regards this practice as cruel and primitive, the RSPCA have been campaigning against it for many years and an official government enquiry recommended in 1985 that it should be made illegal. Should Rastafarianism be part of the religious education syllabus? What version of history would be likely to satisfy all groups, especially those between whom there is traditional animosity (for example, Sikhs, Moslems, Hindus)? Any attempt to create a publicly supported multiculture would have to address many questions of this kind.

Of particular concern would be language—the key transmitter of cultures. What status would minority languages enjoy? A common theme in the literature of multiculturalism is that any disadvantage suffered by non-English-speaking citizens is a form of discrimination, and many local authorities are responding to this by providing information and official forms in non-English languages —the first time in the very long history of immigration to Britain that this has ever happened. Leaving aside the absence of public approval for this (not to mention the potentially enormous costs involved), what might be some of the practical effects of creating a multilingual, public environment that consistently assumes the presence of non-English speakers and readers? Clearly, the incentive to learn English would be reduced, and with it the ability to cope with a range of social demands. Take, for instance, safety in the workplace. Partington,[10] in discussing this issue in Australia, has drawn attention to the chaos and danger which could ensue if there was a lack of a common language: 'To have every industrial notice in all hundred and more community languages in Australia would ensure confusion in which few, if any, notices were read at all, while at the moments of danger a common spoken language is vital.' More crucially, the threat to a common, national language which all citizens are expected to acquire—a threat which at least some versions of multiculturalism carry with them—could ultimately threaten national coherence.

There is little doubt that the attempt to create and foster an official, multicultural order would create considerable controversy, not to say conflict—a development scarcely in the interest of good race relations. Nor would the difficulties arise simply from the intrinsic problems of reconciling conflicting beliefs and practices into some sort of public, cultural mosaic. There would also be the very real danger of the racial bigot (and the groups which articulate his concerns) using the prospect of state intervention in cultural matters to rationalise his bigotry and gain support from the uncommitted.

Also, a central issue in the argument would be where the burden of responsibility lay. The justification for multiculturalism is that minority cultures are disadvantaged in the larger society. This may be so, but who is responsible? Is it the indigenous citizen, or the citizen who, knowingly and deliberately, decides to abandon the country in which his culture enjoys dominance, in return for a life in which he knows previously that his mother-culture will necessarily be a minority phenomenon? The question has only to be asked for the answer to be clear. It seems reasonable to ask, in an open society where everyone enjoys the privileges of civil liberties, equality under the law and the franchise, and where every citizen, under the law, can practise any culture he wants, why there should be unprecedented radical changes in public aspects of the cultural environment, changes that not only carry the possibility of controversy and conflict but which the majority population gives no sign of wanting? The successful tradition of absorbing immigrants that Britain has developed is violated by the concept of a state-funded multiculture. If there be such a phenomenon as the man on the Clapham omnibus, these, one feels, are the sort of arguments he might well employ.

The intellectual might point to the problem of the separation of society and the state. One of Britain's greatest assets is the tradition of keeping separate the private and public domains. It is a guarantee of that freedom of the individual we take for granted. Crucial to our understanding of ourselves is the notion of the reasonable person who lives and lets live, who believes that such matters as the language of the home, religion, dress, diet and, indeed, that range of prejudices we all carry around with us are essentially private matters. The culture of public institutions is a function of history, tradition and the broad cultural consensus which, until very recent years, the citizens took for granted. There is no question of such things being imposed. Those who seek to do so would be regarded as extremists or fanatics—types detested by the great majority of British people. Keeping society and the state separate is vital to this view of the world. It is this principle—a happy amalgam of private choice and public consensus—which the notion of officially sponsored versions of culture violates.

Moreover, there is a singular factor pointing to the dangers of some kind of multiculture—Islam. A significant, and rapidly growing proportion of British/Asian citizens are Moslems. Islam, like other religions, has internal controversies and a spectrum of commitment from less to more extreme versions, and no doubt this is reflected in British Islam. Nevertheless, as someone who worked for nearly six years in a Moslem area in Britain I have no doubt that orthodox, fundamentalist Islam is alive and well and flourishing in Britain. Now a thumbnail sketch of complex and profound world religions is a hazardous exercise, but there are certain general comments we can make in locating the essential differences between Islam and our Jewish/Christian traditions, religions which have shown themselves able to engage in dialogue with the state to produce agreed successful compromises about questions of culture and conscience. Whilst the Jews espouse a religion rooted in moral imperatives and Christians pursue a more academic, perhaps more flexible, system of thought, each has shown signs of development over time. Islam is more static and absolutist than either. Moslems believe that what went before their Prophet was simply preparation for their ultimate, unchanging dogmas which are all the individual needs for salvation or the state for worldly success. Islam has an uncompromising legalism its rivals lack. It tends to be an enclosed system of thought, although not of action. While the Jewish/Christian tradition co-exists in the same nation where other non-religious sources of identity, solidarity and cosmology flourish, Islam claims to be sufficient unto itself and to make all other belief systems redundant. Moreover, although Islam can function in re-volutionary ways it always looks backward for inspiration and models for the present and is ill at ease with Western dynamism and pluralism. The essentially Western notion of individual human rights, for instance, has little meaning in Islam. A respected authority on Islam and the Arab world, Dr John Laffin, recently drew attention to a report on human rights infringements in 1985,[12] which ranks eleven members of Arab League Moslem states as 'not free', and ten, plus Egypt, 'partly free'.

Crucially, in the context of contemporary Britain, these features of Islam are important. First, Islam is an international, proselytising movement which is on the march—conversion of both people and states is a central purpose. Second, the Moslem population of Britain is increasing at a rate far greater than that of other groups. According to Dr Syed Aziz Pasha, General Secretary of the Union of Moslem Organisations of UK and Eire, there are now 2 million of his co-religionists in Britain; official sources indicate that there are now more Moslems in Britain than practising members of the Church of England; and at a conference in the 1970s of the British Society for Middle East Studies, Moslem scholars confidently predicted there would be 10 million Moslems in Britain within 40 years. It is important to remember that we are referring to a population whose Islamic philosophy in social and political terms is profoundly anti-Western.[13]

Third, the separation of state and society, of the sacred and the secular, an impulse which lies at the very heart of Britain's civil liberties and free institutions, has no meaning in Islam. Moslems always wish to create theocratic, all-embracing institutions in which the vital distinction between private conscience and public policy is abolished. How far can there be a state-sponsored cultural system which takes account of those fundamental and conflicting differences?

The questions I raise here suggest that multiculturalism is not an appropriate response to Britain's multi-ethnic diversity.

Integration

This approach assumes that culture is essentially a private matter. It also assumes that the absorption of minorities into the broader majority consensus regarding such things as civil liberties, the role of law, parliamentary democracy, the Welfare State and the separation of state and society is essential. Within this broad framework a very wide range of life styles and religious and cultural forms is permitted. Prejudice is accepted as being endemic in all communities, and discrimination on grounds of race is outlawed. Loyalty to Britain is demanded of all citizens, patriotism being a valuable source of political identity and social solidarity.

Over time, the majority culture is enriched by the admixture of new languages, religions and fresh ideas about cultural matters. Since the immigrant is in Britain from choice, natural justice dictates that he has the major responsibility for adapting his outlook and behaviour to fit in with existing ideas about the individual and the state and to transmit this tendency to adapt to his children. (The report of the Home Affairs Committee on Racial Disadvantage in 1981 voiced this very notion: 'Migration does not just mean a change of residence. It means a change of habits, outlook and values' (x-13).) It is accepted as desirable that, over time, the tendency of immigrant communities to gather in ghettoes will give way to a general dispersion. This will tend to prevent the development of a self-conscious, politically dangerous separatism, and encourage that integration between majority and minority peoples which is the best safeguard against stereotyping and bigotry. Since continued reinforcement from the homeland tends to encourage separatism and delay integration, the strict control of immigration from those areas already heavily represented in Britain is assumed to be inevitable.

I would argue that this integration concept of the multi-ethnic society would have the support of a majority of the population of Britain, including significant numbers of blacks and Asians. This, of course, is no more than a hunch based on lengthy experience in a multi-ethnic area and countless talks and discussions with mixed groups of people all over Britain. However, several of its features would be fiercely rejected by the race relations/anti-racist lobby, which claims a monopoly of concern for the ethnic minorities. Its implementation would certainly reduce the need for, if not effectively abolish, such organisations as the CRE. It undermines the notion, current in Britain for perhaps 15 years or so, that a combination of 'experts' issuing 'policy documents' and blueprints for society can create a harmonious and coherent multi-ethnic Britain. It shifts the burden of responsibility from state to society. Public opinion and existing political machinery, rather than government or council edict, become the arbiters of disputes and the basis of developments. A dialogue at political and media levels becomes the vehicle for creating and maintaining appropriate private attitudes and institutional decisions. The educational system encourages loyalty to a national ideal, while making every effort to respect religious diversity.

This minimal interventionist approach not only challenges professional self-interest in the field of race relations but also creates anxiety in the liberal mind, since it reduces the need for guilt feelings typical of the contemporary liberal confronted with a legacy of Empire. It also threatens to extract race from politics—a serious blow to those anti-racist Marxist elements who have made the exploiting of racial friction a weapon in the class war. The 'rainbow coalition' of minorities forming a consensus against the status quo becomes much less likely. Similarly, it will dismay the mentality which supports the National Front, since the integrated, cross-racial alliances it encourages cuts away the validity of racial superiority doctrines which depend on stereotyping, fear and ignorance.

Central to the concept of integrations is the notion of constitutional loyalty. Parliamentary majority rule depends upon public support. The Westminster model works because the disparate elements making up the United Kingdom have created a consensus about its viability. Although there have been disturbing Celtic rumblings in recent years—and the emergence of appalling violence from a tiny minority in Ulster—there has been a broad and binding agreement since the settling of Wales after the Tudors and Scotland after the 1745 rebellion. Everyone knows that he or she is British (although few will feel the need to articulate this) precisely because he or she approves of the key constitutional arrangements of parliamentary democracy and the hereditary monarchy. They symbolise what the British have gone to war to defend, and they are reinforced in the popular mind every time there is a general election or a royal wedding or coronation. Constitutional arrangements have both expressed and guaranteed national sovereignty and identity.

However, the presence of large and growing minority communities who may choose to reject integration and define themselves in terms of a foreign nationality could constitute a threat to the constitution, particularly where separate political influence is being claimed. History provides many instances where minorities with divergent loyalties have caused national disintegration—Palestine,

India, Cyprus and (currently threatening) Sri Lanka. The holding of passports is no guarantee of national loyalty. There needs to be genuine commitment to the constitution, and existing arrangements governing the separation of society and the state. Failure to grasp this has been a major defect in the arguments for multiculturalism, which encourage a separation mentality, and separatism, which explicitly preaches partition. Moreover, fears about constitutional integrity provide those who favour a policy of repatriation with one of their most appealing arguments. A commitment to integration may well be the last safeguard of agreement and understanding across ethnic barriers.

It is impossible to say how far the principle of integration enjoys popular support. Since, as I have said, the public have never been consulted about what *kind* of multi-ethnic society they prefer, we do not know in any objective sense how popular is *any* of the alternatives I have proposed. However, it would be a mistake to assume that integration might appeal only to the majority. My own postbag and wide-ranging contacts within the minorities suggests cross-racial support. The flavour of minority support is echoed in these words of Mr Nirji Deva who, as I write, is the Conservative parliamentary candidate for Hammersmith:[14]

> . . . We need a policy which encourages further integration. Teaching Bengali in Bradford does not unite, it separates . . . we were not dragged here against our will and there is therefore no moral obligation on this country to treat us differently. We have to swim for ourselves. Given time and effort we will prosper.

References

1. G. Dench, *Minorities in the Open Society*, Routledge and Kegan Paul, London (1986)
2. G. Partington, 'Is the Core Sound?' *Quadrant*, November (1980)
3. Lord Swann, *Education for All*, Report of the Committee of Enquiry into the Education of Ethnic Minority Children, HMSO, London, March (1985)
4. T. Sowell, *The Economics and Politics of Race*, William Morrow, New York (1983), p. 202
5. F. Fanon, *Black Skin, White Masks*, Pluto Press, London (1986)
6. Sowell, *op. cit.*, pp. 247–8
7. G. Partington, 'Attitudes towards Ethnic Groups', *Quadrant*, January–February (1981)
8.

9. Sowell, *op. cit.*
10. H. Brotz, 'Multiculturalism in Canada: A Muddle', *Canadian Public Policy* (1980)
11. Partington, *op. cit.*
12. 'Islam and Human Rights', *The Free Nation*, June (1986)
13. K. Roden, *The Middle East Situation*, Unpublished paper, June (1986)
14. *Sunday Telegraph*, 19 April 1987

CHAPTER 3

Special Needs Versus Human Capital

Nothing in parts II and IV shall render unlawful any act done in affording persons of a particular racial group access to facilities or services to meet the special needs of persons of that group in regard to their education, training or welfare, or any ancillary benefits (Race Relations Act 1976, part VI, section 35).

More broadly, Hong Kong underscores the point that the 'Human Capital' in the general populace is crucial to economic development (Thomas Sowell, *The Economics and Politics of Race*).

These two quotations encapsulate a debate central to race relations. The 1976 Act makes it clear that ethnic minorities are to be regarded as people having legal rights to special treatment. Moreover, the term 'welfare', which would be very difficult to define in law and in practice, suggests that these special needs can refer to a very wide range of provisions. This has been made clear by the decision of several local authorities and public bodies. For instance, a housing association has advertised for a 'black lawyer', a description which clearly involves racial criteria and which excludes the great majority of potential applicants. An LEA sent a group of British/West Indian juvenile delinquents on holiday to their parental country of origin. Interpreters have been installed in hospitals to assist those immigrants who do not speak English. The underlying assumption is that the population is to be regarded as two broad groups; ethnic minorities and the majority. Minorities have claims on public provision over and above those of other citizens. It is important to point out that the word 'race' as used in this Act has been interpreted in very broad terms by the Law Lords. 'Sikhism', which in dictionary definitions and common usage is a religious appellation, has, for purposes of the Act, been interpreted as a racial epithet. Thus

Sikhs, by virtue of being Sikhs, could be regarded as having 'special needs'. Although 'reverse discrimination' is held to be illegal in Britain, in practice, the 'special needs' section of this Act has sanctioned policies which favour the minorities and exclude the majority.

This view of ethnic minorities, although now the official, public and legislative response to Britain's 'multi-ethnic society', is not shared by all. There is a considerable literature, mainly from the USA, which holds that this view is unwise. It encourages welfare dependency, creates conflicts within the minority groups as to which is most disfavoured and so deserving of most benefits, and tends to produce resentment in the majority population. Moreover, it inevitably creates race-relations bureaucracies which have vested interests in their own aggrandisement, and it may well exacerbate racial differences, since many majority people suffer from social deprivation but are given no special consideration. Thomas Sowell has been a noted exponent of this viewpoint. I should say at once that the 'Human Capital' thesis has nothing to do with race. It is *not* a genetic concept. Sowell—who is black—argues that the key factor in a group's economic, social and political progress is its own culture and value system. Thus attitudes to education, skill training, discipline, organisational talents, foresight, frugality, delayed gratification of wants and good health are all factors that crucially influence the fortunes of minorities. Sowell illustrates his view with international examples. For instance, the Chinese in South-east Asia, the Japanese and the West Indians in the USA and the Jews everywhere are all examples of minority groups who have suffered from exploitation and cruelty. However, history shows they have achieved considerably better levels of socio-economic progress than other minorities, and a key factor in explaining variations is human capital.[1]

This is a very broad and over-simple outline of what are several complex arguments, but it points up the essential differences between the two approaches. What I should like to do now is to examine these arguments. This is necessary for two reasons; there has been a conspicuous lack of such debate in Britain; and policy decisions have been made without these arguments being properly weighed. Both public opinion and legislation have been created against a background of very little informed debate.

Group Entitlements

To the layman the notion of a right inheres in the individual. Thus the right to safety from personal attack or abuse or to have one's personal property respected are normally conceived as being personal rights accruing from our generally accepted definition of the ordered society. However, groups also have legal rights. Commercial companies, for instance, can enlist the help of the courts in protecting their rights over their own products; local councils can sue anyone who casts aspersions on the area for which they are responsible; and voluntary associations may take action against any person or organisation that seeks to violate the established rules of the body in question. Until fairly recently the groups tended to be in some sense formally established, and were publicly recognised as having an obvious group identity. However, there is an increasing tendency now for new groups of various kinds to emerge—ethnic groups, the handicapped, homosexuals, women—and these tend to claim specific and exclusive rights. They are also inclined to pursue their claims through the courts—although this is more true of the USA than it is of Britain. Moreover, both individuals and groups are, in their relationship with the state, increasingly subject to official regulations. Thus both legal process and bureaucracy play an increasing part in the life of society. This development has met with opposition. Various interests in Britain have claimed that these developments are inimical to individual and corporate liberties. Decentralisation, private initiative and freedom of contract, and the openness of the marketplace have all been urged in attempts to keep courts and government from encroaching on individual and group autonomy. However, the creation and maintenance of the Welfare State as both the embodiment of society's compassion and, increasingly, the benchmark of electoral popularity is now a major feature of social and political life in the modern world, and the Welfare State inevitably means more, not less, regulation. In order to establish ground-rules for ordering its relationship with the citizen, particularly in the matter of welfare benefits, the government has had increasing recourse to legislation. There is now massive documentation in this area. Moreover, this contemporary trend tends to encourage litigious individuals and groups to assert their rights in the courts. My morning newspaper contained a news item about a group of squatters who have occupied a house for sale. They affixed a notice to the door proclaiming that the 'squat' is protected by section 6 of the Criminal Law Act 1977, and that anyone trying to evict the squatters without a court order could be prosecuted and fined up to £2,000 or imprisoned for six months. A spokesman for the squatters is reported to have said, 'You have to know the legal situation otherwise people take advantage of you'.

As mentioned above, this tendency to invoke the notion of rights as legal entitlements is more pronounced in the USA than in Britain. In the USA, for instance, the idea that ethnic-minority groups have rights that are rooted in history has had considerable success. If an ethnic group can show that a present disadvantage or loss of property or land is the result of past actions by the majority population's ancestors then they may well have legitimate access to the courts to right their grievance. For instance, a claim by present members of the Passamaquoddy Indian tribe in Maine regarding land allegedly taken from their ancestors has still not been resolved. A preliminary judgment has given present members of the tribe money and undeveloped land as compensation.[2] This arrangement has two consequences. It brings into question the private property rights—as well as market values—of current land and property owners, and it foreshadows disputes among the claimant groups about who is eligible to share in the tribes' largesse and its further investment. Ultimately, this tendency may well tell against the basic coherence of society. By permitting groups to employ litigation to resolve disputes the state may well be encouraging the population to fragment along ethnic lines, and court decisions will tend to reinforce this. The concept of the integrated society with every individual loyal to a national consensus is thus undermined.

Although the British are a very different multi-ethnic nation from the USA, nevertheless, the notion of ethnic group rights is very much part of their race relations rhetoric. The commitment of the ILEA to ethnic rights, for instance, has issued in a public avowal that, in principle, ethnic-minority children have the right to be educated in the mother-tongue of their parents; section 11 of the Local Government Act 1966 explicitly accepts the special needs of minority groups by allowing specific Exchequer grants to local authorities in areas with certain minimum levels of New Commonwealth and Pakistani citizens; and, as we have seen, section 35 of the Race Relations Act 1976 embodies the idea of special group entitlements for minorities.

Special Needs As Equality

. . . Racial criteria are not necessarily the right standards for deciding which applicant should be accepted by law schools . . . neither are intellectual criteria, nor indeed any other set of criteria. The fairness and constitutionality of any admission programme must be tested in the same way. It is justified if it serves a proper policy that respects the rights of all members to be treated as equals but not otherwise.

This view, expressed by Ronald Dworkin,[3] has been immensely influential. The notion of equality of outcome to which it inevitably points, for instance, has had a direct effect on those who drew up the Race Relations Act 1976, and its essence is constantly repeated by officers and supporters of the CRE. It is significant that the joint British–American conference organised by the Commission in 1982 resulted in a book whose sub-title was *Achieving Equality in the US and Britain*. Wherever the CRE wishes to illustrate the existence of racial discrimination it always points to inequality of ethnic outcomes in, for instance, jobs, housing and education.

Central to this notion of equality is the belief that people are intrinsically equal both as individuals and groups. The fact that we see great variations in socio-economic status, academic performance and crime is all due to the failure of the established political system to treat people as equals. The social processes which people experience are inherently unfair and divisive. Certain groups are favoured, others disfavoured.

However, one wonders where the justification for this arises. Apart from the religious notion that all are equal in the sight of God, the striking outcome of research into human endowments and attributes is the essential inequality of men. There is now overwhelming acceptance that, as individuals, human beings are born with wide variations in, for instance, intellectual capacities. Any standard psychological text shows this. Physical attributes show a similar pattern, as do personality factors. Therefore the notion that individuals start off equally endowed is clearly fallacious. It follows that even if we had a system whose absolute impartiality could be guaranteed, there would inevitably be wide variations in outcomes. The reasons for this initial inequality form the subject, of course, of perennial dispute. Genetics, constitution and environment have all been supported separately or in varying combinations as the key factors. However, since the question is closely connected with the protagonists' *a priori* ideological position, the argument is more notable for its endless convolutions and special pleading than for its ability to illuminate.

However, the egalitarians are on firmer ground historically. It is obvious that individuals born into families belonging to favoured groups in terms of housing, space, leisure time, exposure to high culture, as well as better health provision have a better chance than less-favoured people to develop potential and do well in the world. It is a simple fact that some groups *have* been unusually disadvantaged for long periods of their history. Slavery, for instance, undoubtedly imposed a terrible burden on black people, and cruel and dismissive attitudes from white masters helped to suppress their human potential and progress. It could be argued that this historic drawback can only be put right by assuming that black people have a special need for favoured treatment in the contemporary world. This argument in favour of reparation for past injustices is again a major theme in the race-relations rhetoric. Equality of opportunity now involves privileged inequality of treatment to bring blacks up to the same level as whites. Equality can be achieved only by a policy of reverse discrimination with favoured education and training opportunities for blacks and quota systems to ensure proportionate socio-economic and educational ethnic representation.

This line of argument has a certain appeal. It enables the guilt that many white people undoubtedly feel about slavery to be discharged and governments to claim that they are in the forefront of civil rights and concern for the underdog. Other black nations can be appeased. The UN and the EEC would undoubtedly approve. Also, assuming that the policy works, the lowering of gaps between whites and blacks would tend to remove the resentment that fuels anti-social attitudes and social conflict.

However there are several flaws in this argument, and these may be summarised as follows. Reparation for past wrongs is unlikely to have a continuing appeal to public opinion. Time tends to cancel memories and the feelings associated with them. Slavery, for instance, has no part in the memory of the indigenous white population and, as an increasingly number of blacks are born in Britain, it is not part of the family experience of West Indians. Colonialism, of course, is, to some extent. However, whether it actually diminished or enhanced the development of colonial peoples is a matter of intense and continuing controversy. The attempt to justify special needs on the basis of colonial oppression is likely to appeal only to the political left. It is unlikely to receive support from the population as a whole.

Historic wrong as a means of explaining current inequalities is based on a selective view of the minorities concerned. It might be argued with regard to black people, but it is clearly violated by the success of many other groups who have suffered oppression for centuries (for example, South-east Asian Chinese and Jews).

Transforming a philosophical or ideological commitment to equality into actual policy decisions can involve a conflict of rights and a possible increase in racial animosity. For instance, the attempt to enforce ethnic equality in America's law schools, as exemplified by the Bakke case in July 1978, led to considerable public reaction against the whole notion of the quota system and is unlikely to have improved race relations. Moreover, admitting blacks to higher education or professional training with lower entrance qualifications than competing whites has two unfortunate consequences: resentment from the excluded whites and those, probably the majority, who support them; and the stigmatising of able blacks as people given privileged treatment in the selection process.

The supporters of the equality argument do not define the meaning of this term. Does it mean proposed equality of opportunity or retrospective equality of statistical results? Equality as equal shares or equality as ethnic representativeness in jobs, housing and education? In practice, the two very different notions are confused: if there are X per cent in blacks or browns in the population then there must be X per cent of the various outcomes; and if there is not, this *itself* proves discrimination. This ignores the other non-racial variables involved. Age structure, fertility rates, geographical location, national and cultural background and length of residence, as well as personal choice, have all been shown to affect outcomes in housing, jobs and education. Also, attempts to demonstrate discrimination by sending prospective employers imaginary applications which differ only in ethnicity suffer from an obvious defect—they ignore employers' fears of the CRE and the prospect of damaging industrial tribunal cases if it is proposed to sack an unsatisfactory black worker.

The assumption that inequality of outcome proves inequality of treatment ignores two demonstrated counter-arguments. In some areas ethnic minorities are over-represented. For instance, Asians in Britain often do better even than whites in terms of owning houses and running one-man businesses; blacks are often superior in league football, world athletics and professional boxing. Second, outcomes reflect personal decision-making. Given the *same* opportunities, people make *different* choices, and these can vary systematically along ethnic lines. Cultural beliefs have been shown repeatedly to influence personal and group decision-making. Child-rearing practices, for instance, display marked differences between the West Indian and Asian communities in Britain, as do patterns of crime, use of leisure time and religious affiliations. People are not, within the confines of a free and open society, passive victims of their own fate. They appear to be active, self-directing organisms. Their achievement of equal outcomes would mean not only an increase of ethnic participation in certain areas of life but also its decrease in others—processes which could be achieved only by compulsion. This is made more complex, since there are significant socio-economic and educational variations *within* each broad ethnic group. Thus, viewed collectively, within the Asian groups in Britain we find that Bangladeshis do significantly less well in school than other Asians; East African Asians perform better in socio-economic terms and are collectively over-represented in the middle classes. Although there appears to have been little attempt to identify variations *within* the West Indian community there may well be systematic variations according to island of origin. Unravelling these quirky, inconsistent socio-economic patterns would raise difficult questions about the state's right to impose equality.

Imperial Guilt

If you want to understand British racism, and without understanding no improvement is possible, it is impossible to begin even to grasp the nature of the beast unless you accept its historical roots—unless you see that four hundred years of conquest and looting, centuries of being told that you are superior to the fuzzy-wuzzies and the wogs leave their stain on you all—that such a stain seeps into every part of your culture, your language and your daily life; and that nothing much has been done to wash it out.

This view, expressed by the Anglo-Indian writer Salman Rushdie,[4] is a constant theme in race-relations rhetoric. It forms, for instance, the sub-text in countless articles published in the CRE's three journals, *Education Journal, Employment Journal* and *New Community*. The Open University text *Race in Britain* also faithfully reflects it and the whole of the anti-racist enterprise leans heavily on its presuppositions. It is no exaggeration to say that imperial guilt and the need to expiate it through the according of privileged treatment of those British citizens who originate in the former British Empire has played a crucial part in determining both the climate of opinion and official responses. As mentioned above, the two major television productions on the Empire in recent years — those of Basil Davidson and Ali Masrui—both faithfully conveyed this notion.

Although few would want to sympathise with Rushdie's tone of accusation and unrelenting and unforgiving bitterness, there is, no doubt, an element of truth in what he says. The British—or at least some of them—did lord it over their subject peoples and act in insensitive and arrogant ways. They did create artificial countries by drawing lines on maps that ignored profound historical cultural and tribal differences. They did create a literature of jingoism. All that is true, but whether it comes near to expressing a whole or a balanced view of the truth is open to doubt. Perhaps we are yet too near the Empire to judge. Any attempt to achieve that sense of impartiality and detachment which are the essence of good history would presumably have to reflect the positive as well as the negative side of colonialism.

The wars of the imperialists (against, for instance, the Ashanti, Kaffirs, Afghans, Mohmands, Zulus, Boers, Egyptians and many more) would need to be balanced against the *Pax Britannica* which gave the world an unwonted security during the long reign of Queen Victoria. The arrogance of some Christian missionaries would need to be assessed beside their sincere concern for those they perceived as being in need of medical treatment, schooling and material support. The destruction of many native constructions and artefacts would presumably need to be weighed against the benefits to all which accrued from the Suez Canal, the Aswan Dam, the Ganges Canal, the Grand Indian Peninsular and the Canadian Pacific Railways. Also the motives of men as complex and varied as Gordon, Livingstone, Rhodes, Kitchener, Baden-Powell, Cromer, Curzon, Lugard, Milner and Fisher—all personifications of Empire at its zenith—as well as their intentions and behaviour would presumably require rather more perceptive and thoughtful analysis than Rushdie's barely concealed loathings could have hoped to provide. We should need a rather more imaginative and sensitive vision to explain why and how in the year 1900 the 41 million citizens of Britain ruled a foreign empire of some 400 million, extending over an area of 11,288,000 square miles. Nor would it be unreasonable to ask about the positive part played by the colonialists in the establishment and maintenance of the rule of law, increased affluence, parliamentary democracy and the controlling of historic intolerence among the subject peoples.

The concept of ethnic special needs, then, takes much of its force or direction from the fashionable notion that a post-imperial people needs to renounce the guilt attaching to its forefathers' behaviour. This can be easily dressed in liberal clothing. Concern for the underdog, shame about past sins and the determination to put matters right are all commendable responses that can be and are projected as liberal and humanitarian, but this is only one aspect. Imperial guilt and attacks on the whole imperial enterprise as capitalist expolitation are, of course, central tenets of the political left. The presence in our midst of former subject peoples has provided them with a field day. Concerns in this matter can be dramatised every day. Any attempt to stop illegal immigrants, to reduce the queues of immigrants at Heathrow Airport by introducing a visa system or to arrest a black suspect are acts that allow the political left a godsent opportunity to create propaganda and incite the minorities. Imperial guilt and the need to expiate it are now powerful weapons in the class war—'racism' and its overthrow have been seized upon by the left not only to justify the satisfaction of 'special ethnic needs' but also to argue for profound institutional and structural changes in society. As someone has said, 'Where Liberals sow, Radicals reap.'

'The Cultural Cringe'

This demotic expression conveys an important idea. It refers to the tendency among Western intellectuals and opinion-formers to view both their own and exotic cultures in highly selective ways. One's own culture always evokes a negative critical response; exotic cultures are perceived as more positive, more attractive and, thanks to the insensitive carryings on of Western imperialists and anthropologists, more worthy of respect than Western societies. This attitude in Britain appears to be rooted in three influences:

(1) The reaction against 'cultural imperialism' which, using political and economic power, spread and exalted the values and habits of a colonial as against a native culture;

(2) The strain of hostility to all things British, characteristic of a particular part of the English upper class—a phenomenon George Orwell noted in the early 1940s, and which found post-war expression in the treachery of Burgess, Maclean and Blunt;

(3) The tendency in modern anthropology to glorify cultures of a pre-industrial kind. Although this can be traced to Jean-Jacques Rousseau and his influence, and the cultural fieldwork we associate with Malinowski, it has taken on a distinctive and very influential form in recent years. According to Roger Sandall,[5] exponents of this version of anthropology lack objectivity. Rather than seeking understanding of another culture by approaching it with an open mind, they are impelled rather by a desire to confirm their own political or ideological hopes. This causes distortions of perception. Thus: 'The laughable must be made grave; the repellent must be made somehow endearing; and the downright revolting must be swathed in a language so latinate and extraordinary, that it is often hard to know exactly what is going on. Words like sacred, sacral, and ritualistic may be called on to produce a vaguely sanctifying effect; and if this is successful, then plain speaking about African tribal life will always seem tasteless and usually irreverent as well.'

These three elements have coalesced to produce an important strand in the movement for the 'special needs of minorities' in Britain. Those advisers to LEAs who write policy documents connected with multi-ethnic education and anti-racism are, for instance, solidly behind the validity of the cultural cringe. I remember, for example, as head of a multi-ethnic school in Bradford, the reverence I was supposed to feel for the culture of Pakistan. The experts constantly insisted on the importance of 'celebrating their culture'. However, when, referred to its aspects I found repugnant

— the treatment of women, male dominance, the mutilation of criminals, ritual slaughter, the suppression of political dissidents this was always regarded as being insensitive. The necessity for what the anthropologist Nigel Barley[6] calls 'a dreadful piety' was taken as read, as was the necessity for a highly critical response to one's own culture.

In that particular context the cultural cringe seemed a particularly inappropriate response. The children concerned were over-whelmingly British-born; their parents so approved of Britain that they had rejected their own country of origin in order to enjoy its benefits. In any case, Pakistani Moslem culture was flourishing out of school, thanks to the freedom all British citizens enjoy. Although the cultural cringe enabled the supply-side experts in the state education service to support their notion of special ethnic needs, it had unfortunate effects on cross-racial relationships. It tended to set up a kind of false reverence and made relaxed, unselfconcious interactions more difficult. There was a constant and probably un-justified fear that one might tread on someone's cultural toes. It emphasised differences of culture and skin colour. Humour was avoided for fear of giving offence. Relations generally were falsified.

An important aspect of the cultural cringe is its relationship with Marxism. Each shares a Manichean view of the world. Only slight alterations in the scenario are necessary for each to accommodate to the other's concepts and language. The exotic and the primitive peoples of the world are clearly easy to identify with the poor and oppressed proletariat. The suspicion of Western intellectuals trans-lates conveniently into detestation of the bourgeoisie, and the alleged destruction of indigenous cultures by Western intruders is a perfect analogue of the exploitation of the Western masses by rapacious and cruel capitalists. These elements merge effortlessly in the left-wing view of the so-called Third World, which is presented in student textbooks not as the result of a formerly colonised people's successful push for independence but as a product of con-tinuing capital exploitation. It is no accident that the most vociferous exponents of the special needs thesis have a consistent tendency to be on the far political left.

A more balanced view of Western development and achievement and of the relationship of the West with former colonies, would, one feels, show just how hollow and dishonest is the cultural cringe:[7]

If the day of the missionary is past, one is less certain that the day of the self-denigrating pilgrim is also past; but it should be. Those who come into dialogue with non-Western cultures in a state of uncritical admiration for what they find there, and of masochistic disavowal of their own cultural heritage are unlikely to obtain a serious hearing and deserve none. A reasoned stand for the human achievements of Western civilisation including the monumental achievement of parliamentary democracy is long overdue.

These elements, then, underlie the case for 'special needs'. The notion of group rights for past wrongs, equality, imperial guilt and the cultural cringe can all be found forming, as it were, the sub-text of the literature on special needs. However, their influence is often rationalised as concern for the adjustment and welfare of immigrants. Thus the reluctance of pregnant Asian ladies to be seen by male doctors, the necessity for ritual slaughter in the diet of Moslem schoolchildren, the desire of parents to send their children back to the Indian subcontinent in term time, the supposed need of British-born Caribbean youngsters to validate their identity by spending time in the West Indies, the refusal of immigrants to learn English can all (and many more) be projected as 'special needs'. Whether immigrants and their descendants actually progress better through this approach is doubtful. No previous generations of immigrants to Britian has been presumed to have 'special needs', yet the Irish, the central Europeans and the Jews all appear to have flourished.

I said at the beginning of this chapter that the concept of special needs has the effect of dividing the population. There are those with 'special needs' (the ethnic minorities) and those without (the majority). 'Special needs', then, implies a distinctive view of the nature of a multi-ethnic society. It implies a 'tossed salad' image rather than a 'melting pot'. Each group's distinctiveness is to be maintained and at public expense. The ideal of an integrated society with all loyal to a national ideal is thus subverted. The only way in which the 'special needs' thesis can be operationalised is through the mechanism of reverse discrimination. The damage this can produce is well caught by the following quotation based on a thorough analysis of the US experience:[8]

The US has become equivocal about its identity. On the one hand America is seen as a 'melting pot' where ethnic and racial differences are lost in the consciousness of being an American united with one's fellow citizens by common principles and values. This view of essential homogeneity dominated the public mind until the 1960s. Since then many have come to regard America as an aggregation of distinctive nationalities and races, a 'tossed salad' rather than a 'melting pot'. Colour consciousness and, in the case of Spanish-language conscious policies, reinforced the image of society as essentially heterogenous. The United States is a potential Belgium, Quebec, or worse yet, Lebanon. The UK begins with a more nearly racially, ethnically and linguistically homogeneous society and thus some of the more frightening possible consequences of racial preferences in the US may not be as likely there *if the temptation to positive discrimination policies can be resisted* (emphasis in original).

I would want to argue that the CRE's commitment to the notion of 'special needs' inescapably means reverse discrimination. No one who has studied the way the Race Relations Act 1976 actually operates and who has looked at the steadily increasing funding going to ethnic minorities under section 11 of the Local Government Act 1966 can doubt that. The CRE's submission to the Home Secretary in 1985 (*Review of the Race Relations Act 1976—Proposals for Change*) says that 'An employer should be entitled where there is under-representation in the work force (as defined in section 38) to carry out a policy of preferring a member of that group for employment in the narrowly confined situation where competing applicants are equally well qualified'.

The Case For a 'Human Capital' Approach

Whereas 'special needs' policies lead to intervention by the state and its agencies in the form of specific monetary support for ethnic minorities, the 'human capital' approach believes in the power of the group's own character and value system to produce socio-economic progress and a place in the power structure. The efficacy of this approach will, of course, depend crucially upon the position of ethnic minorities with regard to human rights. It would be particularly persuasive, for instance, in Britain, since all its citizens enjoy civil liberties, equality under the law, access to the Welfare State and the education system, and the franchise. Equally clearly, the 'human capital' approach could hardly be appropriate for, say, Apartheid South Africa, where there are horrifying imbalances in the distribution of public goods and basic human freedoms. However, having said that, we have to note that the history of minority groups throughout the world is remarkable for the number of occasions that the victimised and the exploited have overcome their disadvantages and flourished. Essentially, the case for 'human capital' arises from historical and comparative studies of the progress of different minority groups. The leading exponent of this view is Thomas Sowell. He has looked in great detail at many groups who have suffered discrimination from exploiting and sometimes cruel despotisms, and has also studied the variations in socio-economic progress of the various immigrant groups that have settled over the centuries in the USA. Two broad conclusions emerge from Sowell's work: (1) human groups have an astonishing capacity for overcoming disadvantage; and (2) different groups appear to vary systematically in their capacity for using and exploiting to their advantage the environment in which they live out their lives. In economic terms, human capital has often played a much more important role in the progress of the people than material wealth:[9]

> Poverty-stricken Italian immigrants who went to poverty-stricken Argentina, in the nineteenth century, made both the country and themselves much more prosperous. Chinese immigrants, with little more than the clothes on their backs, have entered South East Asia—often on foot—and proceeded to create economic advancement for both the native populations and themselves. Germans, too poor to pay their passage to eighteenth century America, nevertheless, after years of unpaid work as indentured servants, went out to the undeveloped frontier and built prosperous farming communities up and down the great valleys of the Eastern United States.

The ability to use those qualities of vision, hard work, self-discipline, thrift and neighbourliness which ensured success does not necessarily depend upon personal merit. Accidents of geography, climate and history can play a vital part. Tropical peoples, for instance, often lack human capital, because of their exposure to debilitating diseases due to the hot climate, as well as the disincentive to effort caused by suffocating heat and humidity. Some people start life with great drawbacks. The key question is, how best are the advantages of human capital which generates the wealth to pay for help for the disadvantaged, spread across populations? Is it best to reward the exercising of human capital, to provide incentives to those who work hard, to produce economic benefits for all, or to engage in a process of redistribution of existing wealth by the state? The latter approach is often justified as an attempt to overcome a circle of poverty—as 'social justice'. The assumption is that those who have wealth must have acquired it by disreputable means or through unfair advantage. Giving money and material benefit to the poor is both morally justified and economically desirable, so it is held. Political dogma is often used as the rationalisation. However, the evidence for the economic benefits of redistribution is hardly convincing. The history of foreign aid since the Second World War does not sustain the case for redistribution. Although rulers may gain short-term political advantages from acting against those with human capital resources, this never adds to the countries' long-term economic benefit or necessarily improves human rights. As Sowell[10] says:

> Much of the poverty, stagnation and even retrogression found in the Third World countries is not the result of an inevitable, vicious circle of poverty for which dramatic aid programmes or draconian domestic policies are the only cures. Indeed, a substantial part of the current efforts of the rulers and Government of such countries often consist of repressing, impeding or even driving out of the country, those who possess the human capital to develop it.

Tanzania is a good example of this. It has received more foreign aid than any other country, yet its output declined 50 per cent over a decade. By 1975 nearly half the 'rationalised' companies seized by the state were bankrupt. Bureaucracy had massively increased, and political persecution and forcible transfer of parts of the population became an accepted part of policy. Much of the tolerance for this kind of obvious failure is linked to the Western fashion for cultural relativism. Reluctance to accept that some cultures are more effective than others (in this context better in terms of their capacity to generate material prosperity and civil rights) means that non-Western cultures are often and rather patronisingly provided with ready-made excuses for these obvious corruptions. No nation or group can grow to maturity until it has learnt to cope with and interpret (and incorporate into its body politic) negative feedback from others, and self-criticism never develops when others constantly provide rationalisations for culpable failures. Human capital implies responsibility for oneself; special needs or 'social justice' tends to erode this attitude and replace it with dependency and expectations of a providing state. Denial of the validity of the human capital principle in explaining the progress of minorities — and the consequent commitment to special needs or 'social justice'—can involve considerable costs. It tends to polarise populations, which in social terms are living cheek by jowel, into the haves and the have-nots. Unfortunately, these basic categorisations often conceal detailed variations across communities. Thus while there may, in general terms, be more poverty among, say, the black than the white communities in Britain, at the local level the reverse may be true. A district, for instance, may contain a high proportion of successful Asian entrepreneurs and a relatively high level of poor whites. This can create friction. The knowledge that racial minorities are regarded as having special needs (for example, in the social welfare and hospital services) and are receiving increased benefits can generate jealousy and resentment. It is very difficult for the authorities to maintain a reputation for even-handedness once the principle of 'special needs' has been accepted. Moreover, the inevitable political and bureaucratic forces created by this policy tend to emphasise rather than play down differences. Sowell has an apt observation: 'Preferential treatment of various racial and ethnic groups has produced political resentment and a growing racist extremist fringe in the United States. It has produced bloodshed in the streets of India.'[11]

In Britain the embodiment of the 'special needs' principle in legislation has led to the creation of anomalies which offend both logic and common sense. Although reverse discrimination and quota systems are said to be illegal, in practice both occur. Thus in Britain it is perfectly proper to advertise for a 'black lawyer' but it would be illegal to advertise for a white one. Employers may make more favourable arrangements for the training and welfare for ethnic minorities than for white employees, and they may make special efforts to recruit blacks and Asians, but may not do the reverse. The annual conference of the Black Section of the British Labour Party may exclude white journalists, but any organisation attempting to ban black journalists would be acting illegally. The case for quota systems—disguised, of course, by reference to 'representative numbers in the labour market'—is undermined by instances in which the minorities appear to be outdoing their indigenous counterparts. We have already referred to the fact that in some areas of work the minorities are, it seems, over-represented, a fact that not only undermines the case for quotas but illustrates the acute difficulties which would be involved in attempting to implement such a policy. The effect of ethnically based value systems and personal choice on outcomes in the labour market would have to be challenged and rejected, a process hardly likely to meet with public support.

Conclusion

This brief outline of the special needs versus human capital debate regarding the progress of ethnic minorities makes it clear that the case for special needs—now embodied in legislation in Britain —should not go by default. There ought to be a public debate on the matter. We have enough evidence, after a decade of the Race Relations Act 1976, to review our commitment to the doctrine of special needs. Do race relations actually benefit? Does the international evidence and the evidence garnered from the fact of previous influxes of immigrants into Britain support the case for special needs? Does it have public support? Does it actually help the minorities in the labour market, or does it create distortions in the selection process and resentment in the majority excluded groups? How far does the notion of 'representativeness' in the labour market—a key element in the 'special needs' argument—respect the free operation of the labour market?

These questions have had very little public airing in Britain, and they deserve to be raised.

References

1. T. Sowell, *The Economics and Politics of Race*, Willaim Morrow, New York (1983)
2. L. Liebman, 'Anti-discrimination Law: Groups and the Modern State', in N. Glazer and K. Young, *Ethnic Pluralism and Public Policy*, Heinemann, London (1983)
3. R. Dworkin, *Taking Rights Seriously*, Duckworth, London (1977)
4. S. Rushdie, quoted in 'Childcare Shapes the Future—the Need for Anti-racist Strategy', *Educational Journal*, Commission for Racial Equality, September (1984)

5. R. Sandall, 'The Rise of the Anthropologue', *Encounter*, March, p. 67 (1987)
6. N. Barley, *The Innocent Anthropologist*, Penguin Books, Harmondsworth (1984)
7. P. L. Berger, 'Democracy for Everyone', *Commentary*, September (1983)
8. K. M. Holland, 'The Recent American Experience: An Example to Avoid', in *Reversing Racism: Lessons from America*, The Social Affairs Unit, London (1984), p. 20
9. Sowell, *op. cit.*, p. 234
10. *Ibid.*, p. 235
11. *Ibid.*, pp. 253–4

CHAPTER 4

Multi-ethnic Education

Terminology

I have used the word 'multi-ethnic' several times, and we must now examine its meaning in more detail.

The type of education which is deemed to be appropriate to the changed ethnic composition of Britain's school population is not identified by a single, agreed term. The absence of consensus is very striking. In 1972 work for the National Foundation for Educational Research (NFER) by Townsend and Brittain referred to 'Multiracial Schools', while the same organization in 1974 published *Race, Schools and Community*, which referred to 'Education for a Multicultural Society'. David Milner's immensely influential *Children and Race*, published in 1975, says 'The education of black children in this country must be bi-cultural education', while the survey by Little and Willey issued for the Schools Council in 1981 speaks of 'Multi-ethnic Education'. In the same year, Maureen Stone's critical study *The Education of Black Children in Britain*, refers to 'Multiracial Education', a term repeated by the Schools Council in 1983, and by Murray and Dawson in their *Five Thousand Adolescents* in 1984 (copyright 1983). A review of the literature by Tomlinson in 1983 employs the term 'Multi-ethnic Education'. The second issue of the CRE's register of current research (1983) makes it clear that researchers use the term 'multiracial/multicultural/-multi-ethnic education' more or less indiscriminately. The 1984 report of the CRE speaks of 'multiracial education', while its 1985 report uses, but makes no distinction between, 'multiracial/-multicultural/anti-racist education'. In 1985 the Institute for Race Relations employed the circumlocution 'multicultural/multi-ethnic education'. The Swann Report plumps unequivocally for

73

'multicultural education'. The most recent text by Madan Sarup is entitled *The Politics of Multiracial Education* (1986).

This lack of agreement among academics, researchers and interested organisations is echoed among LEAs. Berkshire has an 'Advisory Committee for Multicultural Education'. The ILEA's policy, according to their issued documents on the subject, is directed to 'Multi-ethnic Education in Schools', while Bradford's *Towards an Education for All* refers to a 'multicultural curriculum' for education in a 'multi-ethnic society'. Job advertisements placed by Lancashire County Council refer to personnel for a 'multi-ethnic/multicultural education'.

A reading of the literature suggests that the confusion about an appropriate name might not be unconnected with a lack of clear thinking about the object to be named. A central problem is a consistent failure to distinguish between the concepts of race, culture and nation. I have already made some reference to race and culture, but in this context I wish to enlarge a little on what I have already said. In this way the term I select and the reasons for my doing so will be clear.

'Race' refers to a common inheritance and certain physical characteristics. The layman, for instance, will distinguish quite readily between the fair-skinned indigenous inhabitants of Europe, the black-skinned people of Africa, the people of the Orient and, say, Australian Aborigines, and he will tend to use physical attributes for his judgements. The anthropologist will want to argue that the physical features must be capable of being transmitted to descendants of people classified as a racial group; acquired characteristics such as the darkening of a white person's skin colour due to exposure to the sun, would not be passed on to descendants, and could not, therefore, be used as a racial index. Broad racial types have been distinguished, but there is considerable cross-racial reproduction throughout the world, and many people could not be accurately assigned to any racial category. The distinguished anthropologist Raymond Firth says: 'We see in the world today no pure races.'[1]

'Culture' is a term both complex and controversial, and the definer can play an important role in the definition provided. Thus an archaeologist will tend to refer to the material artefacts and the social behaviour deducible from them which can be discovered in the historical record. The collection of objects defined by a particular time and space can be thought of as the culture of a particular group. Sociologists speak of artefacts, world views, symbols and distinctive forms of behaviour such as ritual and worship distinctive of a group and transmitted across the generations. Language, religion and social and political customs are key elements in the culture of a people.

'Nation' is a concept referring to the awareness of a separate geographical identity and common political institutions. Like culture, and unlike race, it is an achieved thing with strong historical associations. Thus the British are a nation since they enjoy both geographical and political unity, a common economic and social life and legal system, and a code of agreed civil liberties. This consensus is articulated and perpetuated, in its formal elements, by the constitution, albeit an unwritten one — although some nations (for example, the USA) do have a written constitution.

Each of these notions is somewhat vague and difficult to pin down precisely, and common usage often confuses them. For instance, we can still observe instances where 'race' is used as a synonym of 'nation' — as in 'the inheritance of the British race' or 'the genius of the French race'. Again, 'race' and 'culture' are sometimes confused. Thus the Jews are often referred to as a race of people, which is misleading, since there is considerable physical variation according to place of origin. In Europe there are distinctive differences between northern and southern Jews, and there are Berber Jews, dark Italian Jews, Chinese Jews and the Black Falasha Jews of Ethiopia. In fact, Jews are more properly a cultural than a racial group, defined principally by common religion and traditions.

The difficulties involved in determining the boundaries of race, culture and nation are well illustrated by the legislation regarding minority groups in Britain. Whereas the key Act is the Race Relations Act 1976, the Law Lords have established that Parliament intended 'race' to refer to Sikhism — in the face of every known dictionary definition and against the opinion of both High Court and Appeal Court judges that Sikhism is a religion, and therefore a cultural rather than a racial notion.

However, if we adopt a *de facto* position and use the relevant literature, particularly the Swann Report and the policy documents of those local authorities involved, it becomes clear that a broad-ranging, umbrella term is necessary to describe the concept with which we are concerned. It is clear from the Swann Committee recommendations (pp. 767–76) that questions relating to race, culture and nation are all involved. Race and race relations are to become a significant, high-profile issue in the classroom; there is to be a new-fashioned curriculum created from a range of cultures; and anti-racism, a structural concept, is to operate not only to reform attitudes but to effect radical institutional change. The all-embracing nature of developments envisaged by Swann may be gauged from the following recommendation based on its key chapter, 'Education for All':

> The fundamental change that is necessary is the recognition that the problem facing the education service is not how to educate children of ethnic minorities but how to educate *all* children [original emphasis]. It is necessary to combat racism, to attack inherited myths and stereotypes, and the ways in which they are embodied in institutional practices . . . Multicultural understanding has to permeate all aspects of a school's work.

I suggest, therefore, that we need a word that encapsulates notions of race, culture and nation, and which reflects the totalist nature of the changes produced, i.e. ethnicity. This is by no means the perfect word — none such exists — but it is broader than any of the three separate concepts I have mentioned and includes elements of each. The appropriate term we need, therefore, is Multi-ethnic Education.

Curriculum

Multi-ethnic education is a curriculum concept in the sense that it is concerned with the content of education. Its various advocates have made it clear that all school subjects are to be recast and given a multi-ethnic character. The Schools Council, for instance, put forward the following very influential notion:[2]

> Multicultural Education for All pupils: The *permeation* [original emphasis] of all school curricula, materials and examinations with a multicultural perspective, to avoid presenting a solely white, Anglo-Saxon view of the world.

This same standpoint has been adopted by the Schools Council's successor, the Schools Curriculum Development Committee (SCDC) — a not-surprising instance of interquango agreement, since the same person, Alma Craft, has had charge of this aspect in both organisations. The same theme is reiterated in a series of booklets, *Race, Sex and Class*, issued in 1983 by ILEA; and the Council for National Academic Awards has made it clear that validation of courses requires a multi-ethnic perspective to be present in all proposals. Teacher-training institutions, after being admonished by the Rampton Committee, the House of Commons Home Affairs Committee and the CRE for a certain tardiness, have responded with commendable vigour. According to Professor John Eggleston, '. . . multicultural and multi-ethnic issues dominate the whole curriculum and this aspect of teacher training has become the most fully and comprehensively taught of all in most institutions'.[3] Therefore multi-ethnic education is all-pervasive and more or less obligatory.

However, it is a very difficult notion to come to grips with. Although the literature is marked by considerable enthusiasm and support for multi-ethnic education, it is extremely difficult to know precisely what this is. The most striking thing is the absence of agreed criteria. For instance, there appear to be no agreed, worked-out and rationally defensible reasons for the assembling of the new, reformed syllabus. There is much criticism of existing curricula along the lines of their being 'white, Anglo-Saxon', and sometimes 'Christian', but very little in the way of rational justification for *particular* changes.

This insecurity is mirrored in the Swann Report: 'This concept is far from being clearly defined and explained.' The second NFER review of research carried out for Swann says: '. . . The very lack of definition of multicultural education has permitted not only the widest theoretical interpretations and broadest policy objectives, but also a considerable mismatch between these and educational practice'. (This is typical educational jargon: it means 'the whole thing is an unconvincing mess'.) The West Indian researcher and sociologist, Maureen Stone,[4] has said 'Multiracial education is conceptually sound . . . its theoretical and practical implications have not been worked out'. Professor John Rex,[5] after looking at developments in four LEAs with large ethnic populations, concluded thus: 'There is no consensus on what multicultural education actually means.' Nor is there agreement on the possible effects of multi-ethnic education. Even Bhikhu Parekh,[6] who, among other things, is a Commissioner at the CRE, has ventured the following opinion regarding the relative educational failure of West Indian pupils:

> . . . The impact of the ethnocentric curriculum and text books is not as great as is sometimes suggested by those who have made them their chief targets. There is no evidence to show that they have held back black children, nor, conversely, that the so-called multicultural curriculum has improved their performance

The confusion is shared internationally. Tomlinson's review[7] points to studies of multicultural education in countries as diverse as the USA, Canada, Australia, Sweden, Israel, Fiji and Hawaii. One researcher (Bullivant) concluded:

> . . . In all cases studied immense confusion exists about what multiculturalism and multicultural education means. Definitions and conceptual models compete with one another . . . and, in general, a good deal of the curriculum is in a mess (p. 91).

In addition to specific doubts, more general reservations can be discerned from a reading of the literature, and these take the following forms:

(1) Multi-ethnic education is simply yet one more example of how an educational system obsessed with change can periodically produce irrelevant lame ducks. The collapse of a consensus among the political, bureaucratic and professional groups which run the state system—although not, it seems, among the public at large—about the school curriculum has created at least a partial vacuum at the heart of children's education. This has been filled by progressive and politicised 'subjects' such as Peace Studies, Development Studies, World Studies, Anti-sexism, etc. These do not reflect what most parents or teachers want but what various kinds of pressure groups approve of. Multi-ethnic education is of this nature.

(2) Multi-ethnic education violates public opinion regarding the necessity for minorities to adapt to the existing British consensus regarding cultural matters. Instead, an officially

approved, vacuous cultural mish-mash having no real intellectual coherence or practical shape is being foisted onto the
schools.

(3) Multi-ethnic education overemphasises 'culture', a term
difficult to pin down and which is associated with controversy.
There needs to be an emphasis not on content but on individual
attitudes and structural defects. It is the anti-racist attack on
those allegedly racist institutions which articulate and
perpetuate the *status quo* that matters. Multi-ethnic education
distracts attention from this crucial purpose.

(4) Multi-ethnic education is, itself, a subtle form of racism. Its
basic purpose is to 'buy off blacks' by pretending to include
parts of 'their culture' in the school curriculum. This is futile and
patronising. The educational system is being used to solve the
basically political issue regarding 'black identity'. Multi-ethnic
education is a disguised way of perpetuating white domination
under the guise of liberal notions and pluralism.

These views come from sources which span the Conservative
–Marxist spectrum of political affiliations, and from both majority
and minority spokesmen. However, they have done little to dampen
enthusiasm or prevent the inexorable advance of multi-ethnic prescriptions and practices. In a lengthy review of multi-ethnic
publications and videos a leading exponent, Gillian Klein,[8] speaks
of 'the publication explosion', and enthusiastically welcomes developments in social studies: 'There is a gratifyingly increased
multicultural perspective in mainstream professional journals on
education, librarianship, social work and sociology'. Indeed, the
multi-ethnic doctrines should have no limits: 'But the field of
multicultural education should have no boundaries.' This heady
rhetoric appears to have very little in the way of rational
justification—although in someone who is actually paid to disseminate the multi-ethnic gospel it is perhaps not surprising. I am re-
minded of the comment of a philosopher who has considered
multi-ethnic education: ' . . . Crudity of conception is already a
feature of the discussion of problems in this field.' In place of
analysis what we usually find in multi-ethnic advocacy is *a priori*
reasoning, prescription and exhortation.

Attempts at Theory

Although the debate on multi-ethnic education has been marked by much sound, fury and intellectual wrangling, there have been some attempts at providing some kind of rational basis. A number of academics have raised questions and proposed developments which deserve attention. Jeffcoate,[9] for instance, has written at great length on this question over many years. He believes that multi-ethnic education relates to attitude change rather than the acquiring of knowledge. Items from various parts of the world ought to be included in the curriculum; information about other cultures and races should be conveyed but should not be assessed against British criteria—a position of cultural relativism needs to be encouraged. He is dubious about using the curriculum to change black children's presumed low self-esteem, and insists that the curriculum is not principally a vehicle for 'anti-racism'. Multi-ethnic education is a form of moral education concerned with creating greater understanding across races and cultures and promoting equal opportunities. Perhaps the most interesting of Jeffcoate's points is that he believes that those pupils in schools who have racialist views should have the right to put those views and to be listened to. This is in sharp contrast to most other academics in the field, and conflicts directly with the 'no platform for racists' policy of the National Union of Students.

Williams[10] claims to have discovered, from a search of the literature, three different types of justification for multi-ethnic education. There is the 'technicist' approach, which emphasises equality of opportunity through the effective teaching of basic skills and improving of the pupil's self-esteem; the 'moral' approach, whereby prejudice and discrimination are made less likely through the use of appropriate material to promote active discussion among pupils; and the socio-political approach, which emphasises the function of the curriculum in creating the skills necessary to struggle for political rights.

Jeffcoate and Williams demonstrate that the paucity of cool heads on this subject is not absolute. The issue *can* be debated rationally and counter-arguments entertained. However, perhaps the most fundamental questions have been raised by Walkling, Zec and Partington. The first two are philosophers, the third an educational academic, historian and former head teacher of a comprehensive school.

Walkling[11] has tackled the problem of worthwhileness in judging items for inclusive in a multi-ethnic curriculum. Clearly, with so many different cultural groups now living in Britain there are bound to be disagreements about what changes in the curriculum ought to occur. There needs to be some kind of rational procedure, some agreed criteria for making defensible choices. This raises two key issues: what should be the changes in *content* and in *conceptual* or procedural differences in thinking? Since different cultural groups not only differ in what is valuable in the education of the young in terms of items of knowledge but also in ways of perceiving and conceptualising experience, each of these two intellectual aspects has to be considered in making practical curriculum decisions.

This gives rise to a series of pertinent questions. First, with regard to content there needs to be a debate about *tolerance* and *selection*: how far should all items judged valid by all relevant cultural groups be considered, and how far is some kind of selection required? Second, how should the modes of thought involved in education be influenced by variations across different ethnic groups: should there be a relativist or an absolutist position adopted, i.e. should we accept that there is no single way but many equally valid ones of conceptualising and thinking about the world, or can we accept the notion of a cross-cultural, generally applicable structure of thought and knowledge? Third, should the purposes of education be influenced by a desire to *transmit* the established culture or to *transform* it? These six conceptual categories—tolerance, selection, relativism, absolutism, transmission and transformation—produce the following eight-part matrix:

(1) Tolerant, Absolutist, Transmissionist;
(2) Selective, Absolutist, Transmissionist;
(3) Tolerant, Relativist, Transmissionist;
(4) Selective, Relativist, Transmissionist;
(5) Tolerant, Absolutist, Transformationist;
(6) Selective, Absolutist, Transformationist;
(7) Tolerant, Relativist, Transformationist;
(8) Selective, Relativist, Transformationist.

Each of these three-part alternatives can be applied to the curriculum to yield rationally determined (although not, of course, equally valid) decisions. Walkling considers item (5) to be the only truly valid set of criteria for determining the multi-ethnic curriculum. This enables items from different cultures to be included, allows the notion of general principles of rational thought and encourages variations in the curriculum in accordance with changes in society.

Zec[12] considers the part that relativism ought to play in producing a viable and sustainable form of multi-ethnic education. He distinguishes between a 'weak' and a 'strong' relativist position. A weak relativist position produces objectivity in judging other cultures and empathy or compassion in relating to its members. Strong relativism, with its emphasis on the internal, culture-bound nature of cultural criteria, tends towards separatism and a denial that different cultures can successfully flourish in the same educational system (the logical outcome of a strong version of relativism is educational separatism or Apartheid). Ironically, much of the talk about 'celebrating cultural diversity' comes from those who favour integrated schools but are strong relativists. The Swann Report, for instance, appears to endorse the Schools' Council commitment to the principle 'cultures should be empathetically described in their own terms . . .' (Should one, one wonders, judge Apartheid culture in Boer terms?) Zec successfully exposes and rejects the irrationality of this position:

> It seems that to accept relativism is to accept the view that, in a multicultural society the only choice is between on the one hand the maintenance through education of a dominant culture (which is undesirable because élitist, anti-democratic, etc.), and on the other hand the institution of separate but equal educational programmes for the transmission of their cultures to co-existing cultural groups (which is also undesirable because it smacks of Apartheid).

That is, strong relativism produces not multi- but mono-ethnic education. To put the matter another way, without the possibility of universal maxims about the status of different cultural beliefs and practices, which enable judgements across cultures to be made, then no kind of harmonious cultural diversity is possible in the same society.

Now Walkling and Zec bring a cool, philosophical mentality to bear, and this is a very welcome thing. They help, as it were, to clear the air and compel us to depend not on emotional or political enthusiasm but on rational thinking. However, their accounts make assumptions about the necessity or desirability of multi-ethnic education which are not adequately demonstrated. For instance, each implicitly supports the notion that unless the schools reflect black and Asian cultures (for want of better terms), then the children concerned will feel rejected and lack self-esteem. Moreover, there is an underlying assumption that minority cultures can only be maintained through the formal schools system. The evidence for this assumption is not forthcoming, and it is explicitly denied by the experience of previous immigrant cultures in Britain such as the Irish, Jewish and central European ones which have always flourished out of school. Moreover, they give insufficient weight to the uniqueness of Britain's present multi-ethnic situation, and are perhaps too ready to see current developments simply as part of a continuous historical process.

Partington[13] has the benefit of living and working in Australia, a society in which notions about multi-ethnic matters are perhaps more developed than they are in Britain. The presence there of an indigenous ethnic minority—the Aborigines—has meant the development of a very influential multi-ethnic lobby. The spokesmen for this lobby espouse a version of multi-ethnic education that can be described as 'reactionary'. They argue that the skill of literacy and numeracy for ethnic minorities is a form of 'cultural genocide'. The authorities have a duty to enable Aborigines not to aspire to development but to cultural preservation within a separate social and political context. The controllers of Aborigine education should be Aborigines themselves, the curriculum being made up of items of knowledge and of beliefs grounded in Aborigine culture. A similar approach can be discovered in Canada with regard to Indians and Inuits.

Echoes of this can also be found in the multi-ethnic literature and actual practices in Britain. The 'Black Studies' promoted by ILEA, the provision by certain local authorities of official leaflets and forms in community languages and of halal meat in school dinners and the demand for teaching in the 'mother-language' all revert to what Partington has called 'a species of romantic primitivism', and he effectively underlines the contradictory position of its adherents. For instance, while certain multiculturalists decry the less-than-representative proportions of the ethnic minorities in prestigious jobs, they deny the value of an instrumental curriculum providing the skills necessary for entry into these jobs. He also makes clear the way in which professional self-interest, articulated as concern for the underdog, can function to promote ideas whose purpose is basically to create a demand for multi-ethnic 'experts'.

However, Partington is not averse to the principle of ethnicity applied to the curriculum. What he challenges is the idea that it should be a first-order consideration. A liberal education would first want to ensure that certain universal criteria are met before specific sectional interests are considered. Narrowness or ethnocentricity cannot be overcome, or challenged, by replacing one form of shortsightedness with another. If we include items in a curriculum *just because* they are of West Indian or Asian provenance we perpetuate the very thing to which we are assumed to be opposed. Ethnocentricity does not have to be Anglo-Saxon, it can focus on any culture.

People such as Walkling, Zec and Partington render a valuable service, since they make necessary conceptual distinctions, distinguish between reason and ideology and raise crucial questions.

Objections

Having considered problems of definition and some general objections to multi-ethnic education, and having pointed to the most fruitful theorists in the field, I now wish to list a number of objections that have occurred to me partly due to a reading of the literature but principally because of my practical experiences of working in multi-ethnic schools.

(1) The claim that established school curricula are narrowly Anglo-Saxon (a key weapon in the multi-ethnic education armoury and implicitly supported by Walkling and Zec) is questionable. The briefest look at any typical school curriculum will indicate a mosaic of influences. The Bible, for instance, is an essentially foreign influence taken over from the Jews. Literature and science have roots in Greek and Roman experience. Our mathematics has been influenced by Arabic notions imported after the Crusades. Geography syllabuses have always included the study of far-away places and exotic peoples. Our greatest dramatist provides experience of cultures and characters that lie far beyond the

everyday life of English people—consider *Julius Caesar, Othello, The Merchant of Venice* and *Hamlet*, and all that they represent in the way of other cultures and thought. The sympathetic portrait of Saladin, the Moslem hero, in history textbooks is familiar to anyone who has been through an English school. Art teaching has included exotic influence for generations, including the art of Africa, India, and the Near East,* and no one can accuse the English language of narrowness and rigidity; it is an amalgam of an astonishing range of influences. Robert Burchfield says:[14]

When one turns to vocabulary one cannot but be impressed by the amazing hospitality of the English language . . . Foreign words have been welcomed at all periods . . . Any good piece of modern English writing is likely to contain an even proportion of words of native and foreign origin . . .

This openness to the world ought not to surprise us. The historic role of Britons as seafarers, explorers and empire-builders has encouraged immensely powerful cross-cultural forces. The work of the great Victorian architects in India, the bringing together of English and Arabian cultures by Sir Richard Burton, of English and Indian influences by Rudyard Kipling, of English and Balinese music by Benjamin Britten and of English and Russian ballet are just a few indications of just how permeable British culture has been. A gradual process of absorption of influences has created an English school culture which, I could argue, is by no means egocentric. There is no reason to assume that the same process will not gradually absorb into the school curriculum our new ethnic cultures — without the benefit of either official 'policies' or professional self-interest.

   (2) Multi-ethnic advocacy inevitably tends towards demands for the community language to be both on the curriculum and the medium of instruction—the American experience with the Spanish-speaking community is a pointer here. Walkling says of his proposed curriculum model that it makes possible '[the] use of the mother tongue for initial instruction', and some LEAs already have Asian languages on the curriculum. Indeed, one Wolverhampton school not only has Punjabi on the curriculum, it is a compulsory subject.

* I owe this insight to Roger Scruton.

Now there undoubtedly is a case for community languages such as Punjabi, Urdu, Pushtu or Gujerati to be placed on the curriculum where there is parental demand and the resources are available. There are, however, obvious dangers. First, if we allow one community language as a school subject then we set a precedent for a demand for *all* such languages to be taught—and there are now probably at least 160 such languages currently spoken in Britain. If we accept only certain languages for inclusion, then we risk jealousy and resentment from those whose languages are not selected. Also, the prospect of teaching *all* such languages is an administrative nightmare, and the cost would be astronomic. The virtue of confining language teaching to the traditional ones (for example, French, German, Spanish, etc.) is that they are not associated with minority groups living in Britain, so there can be no inter-racial squabbling between different minority groups. Of course, precisely the same objections can be made of the multi-ethnic curriculum in general—whose cultures ought it to reflect and what about those cultures that, perhaps for practical reasons, are rejected? Have Caribbeans or Asians any greater right to see their community cultures reflected in the school curriculum than, say, the Irish, Poles, Hungarians or Jews—all of whom have substantial and established communities in Britain?

Teaching *in* the mother-language runs the risk of imprisoning ethnic minority children in their community language, and an uncertain grasp of English cuts people off from the whole social order, with all that that implies for ghetto mentalities. Language is fundamental to social integration and political unity, and history is filled with instances of serious conflicts over the issue of language. Britain's transformation into an astonishingly polyglot nation may mean, logically, a greater commitment to a common language, not a reduced one. (The language issue is considered in Chapter 7.)

(3) The multi-ethnic curriculum ignores a key influence in the child's development—housing patterns. Since the end of the dispersal policy, which aimed to create balanced multi-ethnic intakes as a microcosm of the general population, the tendency for schools to cater for mono-ethnic intakes has increased considerably. This is simply because immigrants and their descendants tend to congregate in the same district, and schools, due to the comprehensive system, have to reflect this. The possibility of either majority or ethnic-minority children absorbing wider cultural influences

through the medium of cross-racial friendships has been significantly reduced. If ethnic-minority children, attending increasingly mono-ethnic schools, are to cope with their bi-cultural realities and identities, then this argues for more, not less, emphasis on things British in the school curriculum. If you are an Asian child going to an all-Asian school (there are at least 20 such schools in Bradford alone, and their numbers are bound to increase rapidly) is it better to learn English cuisine or Indian, which you already know since your mother practises it every day in your home? If, in the name of multi-ethnic education, English schools fail to pass on such knowledge, where else will such a child acquire it? And what are the implications for such a failure for his capacity to cope with his British experience? Might not schools be functioning to create a ghetto mentality if attempts are not made via an essentially British curriculum to compensate for the lack of balance in the child's experience?

However, the dangers inherent in the creation of ghetto schools are not only not acknowledged by multi-ethnic advocates, some have actually applauded the development of schools separated by skin colour. A seminal influence in this field, the social psychologist David Milner,[15] say: 'So neighbourhood schooling is a prerequisite, whatever concentrations of black children in individual schools might result . . . But there is nothing wrong with black ghettoes.'

I find it difficult to understand the mentality which makes this kind of statement. Milner appears not to be aware that the very word 'ghetto' is pejorative, carrying associations of separation, confinement and rejection by a dominant culture. Of course, his enthusiasm for the comprehensive school might be connected with his support for the ethnic neighbourhood school, although how the cause of social harmony is to advance by a system which has served to emphasise rather than reduce the divisions of social class and which, according to Milner's aspirations, will now function to emphasise ethnic differences is difficult to see. Children in school learn a great deal from one another, not least how to get on together. How children raised in ethnically distinct schools (which, moreover, reject the integrating function of a common British curriculum in the name of 'cultural pluralism') are to feel part of the social order and cope with inter-ethnic relationships is also difficult to envisage.

Of course, no one is suggesting that people can be prevented from living anywhere they like in a free society. If ethnic groups choose to live together in distinct housing patterns, so be it. However, the consequences of that for the school curriculum seem to be the very opposite of those envisaged by the multi-ethnic educationists.

(4) Underlying much multi-ethnic rhetoric is the notion that unless ethnic-minority cultures are preserved and transmitted by the schools they will wither and die. This is to fly in the face of the evidence. The Irish, Jews and central Europeans are all examples of successful immigrant communities which have kept their original cultures alive and flourishing, without any attempt to see them self-consciously fostered in the state schools. Moreover, there is no evidence for public support for the state to promote foreign cultures in the schools. In truth, cultures can only live and continue in the social context in which they are practised. Can they be tagged onto, or absorbed into, existing cultures by government decree? How many teachers, or educational experts, does Britain have capable of mastering all the minority cultures that now exist so as to create a genuinely imported and representative cultural mosaic as the basis for the school curriculum? Perhaps the new cross-cultural curricula are to be fashioned by teams of experts from the different communities. One wonders how the Moslem and Hindu representatives on such a committee might wish to see the partition of India taught, or how slavery should be conveyed assuming a debate between a Jamaican and English academic. If the traditional principle of the minority cultures gradually *influencing* established curricula over time via local and informal school-based processes is to be replaced by some kind of official, prescribed formula, we can only hope that the committee responsible has better luck than the one that created a camel while aiming for a horse.

(5) Advocates of a multi-ethnic curriculum often appear unaware of the relationship between the formal educational process and the maintenance of social and political cohesion. Reflecting a diversity of cultural styles may appear to be both enriching and humane and, in principle, emminently defensible. What, however, of its predictable, consequential effects? Are established social institutions based on the principle of cultural pluralism, or do they proceed on the basis of a common public culture, with minority lifestyles being an essential, but private, matter? Do they not, for instance, assume a common, national language and access to a common set of presuppositions about procedures and beliefs in the management of

human needs? Is there not, for instance, an essentially Western, capitalist, mixed economy to which everyone has access either as worker, manager or investor? Could support for cultural pluralism permit, say, the introduction of Moslem notions about the evils of usury or the integration of state and society? How far can respect for diversity by the state through the schools system go, before the process becomes divisive?

This can be illustrated as follows. A school in a heavily Asian area with an all-Asian intake of pupils might well decide that its curriculum should be essentially Asian in character, with the culture, the language, the religion and the history of Pakistan providing the basis for curriculum selection. A sufficient number of schools will create pressure on the public examination boards to consent to this, and the GCSE, with its emphasis on school-based continuous assessment and a willingness to stress width in the curriculum, would tend to encourage this kind of development. Once this happens, such schools would function not to assist integration but to stress differences. Political loyalties would then become an issue. How far would the products of such schools feel any fundamental attachment to Britain, its traditions and institutions? This needs to be placed within a context in which immigrants from Pakistan continue to arrive and British-based Pakistanis are involved in regular contacts (including actual visits) to the homeland. Inevitably, this, in turn, means constant pressure on the existing British–Pakistani to reinforce the mother-culture rather than to adapt to the demands of life in Britain. The possibility of political aspirations being expressed through separate ethnic channels rather than through established cross-cultural parties and organisations is clearly enhanced through such a proces. How would that affect our sense of national unity?

These anxieties tend to be ignored by protagonists, but they have not been entirely avoided. Both James[16] and Craft[17]—a noted exponent of multiculturalism—have drawn attention to the need to balance cultural diversity against political and social cohesion.

(6) If we assume that the school's curriculum ought to have regard to the wishes of the parents, then multi-ethnic education has little in the way of a mandate from the consumer. It is important here to stress that multi-ethnic educational embraces the *whole* curriculum and *all* pupils. It is not simply something to do with the ethnic minorities—the Swann Report was very deliberately entitled

Education for All. Now we know that the Swann Committee made no attempt, in coming to its conclusions and recommendations, to assess the acceptabilty of its approach to the approximately 95 per cent of parents who constitute the majority. More surprisingly, there were no opinion surveys among ethnic-minority parents either (see Chapter 6). Indeed, if one had to point to the way in which the state system of education reflects not the views of parents but rather of the educational establishment to which it is attached, then the Swann Report would be a relevant document.

Swann did conduct a number of what are described as 'forums' with parents and young people, but we are given no indication of how many parents actually attended; and of the 249 organisations that submitted evidence, only one had the word 'parent' in its title—the Afro-Caribbean Parents Educational Support Group (Waltham Forest). Of the 369 individuals who submitted evidence, 24 were name as parents; of these (from their names), 17 were of Asian origin and the others had English names. Although members of the committee met representatives from 132 organisations, none was a parents' organisation. Of the 213 individuals who met the committee only one was described as a parent—Mr B. Henry, of the Black Parents Education Group, Deptford, London.

More evidence of how parents have been excluded from the debate can be found in the 1983 CRE register of current research: of the 40 projects mentioned in its education section, none contains a reference to parents. In a book published in 1984, Tomlinson,[18] in referring to ethnic-minority parental opinion about what happens in school, says 'There is to date, however, limited research evidence'. However, she does provide a summary of what is available. From this there would appear to be no demand from either West Indians or Asians for multi-ethnic education. What is clear is that such parents appear to have very much the same expectations of the education system as do indigenous English parents:

> In general research suggests that whatever the class position, educational levels and colonial backgrounds of migrant parents, they mostly share high expectations about education, and they view schools as places where their children's life chances should be enhanced . . . Rex [a noted multi-ethnic expert] pointed out in 1971 that an open education system may be the one means whereby occupational and

status mobility is made possible for migrants in any country, and education has always been regarded by migrants from colonial countries as a way into the established social order of the 'mother country'.

Maureen Stone,[19] a British/West Indian academic, say: 'West Indian parents want a traditional, basic curriculum and do not want multicultural innovation.' Asian parents share a similar instrumental view of the role of the school; they expect it to provide their children with the means of rising in the world. To quote research referred to by Tomlinson:[20]

> South Asians are proving more successful in penetrating the higher levels of the British education system than their white working-class peers —which suggests a functional view of the school's purposes, rather than a social engineering or attitude change perspective, both of which principles underly multi-ethnic innovation. Provided religious sensibilities are respected, Asian parents have a view of the content and purpose of education which differs little from their indigenous white counterparts. If they have a complaint, it is along the lines of that discovered by a researcher as early as 1969, ' . . . too much play, too little homework, and lack of discipline in schools.'

As someone who has been the head of a virtually all-Asian school for six years, I can confirm this. Perhaps the best reflection of the real concerns of ethnic-minority parents regarding the school curriculum is Maureen Stone's judgement on multi-ethnic education:[21]

> It takes schools away from their central concern which is basically teaching or instructing children in the knowledge and skills essential to life in this society. It effectively reduces choice and creates dependence on experts and professionals which undermines the individual's own capacity to cope. Matters of individual responsibility and group culture should not be primarily the concern of schools but of the family and the community.

An illustration of how the false myth that ethnic-minority parents want multi-ethnic education for their children can be perpetuated is provided by the Community Relations Commission (CRC). In 1977 the CRC published a report on enquiries it had made, *inter alia*, into parental opinions about the school curriculum.[22] The folowing is a summary of the findings about what parents thought about how far minority cultures were taught in schools. There was a sample of 600 parents from the West Indian, Cypriot, Indian, Pakistani and East African groups:

Taught nothing of country of origin	35%
Not enough taught	29%
Very good/taught enough	10%
Alright [sic]/OK	5%
Not bothered	5%
They learn it at home	2%
No need to know	2%

Two preliminary observations are needed: the researchers mix up questions of fact—as in question 1, or rather the parent's perception of the facts (parents rarely know what their children are actually taught in school), with value judgements. Second, only 88 per cent of the parents provided information, i.e. 528, which suggests that 12 per cent or 72 parents were not concerned either way:

(1) Now since 35 per cent (of 528) thought nothing was being taught, 65 per cent thought something *was* being taught, i.e. *343*.
(2) Of this 343, 29 per cent or *99* parents were dissatisfied.
(3) Now 24 per cent, plus the 12 per cent who did not respond, were satisfied or not bothered. This gives 36 per cent of 600, or *216* parents.

This is how the CRC reported this: 'Most parents reported that their children were not taught anything, or not enough of their own culture' (p. 39). Despite this, the same researchers found 'that ethnic minority parents have a high opinion of the schools their children attend and of the teachers who work there, as do other parents' (p. 102).

No one who has looked at the origins of the multi-ethnic education bandwaggon can doubt that it provides compelling evidence that the state education service is, indeed, a supply-based rather than consumer-oriented process. That parents ought to be consulted *before* radical educational change is carried out is not an influential theme in the culture of the state education establishment.

(7) The defenders of multi-ethnic education frequently refer to 'their culture' in connection with ethnic-minority children attending British schools. Unfortunately, this term is never defined. The assumption, however, appears to be that such children are still wholly attached to their parents' or, increasingly, grandparents' coountry of origin. However, since the great majority of the children were born in Britain, this is a dubious assumption. Cultures are largely a function of a specific place, of its geography, landscape, climate and history. If you change your country of residence then, in some degree, you change your culture and, even more, you change that of your descendants born in your adopted country. There would have to be a very serious and sustained effort to seal off the children concerned in a heavily enclosed environment for this process not to occur.

In reality, the great majority of ethnic-minority children attend day-schools, which are necessarily rooted in the culture of large British towns and cities. This does not mean that the parental culture cannot be preserved in the home, but it does imply that the child is inevitably bi-cultural. The Asian child who speaks Gujerati, Hindi or Urdu at home, eats Asian food, watches Asian videos and attends the mosque every evening will speak English at school, read the *Beano* or *Dandy* and support the local football team. Precisely the same kinds of cultural transition, though not perhaps so pronounced, will be successfully transacted by British/Caribbean children. To speak of 'their culture' is to imply that the child goes to school in Karachi or Port of Spain, and that is to fail to understand the child's actual, everyday cultural realities.

(8) The ideological dangers of pursuing a multi-ethnic approach in specific subjects has been made clear by Her Majesty's Inspectors (HMIs). In 1985 they published *History in the Primary and Secondary Years: An HMI View* (HMSO). Now a mark of HMI reports is their blandness. HMIs are acutely aware of the political and ideological pressure focused on the state system of education, and they are always anxious not to appear partisan in any way. The language of their reports reflects this, often to the point of banality. It is no exaggeration to say that, particularly when dealing with highly charged subjects such as history, they desperately attempt to look not simply both ways but several ways at once. We can be sure, therefore, that when they offer criticism they feel very strongly indeed.

After looking at a great deal of evidence, the HMIs attack as 'neither morally or historically justified' the assumption made by many teachers involved in multi-ethnic history and complain of:

(1) An emphasis on West Indian history at the expense of European history;
(2) Multi-ethnic history stressing 'problems, conflicts and exploitation';
(3) The assumption 'that any black pupil will be interested in the history of any black culture or individual';
(4) The attitude that present generations 'in some way share a heritage of guilt for the mistakes of their predecessors'.

They also warn teachers against naive and tendentious definitions of words such as 'imperialism', 'bourgeoisie', 'massacre', 'rebel', 'peasant', 'civilisation'. These strictures make it clear that, far from harmonising disparate material aimed at cultural understanding and tolerance, multi-ethnic education can, in reality, function to conceal the real, ideological purposes of the teacher, and perhaps the LEA, which promotes and supports such teaching.

The prevalence of this view of history can be gauged (at least in Inner London, the biggest of Britain's LEAs) from the following statement as early as 1981 in *The Times Educational Supplement*. It comes from Tom Hastie who, as warden of a teachers' centre, had contact with a wide range of schools and teachers:

> I frequently groaned when yet another social studies teacher asked me for information about resources for yet another scheme of work on slavery. I groaned as an historian, for I knew that the study of slavery would be limited to the Atlantic slave trade, and would be merely a white-bashing exercise, with a minimum of historical accuracy. We are confronted here not with the teaching of history, but with sheer propaganda and indoctrination.

Now it might be objected that what we have here is an abuse of multi-ethnic education, not the real thing, but that would be naive. Given the structure of the state education service, with considerable powers (not least over the curriculum) in the hands of local authority politicans who effectively control teachers' careers, and given the clear evidence that some teachers at least are not willing to make the vital distinction between education and indoctrination, the inspectors and the teachers' warden are not revealing an abuse of multi-ethnic education. They are simply pointing to some of its inevitable consequences in the prevailing system.

The Self-concept

In addition to radical reform of the curriculum, multi-ethnic educationists also urge a further justification for their viewpoint. A key notion, they argue, is the concept of the self. Educators now subscribe to the notion that our sense of who we are, our personal identity, is largely formed on the basis of the ways we interact with others. As a result of feedback from others, the child gradually builds up a picture or understanding of his essential attributes, powers and weaknesses. Other people act as a kind of looking-glass, and we incorporate this picture as the image of who we are into our general view of ourselves. As we grow and develop interactions with others—particularly with significant people such as parents and teachers—this feedback process is augmented and made more specific by and through the social role we occupy. The expectations associated with these roles act as information about who we are in specific circumstances. Being a pupil in school, for instance, means creating a view of ourselves that is dependent upon the expectation of us by our role partner, i.e. the teacher. The extent to which we respond appropriately to the teacher's expectations will determine how far we create a stable, consistent image of ourselves as pupils. In the course of human development an increasing number of roles has to be performed (for example, sex role, pupil, son/daughter, student, worker, marriage partner, middle aged, elderly person). All this means changes, over time, in how we evaluate ourselves. A vital element here is self-esteem. The extent to which we develop feelings of our own worth and feel valued by those around us will be a critical variable in determining both our feelings and behaviour. High self-esteem tends to create the well-adjusted, integrated individual. We behave appropriately and are accepted by others. Low self-esteem creates feelings of rejection, inappropriate responses to expectations and, possibly, anti-social behaviour.

These deterministic notions about the self have influenced life in schools in a number of ways. First, they have reinforced the argument against streaming or classifying children according to academic ability. Streaming, in this perspective, is seen as damaging because children in low streams perceive the low-status label their class bears as negative feedback about themselves, and this creates low self-esteem. Second, this theory of the self has fostered the notion that schools should be involved in some form of psychotherapy or counselling, notably that prescribed by humanist psychologists such as Kelly, Maslow and Carl Rogers. This is justified on the grounds that the character of the self-image affects both academic performance and social behaviour. Third, this theory has been enlisted by those who espouse an egalitarian philosophy. If recognition of excellence damages those children whose abilities mean that they cannot compete with cleverer pupils then the abolition of both competition and the pursive of excellence is a desirable end. Fourth, the theory provides an explanation of the dynamics of the self-fulfilling prophecy. If the teacher's expectations of the child are low, this will be incorporated into the child's self-image as negative feedback, and he will respond accordingly, i.e. he will fulfil the teacher's predictions by performing poorly, and the reverse will also apply.

These arguments have formed an important thread in the debate about the education of the ethnic-minority child. It has been argued—notably by Milner[23]—that 'black' (which usually means both Afro-Caribbean and Asian) children have, speaking generally, low self-esteem as the result of prejudice and living in a world where 'black culture' and black role models are scarce commodities. In order to boost self-esteem and therefore performance and behaviour we need more 'black' teachers and should incorporate ethnic cultures into the school curriculum:

> There may be a case for providing instruction in both English *and* immigrant languages for all pupils. This is one way of increasing communication between pupils and between teachers and pupils, but most important, it serves to acknowledge the worth of the immigrant language and cultures. Equal weight should be accorded to immigrant cultures as to English cultures in the teaching of history, geography, art, literature and every other subject. In the primary school the potential for including bi-cultural materials in learning to read and write, number work, art, drama is enormous . . . cumulatively the endorsement of his own culture by its inclusion in books, teaching materials—indeed in the whole life of the school—must confirm its value in the eyes of the child.

This view has had enormous influence, and almost all the literature on the multi-ethnic curriculum embodies its assumptions. However, it is open to two lines of criticism. First, the theory of the self on which it is based is by no means self-evident. It is reductionist in its view of the human person and tends, therefore, to regard people as passive receptors of information rather than as sentient, intelligent individuals who interact with and interpret their environment in positive and unique ways. The creation of the self may be a much more active, self-determined process than its advocates suggest. No one who has been either a parent or teacher has any doubts that most children are not simply passive observers of the world around them. They actively participate in the process of deciding who they are. Abelson, in *Persons: a Study in Philosophical Psychology*, takes a view of people much more in accordance with common observation, particularly of what we know of human beings faced with adversity: '[People may be seen] as free agents whose actions and avowals are explained by . . . reasons, purposes and values . . . in brief, a human being is a person, not an automaton.' Also, as a psychological theory, the 'looking-glass self', insofar as it refers to children of school age, suffers from a certain inconsistency. Psychologists are in general agreement that in the development of key attributes such as personality, social adjustment and intelligence, the really decisive influences occur in early life, i.e. before school begins. Why is this not so for the self-concept? In reading the literature it is not difficult to gain the impression that children's self-concepts are entirely what the school determines they should be. This ignores not only the influence of life before school but also the continuing influence of parent, home and, indeed neighbourhood values and peer group. Since the great majority of schools are day-schools most children spend most of their time out of school. (The 'average' child now probably spends more time watching television than attending school.)

Moreover, this view of the self tends not only to restrict the influences impinging on the self; it also omits the function of subjective interpretation of experience in human consciousness. People, including children, may not only rely on adverse feedback as an influence in selfhood; they may use their powers of reasoning to question, discount or reinterpret it in a more positive direction. While the damaging effect of a constant rejection and hostility is beyond question, the fact is that very few children grow up in a school environment that could be characterised in that way. Almost all children receive a mixture of negative and positive feedback. Children, too, are sustained by group culture embedded in the home, family and district. Notions arising from religion, literature and oral stories, politics, history and tradition may be transmitted via these agencies, and all may help to create and maintain positive self-images in children. An obvious weakness in deterministic theories of the self is that they cannot begin to explain how, throughout history, some despised and rejected groups have survived and flourished, for example the Chinese in South-east Asia, the Japanese in the USA and the Jews everywhere.

In truth, these theories of self do not represent a consensus. In a recent dictionary of psychology[24] we find: '[The Self] may be defined in a number of ways, none of them entirely satisfactory.' The relation of the theory to black people has been powerfully expressed by Maureen Stone: ' . . . To see black people and their children as passive beings, simply reacting to structural forces is a limited view which denies the facts of history and is supported neither by common sense nor by rigorous sociological analysis.[25] Second, the conclusions which Milner reaches on low 'black' self-esteem are not based on research that is entirely convincing. Milner, a social psychologist, used a sample of 300 children from two large cities with substantial ethnic-minority populations. The study was carried out in local schools with equal number of West Indian, Asian and English children aged five to eight. Each child was required to respond to four questions about two dolls or two pictures, which always depicted a member of the child's own racial group and of the other principal racial group in the child's immediate environment. Each child was asked to choose the doll or picture he or she preferred and the responses were used as the basis for drawing conclusions about the child's racial identity and preferences, tendency to stereotype and social aspirations. Essentially, Milner assumed that the choice of doll indicated the children's attitudes, particularly those relating to the worthiness or esteem of their own racial group. Since both West Indian and Asian children chose white dolls or pictures to a significant extent, it was assumed that this indicated a tendency to reject their own group in preference to the white, English group.

Again, it is important to stress that this work of Milner has had considerable influence. The Schools Council, the NFER and Swann all reflect this, as does almost all the material issued by those LEAs committed to multi-ethnic education. The same is true of teacher-training institutions, and it is no exaggeration to say that Milner's dolls have attained the status of a classic in the literature of multi-ethnic education. Also, they have had far more than a theoretical influence. They have had a direct influene on teachers' understanding and classroom practice. It is important, therefore, to take Milner's views seriously, and to examine them with a critical eye. What follows is a combination of criticism offered by Maureen Stone together with my own reflections:

(1) The researcher was a white adult, and children have a marked tendency to please significant others interacting with them. The socially desired response is a well-known contaminating variable in this kind of research. Milner, to be fair, acknowledges this, but ignores it in his conclusions. The result *might* have been different with a black researcher.

(2) Black dolls may have been in scarce supply in the child's school and home. The great majority of dolls produced for sale in shops are white—as indeed are most photographic or painted images of children. The children's exposure to dolls and pictures in their social environment could well have influenced their response to the dolls in the experiment.

(3) Black dolls *may* be more adversely depicted in children's story books and on television than white ones. The children could have been responding to this rather than to the image of black people whom the researcher assumed the dolls evoked in their minds.

(4) Neither dolls nor pictures are people. The assumption that young people transpose the two is at least arguable. Children's play is very complex and, although Milner reports that the children responded to the dolls 'as if they were people', the fact remains they were not 'real people'. Moreover, we do not know whether the children responded differently to the dolls and the pictures.

(5) The situation was researcher-directed—he provided both the material and the questions. The children were compelled by the constraints of the situation to make quick and very limited choices. Doll preferences would clearly have been more validly assessed in a free-play situation, with an invisible, non-directive

researcher noting the tendency of children actually to pick up and play with particular dolls.

(6) Milner looked at misidentification among West Indian children in a follow-up study but he does not make clear how far they were the same group of children. Moreover, in this study no fewer than 43.75 per cent of the black children who had originally chosen white dolls now chose black ones. Only 18.75 per cent identified with white dolls on both occasions. Milner does not speculate on the reason for this shift in preferences, but it does suggest research lacking stability over time, i.e. reliability.

(7) It is clear from his own comments and from his approving references to such well known anti-racists as Sivanandan, Ann Dummett, Rex and Moore, and to the periodical *Race Today*, that Milner is a committed anti-racist (see Chapter 5). Throughout his book he accepts the proposition that Britain is riddled with endemic racism. It was from within this perspective that he generated the purpose of this research: 'The central concern of the study conducted by the author was to investigate the effects of racism on the children of West Indian and Asian immigrants to Britain.' The racist nature of British society was assumed, the intention of the study being to demonstrate its effects on ethnic-minority children. However, no attempt was made to establish whether the schools the children attended actually practised racism (they clearly did not do so in their admissions policy) or, indeed, treated the black and brown children in any way differently from white. In short, the cause of the outcome had already been assumed.

(8) The research reflects the unproven theory of blacks being passive victims of hostility. Black personality is explained in terms of self-hate and racial misidentification. Other possible ways of interpreting the evidence are not considered. Milner himself points to the origin of (and central weakness in) this approach in speaking of black Americans: 'But where in all this are the normal, well-adjusted black Americans, who are identified with their race but have sufficiently resilient egos to withstand imposition of inferiority on them? Very little has been written about them, the main emphasis having fallen on those with identity conflicts and emotional difficulties' (p. 153). That is, this pathological notion of poor black self-esteem is not based

on a representative sample of black people. This is perhaps the Freudian fallacy in a new guise.

The truth is that the research on the self-concept of black children in Britain and the USA is, at best, not convincing. After reviewing the literature Stone says: 'As to the research discussed here, it is generally inconclusive and contradictory.' A later review by Tomlinson[26] concluded:

Research findings are contradictory and the relationship between self concept, self esteem and school achievement is still largely an unknown quantity . . . Both American research and British studies of self esteem among minority pupils have produced contradictory findings . . . Studies . . . undertaken towards the end of the 1970s have suggested that there is little or no difference between the self esteem and acceptance of their own identity of black and white children.

This optimistic comment is given empirical support by Murray and Dawson.[27] Here the researchers looked at a sample of 626 West Indian, 638 Asian and 3,790 English adolescents from ten comprehensive schools in Manchester. The conclusion is emphatic ('There is no difference between the groups on the self-esteem measures'), and the researchers were decidedly optimistic in their view of West Indian and Asian academic performance. Certainly, for what it is worth, lengthy classroom experience of ethnic-minority children provided me with no evidence that black children suffer from either a damaged self-concept or low-self-esteem.

Third, the assumption that the black child's assumed low self-esteem can be improved by changes in the curriculum has nowhere been demonstrated, nor has the relationship between a multi-ethnic curriculum and improved academic performance. Yet both these assumptions are accepted as unassailable by the advocates of the multi-ethnic curriculum. ILEA, for instance, constantly and enthusiastically makes this assumption, in particular in its support for 'Black Studies' and for ethnic-minority languages on the curriculum and as media of instruction. Milner,[28] whose commitment to this notion was apparent from his 1975 book referred to above, repeated it in 1983. Multiracial/cultural education is, he says, ' . . . an educational and human right, an aspect of equal educational opportunity and basically sound pedagogy'.

There is no space available to examine this assertion with the thoroughness it deserves. Suffice it to say that it contains two assertions about rights and equality which are at least questionable, and a statement about effective teaching and learning for which there is no evidence. Tomlinson concluded that although the curriculum –self-esteem thesis underlying changes in curriculum, language and teacher-training might appear logical, it was an 'empirically unestablished notion', and 'The relationship between minority group pupils' perception and understanding of themselves is by no means fully researched or understood'. Stone goes even further. After studying multiracial education in a number of schools, she dismissed it as irrelevant to black children's needs —either psychological or educational. Moreover, it causes schools to exacerbate the West Indian child's problems: 'It takes children away from their central concern which is basically teaching or instructing children in the knowledge and skills essential to life in this society.' The most recent (1986) research on black children's academic performance points to perhaps their real needs. After looking at the records of black children London schools Dr Christine Mabey[29] concluded that there should be a major re-emphasis on the basics:

> The emphasis on and the quality of teaching of basic skills needs to be improved . . . The most important single factor in determining examination levels was the degree of performance in reading.

In truth, the linking of the child's self-concept with the multi-ethnic curriculum and improved academic performance via reinforced self-esteem is not only theoretically unconvincing; it is an approach that may well be associated with the relative academic failure of black pupils. What leads to increased self-esteem is success. It is the child's increased mastery over its environment through increased knowledge and new skills which increases confidence and generates feelings of worth. Moreover, given the nature of the society in which we live, both personal fulfilment and active participation in the job market depend on educational success. This means that schools, particularly with regard to minorities who need to prove themselves to a sometimes sceptical majority, have to emphasise their instrumental character. Those schools which effectively teach black children the three Rs and obtain high levels of examination success are far more likely to meet their real needs than those pursuing an approach based on dubious psychology and confused ideas about the self and multiculturalism. There is good evidence that ethnic-minority parents understand and support this.

Conclusion

I believe that the following conclusions are valid and should make us extremely cautious about accepting the idea of multi-ethnic education:

(1) The absence of an agreed nomenclature suggests an underlying confusion.
(2) Even assuming a consensus about meaning, there are fierce disagreements about the purposes of multi-ethnic education and its value for ethnic-minority children.
(3) There appears to be no convincing framework of ideas for determining what constitutes a valid and acceptable multi-ethnic curriculum. The criteria have not been established and, given the lack of consensus about meaning and purpose, it is very unlikely that they ever could be.
(4) A multi-ethnic curriculum reflecting immigrant cultures and financed by the public violates the well-established principle that, in a free and highly developed society, such cultures are the responsibility of those among whom they flourish. There is no evidence of majority support for this proposed change. Moreover, the process of determining the cultural balance of such a curriculum could lead to conflict among the minorities about how far each distinctive culture should be reflected in the work of the school.
(5) The belief that the typical English school curriculum is narrow, inward-looking and exclusively Anglo-Saxon—a key assumption in the multi-ethnic canon—is difficult to sustain in view of Britain's history and the abundant evidence of cross-cultural influences.
(6) The advocates of multi-ethnic education lack understanding of the link between social and political cohesion and a common school curriculum. Britain's transformation into a multi-ethnic nation—to an extent unique in its history—may well make a broadly similar education in the young more, not less, necessary.

(7) The psychology of multi-ethnic education is unconvincing. The link between the supposed black self-concept, curriculum content and educational achievement has never been demonstrated. There is increasing evidence that the assumption of low self-esteem among black pupils is false.

References

1. R. Firth, *Human Types*, Abacus Press, Tunbridge Wells (1975)
2. A. Craft, 'Equality, Cohesion and Diversity', *Schools Council News*, No. 43, Autumn term (1983)
3. J. Eggleston, 'Ethnic Naivety', *The Times Educational Supplement*, 11 March 1983
4. M. Stone, *The Education of the Black Child in Britain: the Myth of Multiracial Education*, Fontana, London (1981)
5. J. Rex, 'The Development of Multicultural Education in Four LEA Areas', in Lord Swann, *Education for All*, Report of the Committee of Enquiry into the Education of Ethnic Minority Children, HMSO, London, March (1985)
6. B. Parekh, 'Educational Opportunity in Multi-Ethnic Britain', in *Ethnic Pluralism and Public Policy*, Heinemann, London (1983)
7. S. Tomlinson, *Ethnic Minorities in British Schools*, Heinemann Educational, London (1983)
8. G. Klein, 'No Bandwaggon', *The Times Educational Supplement*, 6 May 1983
9. R. Jeffcoate, *Positive Image—Towards a Multicultural Curriculum*, Readers and Writers Publishing Co-operative, London (1979)
10. J. Williams, 'Perspectives on the Multicultural Curriculum', *The Social Science Teacher*, Vol, 8, No. 4 (1979)
11. P. H. Walkling, 'The Idea of a Multicultural Education: 1', *Journal of the Philosophy of Education*, Vol. 14, No. 1 (1980)
12. P. Zec, 'Multicultural Education: What Kind of Relativism is Possible?' *Journal of the Philosophy of Education*, Vol 14, No. 1 (1980)
13. G. Partington, 'The Same or Different? Curricular Implications of Feminism and Multiculturalism', *Journal of Curriculum Studies*, Vol. 17 (1985)
14. R. Burchfield, *The English Language*, Oxford University Press, Oxford (1985)
15. D. Milner, *Children and Race*, Penguin Books, Harmondsworth (1975)
16. A. James, 'The Multicultural Curriculum: New Approaches', *Multicultural Education*, Vol. 8, No. 1 (1982)
17. M. Craft, *Education for Diversity*, Inaugural lecture, Nottingham University (1982)
18. S. Tomlinson, *Home and School in Multicultural Britain*, Batsford, London (1984)
19. Stone, *op. cit.*
20. Tomlinson, *Home and School in Multicultural Britain*
21. Stone, *op. cit.*
22. *The Education of Ethnic Minority Children*, Community Relations Commission (1977)
23. Milner, *op. cit.*, pp. 203–4
24. C. Evans, *A Dictionary of the Mind, Brain and Behaviour*, Arrow Books, London (1978)

25. Stone, *op. cit.*
26. Tomlinson, *Ethnic Minorities in British Schools*
27. C. Murray and A. Dawson, *Five Thousand Adolescents*, Manchester University Press (1983)
28. D. Milner, *Children and Race—Ten Years On*, Ward Lock, London (1983)
29. C. Mabey, *Educational Research*, Vol, 28, No. 3 (1986)

CHAPTER 5

The Anti-Racist Lobby

Structure

Just what is the 'anti-racist lobby'? This can be answered on two levels: the structural and the ideological. Structurally, we can say that the lobby exists at both official and unofficial levels. At the official level we have the CRE (Commission for Racial Equality) and the various local publicly funded CRCs (Community Relations Council). Unofficially there are many groups propagating the notion that Britain is a racist society—the National Association for Anti-Racist Education, the Campaign Against Racism in Education, War Against Racism, the Association of Black Social Workers and Allied Professions are examples. Some idea of the number of organisations involved can be gained from the list of grants provided by the CRE in 1984. These number 153 national, regional and local organisations, and they received a total of £1,471,889. In addition to this, 84 CRCs operating in every region in England and Scotland received annual grants.

This organisational phenomenon is coupled with a sizeable academic and research thrust. There is now in Britain a body of academics working in colleges, universities and research foundations which, to judge from the material it produces, espouses the ideology of the anti-racist lobby. Instances of this are a review of the literature produced in 1983,[1] *Race, School and Community*, a study of research and literature produced for the National Foundation for Educational Research (NFER) in 1974,[2] an Open University 'reader' edited by Charles Husband, *'Race' in Britain: Continuity and Change*, issued in 1982 and reprinted in 1982/4/5[3], and the most recent production, *The Politics of Multiracial Education*, by the Marxist teacher–trainer, Madan Sarup.[4] The CRE register of current research on race relations in Britain lists over 100 researches.[5]

The effect this activity can have in creating the *a priori* assumption that Britain is a 'racist society' can be judged from the assertion in the Rampton Report that a major factor in the poor average performance of West Indian pupils in school is 'racism '— although no scientific evidence is produced to support this pre-existing assumption, anecdotal assertion being elevated to the status of valid and reliable evidence.[6]

There are, too, several regular periodicals in which the anti-racist thesis is systematically repeated and developed. The CRE publishes three regular journals and there are regular publications from the Runnymede Trust, the Institute of Race Relations, ILEA and, of course, the regular *Race Today*.

Ideology

Ideologically, anti-racism is rooted in that classical political philosophy of the seventeenth and eighteenth centuries that we call liberalism. Rather, its adherents often justify their aims and practices by reference to liberal notions about the freedom of the individual, 'social justice', democracy and the rights of minorities, as well as by a consistent commitment to governmental action to put right alleged injustice. However, an examination of anti-racist literature quickly dispels any notion that reference to Adam Smith, the founding fathers, John Stuart Mill or the French Enlightenment provides an adequate reference point. Anti-racists invariably see the world not so much in liberal terms as in terms of a neo-Marxist hegemony. Talk of good race relations, social harmony and respect for minority cultures so often appears to mask, or to act as a kind of channel for, the ideology of the class war, settling old colonial scores and propagating the need to re-educate the bourgeoisie. The work of Franz Fanon, the black Martinican philosopher and psychoanalyst, rather than that of the classical liberals, provides the rationale of much anti-racist rhetoric. Fanon, an embittered product of French rule in Algeria, became—as an understandable reaction to French colonial cruelty —violently anti-white and anti-capitalist. Although perceiving its political weakness in the wider world, he expressed the notion of 'négritude'. This was an attempt to glorify all things African, as a revolt against colonialism. There is an underlying assumption of a common negro inheritance and destiny.

A typical Fanon sentiment is to be found in his *Black Skin, White Mask*[7]

> When it does happen that the negro looks fiercely at the white man, the white man tells him, 'Brother there is no difference between us', and yet the negro *knows* there is a difference. He *wants* it. He wants the white man to turn on him and shout 'Damn nigger!'. Then he would have the unique chance to 'show them' . . . the former slave needs a challenge to his humanity, he wants a conflict, a riot . . .

This kind of analysis of the black experience and mentality has been criticised by many black intellectuals. They have rejected the notion that culture can be identified with skin colour and have questioned its relevance to present-day political realities. (The Senegalese novelist, Sentane Ousmane, has said that 'Negritude neither feeds the hungry nor builds roads'.). Nevertheless, the combination of bitterness, belief in the virtues of revolt and the rejection of capitalism is found in the work of very influential people in the vanguard of anti-racism in Britain.

For instance, Chris Mullard, a Marxist sociologist, owes much to Fanon's influence. Mullard, until recently a lecturer and professor of sociology at the London Institute of Education, has been heavily involved in teacher-training and is regarded as an expert in matters to do with race relations. (As I write, he is Professor of Race Relations at Amsterdam University.) He has contributed to an SSRC-funded research project on *The Social Management of Racial Policy and Practice*, and has been involved in *Towards a Non-Racist Curriculum*, a collaborative research project between the London Institute of Education, ILEA and the DES. He was also the director of the recently completed enquiry commissioned by Brent Council into the education of black children, and is to be employed by the same council to develop an 'anti-racist' curriculum, to advise on the development of section 11 of the Local Government Act 1966 in the area, and to train Brent staff in 'anti-racism'. The unit that Mullard runs is also collaborating in a publicly funded research project with LEAs in Avon, Birmingham, Bradford, Brent, Derbyshire, Hampshire, Haringey, Inner London, Leicestershire, Manchester and Sheffield. The aim is to transform the whole school curriculum in these areas.[8] Mullard gave evidence to the Swann Committee and speaks regularly on the Swann conferences organised by colleges, universities and LEAs. His status and influence in the anti-racist lobby is unquestioned, and his basic political stance and his debt to Fanon is evident throughout his work. Consider, for instance, the following passage:[9]

> . . . All the time I was writing *Black Britain*, I found not solace, comfort or tolerance, but tension, a disturbing desire to break, smash and riot, to bellow: 'Whitey! One day you'll have to pay' . . . Already we have started to rebel, to kick out against our jailers . . . The battle will be a bloody one . . . Blacks will fight with pressure, leaflets, campaigns, demonstrations, fists and a scorching resentment which, when peaceful means fail, will explode into street fighting, urban guerrilla warfare, looting, burning and rioting . . . To these I say 'Watch out, Whitey, Nigger goin' to get you!'*

A similar crudity of expression and political stance is to be found in the work of Ambalvaner Sivanandan, a Tamil Marxist from Sri Lanka who came to Britain in 1958. In 1964 he joined the influential Institute of Race Relations as a librarian. Since 1972 he has been its Director. Although he is little known outside the anti-racist lobby, Sivanandan has had great influence. Professor Stuart Hall[10] has said of him: ' . . . It is worth saying that he is one of the handful of black intellectuals who has actively sustained the black struggle in Britain over more than two decades.' David Dale,[11] in a critical essay, says: ' . . . Sivanandan's writing is a central reference point for anti-racists.' ILEA refers approvingly to his work: his pamphlets *Race, Class and the State* became, according to Professor Hall, the left's 'adopted wisdom overnight', and his collected writings have been published by Pluto Press. He is co-editor of the journal *Race and Class*. Again, like Mullard, no-one can doubt his seminal influence, both in the theorising of anti-racism and in policy-making in those areas where the LEAs are committed to anti-racism.

Sivanandan has published a great deal, and anyone who wishes to gain an insight into the nature of his thought and action should read the excellent essay by David Dale mentioned above. However, two sources in particular seem to epitomise the man's style and beliefs.

---

* In his report, "Brent's Development Programme for Racial Equality in Schools", Sir David Lane, after commenting that Professor Mullard had "had considerable influence on the Committee's findings", says this, " . . . I have read some of Professor Mullard's writings, which contain aggressively anti-white sentiments; for the sake of all Brent children and of the D.P.R.E. I hope he will not again be invited to play a leading role on the borough's education scene" (p.11, Home Office, 1988).

The first is a revealing interview with Dhiren Bhagat and reported in *The Spectator* (23 August 1986). The following is part of the transcript of the interview:

> You ask me why is it that the Director of the Institute of Race Relations didn't know that I was a trouble maker . . . because he thought I was a nice coolie boy who would behave himself and say yes sir no sir, three bags full sir. And I did. For four years . . . They didn't even look. They're be high class people. They wouldn't look at little me. They were so cocky. That is what I mean by paternalism. Paternalism forgets you are a human being. Paternalism says: 'Well I am responsible for you like I am responsible for a dog . . .'.

The second source is Sivanandan's *How Racism came to Britain*.[12] This is a cartoon book with bubble language, and purports to be an objective account of British colonialism and relations between black and white people in the Empire. It is clearly aimed at children and adolescents, the layout, illustrations, use of space and short, catchy phraseology being modelled on comics and teenage magazines. Its intellectual level is captured by its illustrations and the crude, anti-white and anti-police sentiments surrounding them. A typical example, used to illustrate the notion of 'Bias in the judiciary', shows a judge in full bottom wig saying: 'I s'pose you are innocent until proven guilty . . . As long as you are white that is! If you are white *and* wear a blue uniform, however, well then as we all know . . . you are innocent even when proven guilty. Got it?'

Elsewhere Sivanandan has echoed Fanon's notion of the 'black community' to include British-Asian citizens:[13]

> That community of Black, of Afro–Caribbean–Asian had been created in the post-war years by a culture of resistance to racism in the factories and the neighbourhoods of the inner city in which Afro–Caribbeans and Asians had been condemned to live . . . as denizens of the same ghetto, they found common cause against a racism that denied their basic needs in housing, schooling, and social and welfare services, and brought them up against racist landlords, racist teachers, racist social workers and racist policemen.

The cartoon history caused great offence. Its distortion of complex historical truths, its crude anti-white and anti-British sloganising, its barely suppressed hatreds and its systematic use of a slick propaganda format to appeal to and win over impressionable young minds were all commented on critically. *The Times* called it 'a book of great wickedness'; Baroness Cox said that it is ' . . . grotesquely dishonest and blatantly intended to stir up racial conflict'; another member of the House of Lords spoke of 'this monstrous document'; while Sir Keith Joseph, then Secretary of State for Education and Science, wrote in a policy document of 'those who . . . want to subvert our fundamental values and institutions'.

However, the real significance of Sivanandan's anti-racist propaganda can be gauged not so much from the reaction of those for whom an honest attempt to seek and tell the truth is the basis of writing history. What really matters is that the book was eagerly embraced by many teachers and others who claim allegiance to the anti-racist cause. The All-London Teachers Against Racism and Fascism (ALTARF) recommended it as a 'highly readable yet serious book' suitable for twelve-year-olds. Moreover, the first impression quickly sold out and a second was produced. It was also translated into Dutch. A preface to the book makes clear that the work involved had official blessing: 'We are indebted to the GLC Ethnic Minorities Grant for lightening our financial burden.'

Finally, as a further pointer to the antecedents of anti-racism there is the work of Madan Sarup. In his preface to his *The Politics of Multiracial Education* Sarup informs us that he is a Lecturer in Education at Goldsmith's College, University of London. The course on which the book is based is a compulsory one; the would-be teachers for whom Sarup is responsible *have* to listen to his anti-racist discourse, an institutional and professional constraint which must bestow unusual status on his opinions and analysis. Sarup informs the reader that he is an adherent of the Marxist – Leninist school of thought. Like Mullard and Sivanandan, and echoing Fanon, Sarup assumes, against all the sociological evidence to the contrary, that there is a homogeneous 'black community' in Britain. Moreover, this 'black community' is involved in a bitter struggle against the British state and its institutions. British traditions, history and world view are all condemned as 'imperialist', 'racist' or, perhaps slightly less culpable, 'reformist'. Although formally functioning as an academic, Sarup appears not to be constrained in his advocacy by the normal rules of detached, academic discourse. He makes no bones about his basic purpose — recruitment for the cause:

Teachers should intensify the struggle on a large number of sites. They should be developers of 'critical consciousness' amongst their communities. They must link up with other teachers, not only in their staff room and teachers' centres, but in unions and political parties.

The teacher's greatest enemy is not, as an aspiring pedagogue might imagine, the reluctance of his pupils to work hard, discipline their wayward inclinations and progress in the painful business of mastering the subject—the real enemy is the police: 'A class force serving not the people as a whole but the interests of the bourgeoisie.' Moreover, aspiring teachers need to understand that there is a conspiracy between the social services, schools and the police, the object of which is 'the disciplining of black youth'. Nor do those members of the ethnic-minority communities who aspire to self-improvement escape the lash of Sarup's tongue: 'They form a class of collaborators who justify the ways of a capitalist state to the blacks and are engaged in domestic neo-colonialism.'

Now it might be objected that, in tracing the ideological roots of anti-racism, I have selected extreme protagonists, the crudity and extremism of whose views guarantee their own demise. They cannot, surely, be influential? This objection, although understandable, would be false. The views I have outlined can be shown to be directly linked to actual policy documents issued by certain LEAs. For instance, the 'Anti-Racist Strategies Team' of ILEA in its annual reports[14] makes clear that its views of British society, of British colonial history and of the relationship between black and white people all follow lines to which the writers I have referred would applaud. The school curriculum is perceived as the result of a conspiracy by the Establishment to preserve the political and social *status quo*. The possibility that knowledge can be objective and the result of a search for truth is contemptuously dismissed. The job of the school is to recast the whole curriculum in accordance with the preferred ideological standpoint. Every subject, from mathematics to cookery, is to act as a channel for Marxist, anti-racist propaganda. History is a special target, since it 'is partly responsible for the racism inherent in British society, and it is part of the mechanism by which this racism is perpetuated'; and history is a special instance, too, of the lack of Marxist objectivity the protagonists demand: 'It is in an analysis of history textbooks and syllabuses that the notion of political neutrality is most obviously and starkly a lie.' In this same document the police are presented in terms

Sarup would approve—although the style is somewhat more guarded. One wonders how many of the authors—all teachers—are the product of Sarup's seminary.

The CRE can also be shown to espouse views that Fanon and the rest would readily recognise—not officially, of course, since the Commission is a statutory body, publicly funded and subject to public scrutiny. However, the views of some of its officers, as conveyed in its *Education Journal*, are unmistakably the product of a very distinctive ideology. Here, for instance, is Jane E. Lane,[15] the CRE's civil servant responsible for the education of the under- fives:

> Racism is rooted in our history—in imperialism and the practice of colonialism. As a result of this history exploitation and oppression of black people continues largely unchecked . . . in British culture racial ideology is deeply embedded.

Here, writing in the *Headteachers' Review*, is Horace Lashley,[16] Senior Education Officer of the CRE:

> The structural racism in society mitigates [sic] against the black members of the population playing their full part and feeling like first class citizens. While this reluctance and neglect persists the society is stacking up a bonfire of social unrest and division which can bring no good in future years.

Lashley also speaks of: ' . . . The conventional classist nature of British education . . . Education has traditionally contributed to the perpetration of institutionalised racism . . . The knowledge tenets of Western civilisation have enshrined negative concepts of black people . . . Black youth in British society are clearly the most pertinent victims of cumulative social and educational practice.'

Similar sentiments can be traced to mandatory policy documents by Brent, Bradford, Haringey and several other LEAs—their provenance is clear to anyone who bothers to read the seminal literature. This reference to local authorities brings us to a further strand in the anti-racist movement. Since, as we have seen in the views of Fanon, Mullard, Sarup, Lashley and other academics and professional anti-racists, the lobby is essentially Marxist in its ideology, we might expect its doctrines to appeal to left-wing councils. Such, indeed, is the case. The linking of race with the class struggle, the hostile view of the police, the attack on colonialism and a consistent attempt to show that British institutions are essentially conservative and functioning entirely to maintain the *status quo* are all essential tenets of the anti-racist ideology which are bound to make an irresistible appeal to the political left. This is particularly so of the misleadingly termed 'loony left'. In reality, of course, those who have used the flag of the Labour Party to advance into the ideological battlefield are by no means 'loony'. They are, rather, a newly resurrected embodiment of the Marxist extremism which has always formed part of that umbrella organisation, the British Labour Party. Until recently the Party has always been able to keep this strand in its make-up within reasonable limits, confining its influence to the outer limits of policy-making. One of the reasons the Labour Party has succeeded in neutralising Marxist influence within it has been the failure of the hard left, particularly in the post-war years, to produce a convincing description of the masses in Britain as being a uniformly depressed underclass, exploited by a boss class. This was never very accurate. In recent years, with the rapid improvement in living standards and the perverse and increasingly obvious desire of large sections of the working class to engage in that process of 'embourgeoisement' Marxists fear and despise, these things have tended to expose the fantasy view of class war espoused by all dedicated leftists. The derisory performance of far-left organisations fighting under their own banner in local and general elections make clear their failure to win over the white, traditional proletariat.

This depressing situation, so total as to sap the energies of even the most vigorous of Marx's disciples, has been greatly mitigated since large-scale immigration in the 1950s and 1960s and the creation of large groups of ethnic minorities in Britain's inner cities. Thanks to the spectacular success of the technique of entryism in the Labour Party—and assisted by the worsening situation in the inner cities—hard-left activists have had considerable success, particularly at the local level. Having failed miserably to win over the white indigenous working class, the activists of what has been described as the new model Labour Party could now direct their energies into pushing the cause of the ethnic minorities in the name of anti-racism and race relations. A disaffected 'black' proletariat, containing a disproportionate number of energetic young, unemployed people and living in the highly charged, crime-ridden inner cities was a veritable godsend. As a means of creating that social tension, discord and, ultimately, conflict all Marxists regard as a prerequisite of the revolutionary solutions they dream of, the new multi-racial situation could scarcely offer a better opportunity. The techniques involved are well brought out in an article in *Police Review* in February 1983. A group of black militants and a section of the local Labour Party had formed an alliance to exploit black grievances in north London. Stoke Newington police station had become ' . . . the focus for a racist campaign, a black racist campaign'. The Colin Roach affair (a black man had killed himself in the foyer of a police station) had provided the rationale:

> Within days, banners and leaflets were prepared and distributed. A 'black' paper accused police of shooting Mr Roach. And the [left wing] Greater London Council hurried to grant £1,500 to groups organising demos outside the station.

However, the financing of demonstrations and those myriad Marxist pressure groups committed to subsuming racial conflict under the generalised theme of the class war is only one way in which the hard left operates to achieve success. Another and more powerful thrust is coming from the successful attempts by local councils to institutionalise anti-racism (under cover of 'equal opportunities'), give it official status and confer upon it the prestige of an official department funded from local and central government. Bradford Council has a group of officials known as 'Race Trainers', Brent has 'Race Advisers' and Manchester is busily creating a highly paid group of bureaucrats known as 'Race Officers'. This tendency is likely to increase. Both the CRE and the various CRCs approve of the process, and the government's laudable pronouncements on the importance of good race relations and racial equality allow local councils to feel both virtuous and justified in creating racial bureaucracies. Moreover, officially approved and publicly financed 'anti-racism' at the local level provides councils with the means of ensuring that every council employee expresses only those views about multi-ethnic Britain that are officially sanctioned. This process also has important electoral consequences. In certain urban areas, to be seen to be defending the ethnic minorities is a sure way of capturing and holding the burgeoning ethnic vote.

A less crude but ideologically similar development has occurred in the state education service. Before I describe this, I need to provide the context. The state service is a vast bureaucratic and professional apparatus. It has a virtual monopoly in the education of the young—only about 6 per cent of children do not go to state schools and every polytechnic and university is essentially state-financed, except one. There are nearly 32,000 schools, 9.25 million pupils, 500,000 teachers and the cost, currently, is about £14 billion.[17] Not surprisingly, this enormous, national edifice has gathered round itself a large, growing and impregnable bureaucracy and, like all bureaucracies, it creates its own imperatives. A constant, unceasing clamour for more resources, more personnel and a persistent tendency to create self-perpetuating centres of power are features shared by all other large, bureaucratic empires.

In addition to this bureaucratic thrust, the state service is the centre of enormous political and professional conflict. The schools have become increasingly politicised. The determination of the political left to perceive the school system as a crucial cause of the social class system and its radical reform in an egalitarian direction as a means of achieving greater social equality (a belief that produced the comprehensive system) has created enormous tension in the state system. Conservative educationists have always argued that, rather than creating class inequalities, the schools simply reflect existing social structures. The liberal tradition has tended to side with the socialist view. This fundamental disagreement has made the state schools into an ideological battleground. The huge vested interests involved (the LEAs, the teachers' unions, the Department of Education and Science (DES) and teacher-training institutes and departments) have engaged in ceaseless discussion, debate and conflict. There have been battles over the curriculum, the school ethos, discipline, the raising of the school-leaving age, pay, conditions of service and assessment of teachers, examinations and, most notably, secondary reorganisation in a comprehensive direction. Latterly, there has been quarrelling about sixth-form education, the future of the sixth form and the rise of the tertiary college. Where one might expect an atmosphere characterised by the calm and considered pursuit of learning and a necessary tradition of continuity, there is ceaseless conflict, restlessness and the pursuit of novelty.

This last theme—the consistent hankering after newness in the hope of discovering some sort of panacea to all our educational ills—provides the seedbed for professional self-interest. Within the state service a great deal of power lies with the advisers, sometimes called inspectors, whom all LEAs employ. Formally their role is to provide a link between the schools and both the chief education officer and the politicians who constitute the LEA. They describe what is happening in the schools to various council committees and subcommittees and, in turn, transmit council policy to the schools. They spend much of their time in putting on courses for teachers and head teachers in the name of in-service training. They also form part of the interviewing panel for new appointments. However, their lack of responsibility to head teachers, parents or governing bodies means that they occupy an uncertain, shadowy position in the system. Moreover, despite their highly paid status, they are often regarded by teachers as being peripheral. This lack of identity and credibility inevitably generates anxiety which, in turn, results in a show of furious activity. They work enormously hard. The need to justify a role many professionals regard with suspicion means that advisers are committed, in general, not to pupil progress but to 'development'. This imperative is not difficult to articulate or to justify in a world obsessed with fashion and the surface of things. The well-known 'bandwaggon' phenomenon—a device that links novelty with career building—is very closely associated with the ideology and practices of the advisers. They are constantly on the lookout for new ideas and alleged panaceas, the need for self-justification and career promotion being the driving mechanism.

It is not difficult to understand, then, that the advent of large numbers of ethnic-minority children in the schools provided the professionals with a field day. Here, indeed, was fertile ground. There were, in truth, genuine problems, particularly with the acquisition of English by first-generation immigrant children. There were anxieties about the need to respect religious sensibilities as well as the phenomenon of cultural conflict, and there is little doubt that many honourable and concerned advisers did their best to help matters. However, what began as humanitarian concern rapidly developed, under the influence of the forces I have described, into an expanding professional and politicised bandwaggon. The money to finance this came from the usual local rates and the rates support grant, with additional funds from the section 11 funding arrangement of the Local Government Act 1966. The intellectual justification resided in that amalgam of ideas I have referred to above —liberal notions about the rights of minorities, fashionable guilt about making good the wrongs of Empire and the Marxist view that schools exist to reform 'society' and to challenge the established bourgeois hegemony. Drawing on these resources, the educational professionals developed something known variously as 'multi-racial/cultural/ethnic education', of which anti-racism was a pervasive component. The fact that this development had little or nothing to do with the expressed wishes of ethnic-minority parents was irrelevant. (All the evidence suggests that, provided religious sentiments are respected, such parents have the same wishes for their children's education as all others.) The imperatives of professional self-interest, married to political influences, were sufficient to ensure its success and continuing expansion. Perhaps the most telling comment on this development has come from the British/West Indian sociologist Maureen Stone.[18] After observing the new doctrine actually operating in schools, she concluded thus:

> The setting up of research and development centres for multiracial education in London and Birmingham confirms this view of a professional expansion concerned as much with extending career advancement as with extending curricula.

However, the advisory service, although playing a key role in influencing both theory and practice in the schools and colleges, is only one means through which professional and ideological forces help to fashion specific educational outcomes. There is also a very considerable input emanating from official bodies such as the Schools Council (now the School Curriculum Development Committee), which set up a campaigning movement for Multicultural Education and Anti-racism under Alma Craft, who now performs the same role for the Schools' Council successor body.

An additional thrust comes from the intelligentsia employed in teacher training. Some of the work in these institutions is undoubtedly valuable, but, again, a major theme concentrated therein is 'development' in education. This results from the questionable assumption that teaching is some kind of science that obeys the imperatives functioning in real sciences, such as physics, which progress through making new discoveries, testing theory against empirical evidence and constantly seeking to extend the frontiers of knowledge. However, what is properly regarded as new knowledge and understanding in science is, in education, often no more than ingenious speculation or fervid hope for improvement. Audiovisual French in the primary school, reading readiness and learning through discovery are good examples of how now-discredited theories generated from within the academic establishment in education attained the status of revealed truth, to the detriment of countless children exposed to them. Again, as with the advisory service, the multiracial nature of a growing number of schools provided a new and profitable field for career development in colleges and university departments. Needless to say, the anti-racist cause has been eagerly embraced by the fashion-conscious and politically aware National Union of Teachers (NUT).

Pressure groups are another factor in the anti-racist movement. The huge and unwieldy nature of the state service means that it is very vulnerable to outside penetration. Those with an axe to grind perceive the schools as fertile ground. Any group or movement aiming to reform attitudes or change insitutions is bound to want to influence the young, who represent future political power. The CND, Women's Liberation, 'gay' rights, the International Movement, the 'Peace' Movement—all these and more have sought in recent years to gain control of at least part of the school's curriculum. Operating through a media system hungry for novelty and conflict, though political parties (particularly at the local level), the LEA advisory services and the educational intelligentsia, pressure groups have had considerable success. The anti-racist movement, riding on the bandwaggon of 'equal opportunities', which chimes perfectly with the egalitarianism that has dominated state education for decades, has perhaps been the most successful educational pressure group of them all.

The anti-racist lobby, then, has political, bureaucratic, academic and professional dimensions. It is ideological in the sense that it arises from a distinctive and highly selective world view and in that it represents considerable self-interest as a public service and a humanitarian concern. It is now firmly rooted in Britain. It has institutional, indeed statutory, bases, it is often publicly funded and its influence is now endemic and growing, not least in the most influential of all our media organisations, the BBC, which has so far made no real attempt to question its credentials and purposes. As I write, I learn from press reports that the Director of BBC Television has now committed the organisation to a principle dear to every anti-racist heart—reverse discrimination, and at the managerial level.

I am not, of course, suggesting that all those who support the anti-racist cause are motivated by self-interest. Nor am I arguing that they are all Marxists. Far from it. Support is drawn from many directions, not least the decent liberal influence concerned for the underdog and his life chances. Nor am I suggesting Britain does not have its fair share of racial bigots, both individuals and organisations. Only an insensitive fool would deny the existence of racial prejudice and the need to defeat it. My purpose is rather to have exposed the basic origins of anti-racism as a campaigning and expanding lobby, and to suggest that its ostensible concerns may have only a tenuous connection with its real purpose.

Claims and Beliefs

'Anti-racism' proclaims itself to be a purer, more fundamental and more effective means of eradicating racial disadvantage. But its methods are so uncompromising and its polarisation of the issues so brutal that it is likely to do more harm than good.

The new creed is a grand, universal theory with little bearing on the hard facts of life in the classroom. It is structuralist and essentially Marxist, calling for a revolution in both institutional patterns and personal attitudes to 'tear out racism by the roots'.

This judgement,[19] delivered in Britain's largest and most influential educational periodical—a journal that no-one would want to accuse of right-wing bias—is one with which I, as someone who has been at the sharp end of anti-racist tactics, would want to support. It pinpoints the chief characteristics of the anti-racist lobby—'uncompromising', 'polarisation', 'brutal', 'Marxist' are apposite terms. They encapsulate precisely the lobby's provenance, mentality, tactics and aims.

However, what, specifically, are the anti-racist claims about multi-ethnic Britain? What do they say is the case? A reading of the literature suggests that the following allegations are central to the anti-racist cause:

(1) Britain is a racist society.
(2) Every white person—and only white—is a racist.
(3) There is a uniformly depressed and exploited 'black' underclass in Britain.
(4) Ethnic variations in the labour market, housing and educational achievement prove systematic racial discrimination.

We need to examine these allegations to see if they convince.

Britain is a Racist Society

This is taken as read. The allegation it contains is repeated *ad nauseam*, and it is far more than a simple belief. It is the very basis of radical changes proposed in the schools of an increasing number of LEAs. A policy document issued by Berkshire LEA[20] (a Conservative authority advised by an anti-racist 'expert') speaks of 'The central and pervasive influence of racism'. This assertion is followed by a proposed list of changes in the schools which have been described as ' . . . nothing less than a revolutionary transformation of the whole of British society'.[21] The extent to which this allegation is to result in educational reform can be gauged from material produced by the 'Anti-Racist Strategies Team' of ILEA. In its annual report for 1983/4 this group gives as its objectives:

> To identify strategies, materials and resources for anti-racist teaching.
> (Reform) in-service training.
> The development of whole-school anti-racist policies.
> To assist in the implementation of school policies.
> Curriculum development geared to anti-racist practice.
> To assist in the production of anti-racist teaching materials.

Detailed proposals are then listed for making the following areas essentially anti-racist in character: early childhood education, maths, geography, history, science, home economics, art and school work on the police. This total approach is proposed by responsible authorities in Brent, Haringey, Manchester, Leicestershire, Sheffield, Avon, Derbyshire and Bradford. Since the Swann Report (more particularly the interim Rampton Report on West Indian pupils—see Chapter 6) appears to support the racist allegation, we can confidently predict (barring radical change in the power structure of state education by central government) the spread of this view of the purpose of school life. So we are not pointing here to an abstraction but are referring to an allegation that will have direct, daily influence on the minds of an increasing number of children in state schools.

Moreover, the notion that Britain is a racist society is supported widely outside the state education system. To judge from their various pronouncements, the Labour, Liberal and SDP Parties, all left-wing local councils and some Conservative ones, the BBC and the IBA, many trade unions and certain elements in departments of state, notably the Home Office and the DES as well as sections of the printed media, all these institutional forces which, taken together, exercise enormous influence, appear to believe, and to be willing to propagate, the proposition that Britain is, indeed, a racist society. In this sense the anti-racist lobby has had great success.

However, widespread acceptance of a belief is no guarantee of its validity. Men and women can come to accept the truth of an assertion for reasons having little to do with supporting evidence. Self-interest, professional opportunism, the fear of losing one's job, intellectual fashion, political pressure and the success of the opinion-formers in winning over public opinion are all factors that can operate singly or in unison to gain hearts and minds. History provides many examples of how false myths can be erected into cast-iron beliefs, and these myths have subsequently been articulated as actual social policy having direct, and often painful, effects on people's lives. The views taken of Jews in Nazi Germany and of black people in the southern states of the USA before the civil rights legislation of the 1950s, the racialist ideology of Apartheid, the response to left-wing politics in McCarthy's America are just the more obvious recent examples of false myths succeeding.

Moreover, there are thoughtful dissenting voices to the 'Britain is a racist society' thesis. After reviewing the evidence, the sociologist, Professor Marten Shipman,[22] concluded: 'The ensuing debate over the status of the evidence leaves the problem of the level of racial prejudice in Britain as open as ever.' Geoffrey Parkins,[23] a respected researcher, after investigating the question, found that 'Racism is not widespread in British society'. Rose and Deakins[24] commenting on a major study of race relations in Britain concluded that: 'The extent of [racial] tolerance cannot be stressed too often, and is indeed one of the major facts of the situation . . . what is needed is not an effort to make people unprejudiced but rather to remind them that they are unprejudiced'. This statement not only differs in its analysis of multiracial Britain from that of the anti-racist lobby, it actually proposes a policy diametrically opposed to those anti-racist policies now being assiduously implemented in so many areas of Britain's national life. It also, of course, implicitly denies the need for an anti-racist movement.

This latter view points to a major problem in challenging the truth of the anti-racist allegation. Those whose professional life, and possibly political credibility, depend upon the perpetuation of a particular belief will naturally do all in their power to sustain that belief and win support for it. The historian Tom Hastie[25] has proposed the following law: 'The alleged level of racism in society varies directly with the number of those paid to detect it.' This is not cynicism but simply an attempt to encapsulate an important truth—once a belief gathers round itself the focus of self-interest, it is likely to be both tenacious and inclined to proliferate. We have to remember that paid anti-racists perceive their philosophy as the basis for a career structure. They have, by their very identity, already pinned their colours to the mast. They are not interested in the objective search for truth, since they claim already to have discovered it. They are concerned with defending their position, as are all professionals. They are bound to adopt a negative standpoint. Giving maximum publicity to any racial discrimination that does exist both confirms their presuppositions and increases the demand for their services. Racism is, quite literally, their *raison-d'être*. If there were none, then, if their jobs were to survive, they would have to invent it. Moreover, we need to remember that, since racial hostility or discrimination are indeed repugnant phenomena, the anti-racists can always claim to occupy the moral high ground, a position from which it is not difficult to appeal to humane instincts. (Perhaps we should recall H.L. Mencken's dictum: 'The worst government is the most moral . . . when fanatics are on top there is no limit to oppression.')

The combination, then, of official status, access to public funds and a claim to moral concern has made the anti-racist lobby extremely influential, and this, in turn, has enabled anti-racists to get their interests onto the political agenda.

Values and Definitions

A further problem in discovering how racially prejudiced are the British lies in the values of those who have tried to measure prejudice. There have been several attempts by 'social scientists' to establish objectively how far racism is endemic in the country. However, as Shipman[26] has pointed out, their efforts are based on certain presuppositions about the nature of society. There has, for instance, been agreement that integration, a consensus about values and peaceful co-existence are self-evident. All the surveys have reflected this position but the context of race relations has not been included, and historical, comparative and sociological dimensions have been ignored. The interpretation of evidence, therefore, has tended to reflect not so much a scientific standpoint as the ideological position of those engaged in the debate. Moreover, again echoing Shipman, there are two further difficulties. First, there is no basis against which British racial prejudice can be measured. Is there such a thing as an unprejudiced society? If not, what might be considered an acceptable or irreducible level of prejudice? Second, questions on race may simply evoke responses based on social class. Discrimination may result not from antipathy towards a minority, but from a perceived inferiority of the subject assessed against social class criteria. At the extremes, for instance, 'skinheads' may disapprove of blacks not because of skin colour but rather from their own need, as members of the lower working class, to feel superior to another group they perceive as being even nearer the bottom of the social heap than they are.

If the fierce and unresolved controversy which followed the publication of the most comprehensive survey of opinion on this question is any guide[27] then it seems doubtful that the 'social scientists' can ever devise an acceptable means of measuring racial prejudice at all. Certainly there is little in the survey evidence to support the anti-racist view that Britain is rotted with endemic racism. Rather, what we have is contending groups disputing the status of the evidence.

Again, there are problems of definition. What exactly is 'racism'? According to dictionary definitions and common usage, it would appear to apply to an individual who believes that the racial group to which he belongs is genetically superior to other racial groups. He may or may not express this conviction in his actual behaviour towards those other groups, and this point needs stressing.

Prejudice is a species of attitude, and attitudes, according to those psychologists who claim to have located, studied and measured them, are complex phenomena. The relationship between belief and behaviour is by no means simple or direct. According to a recent textbook on psychology,[28] an attitude has three components: cognitive, affective and behavioural. The cognitive aspect refers to knowledge and beliefs about (in this context) the inferior group; the affective refers to the feelings created by the knowledge; and the behavioural describes those actions resulting from the combination of beliefs and feelings. The extent to which the prejudiced person is prepared to translate his beliefs and feelings into actual, hostile behaviour is problematic. Much will depend upon the influences acting upon him in particular circumstances, his actual experience of interacting with ethnic minorities and the costs and benefits attached to particular behaviour. If the group, for instance, favours prejudiced behaviour, then he is likely to act accordingly, since the cost of group rejection may be too great for him not to do so. Indeed, the individual might well behave in prejudiced ways simply to attract the approval of those around him. Conversely, the basically prejudiced person may not articulate his deeper feelings if the social environment in which he moves supports the norms of acceptance and tolerance towards minorities.

However, not only psychologists have made pronouncements about prejudice. Neo-Marxists, such as the distinguished historian E.P. Thompson, for instance, have conceptualised prejudice in structural and socio-economic terms. They have argued that it is a functional mechanism that subserves the needs of an exploiting class. The class with power systematically creates and maintains a view of an underclass as being inferior. This stigmatising process provides a rationalisation for the existing power structure and helps to perpetuate the *status quo*. In this way, exploitation of one group by another is facilitated and the unequal distribution of material and other resources can remain, sustained by intellectual support, however spurious. In this perspective prejudice is a form of rationalised, upper-class self-interest. This is undoubtedly the basis of the anti-racist movement's dominance by the political left.

This brief reference to the complex nature of prejudice raises doubts, perhaps, about the usefulness of the word 'racism'. Perhaps we need to employ more exact terminology. The penalty to be paid for seeking to encapsulate and articulate a complex concept with a simple for-or-against noun is muddled thinking and inadequate and misleading communication. Words should echo the actual nature of the things they purport to symbolise. This is particularly so where strong feelings are involved, as they undoubtedly are in anything that touches on race. We could make a start by distinguishing between prejudice and discrimination. The two are clearly not synonymous. However, the conceptual distinction they signal is lost in the generalised, portmanteau word 'racism'.

This is more than a semantic quibble. Failure to use an appropriate and adequate vocabulary can have unfortunate consequences. The word 'racism' implies that the world consists only of 'racists' and 'anti-racists', that one is either for or against the cause. This gross oversimplification tends to locate the argument at the extremes, as it were, so that people feel they must plump for one or other position. The possibility that there might be some middle ground, where more complex and better-informed attitudes might be located is removed and the search for truth dealt a blow. 'Racism' polarises the argument, tends to induce unnecessary guilt in those who doubt the wisdom of anti-racism and is a gift to extremists and those with chips on their shoulders.

The damage this mentality can do is well illustrated in the video film *Policing London*, produced by the Greater London Council, which purports to show how the Metropolitan Police operate. In reality it is highly skilled, anti-police propaganda. The police are shown throughout in a bad light, and are seen as racially prejudiced, hostile to minority groups such as the elderly and women, behaving improperly at industrial disputes and being generally both incompetent and arrogant. The film finishes with a reggae star mouthing the immortal line, 'When police smell, communities must rebel'. The film was accompanied by a poster showing graphic scenes of police brutality to children, women and black people and a booklet. The poster also shows the police as though they are a military body, charging on horseback and waving truncheons against defenceless citizens.[29]

This inflammatory and vile propaganda, which met with almost universal condemnation, was based largely on a report on the Metropolitan Police by the independent Policy Studies Institute. This did, indeed, show that many police officers were prejudiced against 'blacks'. They had used offensive language when referring to them, and the essays they had written displayed partial and ignorant attitudes. However, there was no evidence that the police actually translated this prejudice into discriminatory behaviour; they were, it seems, quite able to distinguish between their private beliefs and public duty and behaviour. Indeed, the report contains many positive references to police behaviour. One spokesman for the Policy Studies Institute said that it would have been perfectly possible to present a glowing picture of the police—if the film-makers' obvious bias had operated in the opposite direction—by selecting only those many approving references to the police in which the study abounds. This complex phenomenon will surprise no one who has taken the trouble to look at the psychology of prejudice.

The point about all this is that the makers of the film, by labelling the police 'racist' and failing to make those necessary conceptual distinctions that a more precise and thoughtful terminology would have allowed, were enabled to produce a blatantly prejudiced and dangerous film. The damage done thereby to race relations, not least by deliberately placing unnecessary chips on young black shoulders, can only be guessed at.

Civil Liberties

Since the surveys carried out by sociologists have signally failed to create a consensus about whether or not Britain is a 'racist society', and since the term 'racist' is highly suspect anyway, a more useful and objective approach to the allegation that Britain is a 'racist society' might be through a consideration of civil rights and liberties. Whenever minorities seek to demonstrate the prejudice and hostility of the majority people and state they point to deficiencies in civil rights, and seek to redress wrongs by demanding equivalent access to civil liberties. The campaign for equality of status for black Americans was identified as the Civil Rights Movement. In examining the status of ethnic minorities in Britain, then, it would be useful perhaps to compare their civil liberties in this country with those permitted to minorities in societies which, by common consent, are avowedly prejudiced and racially discriminatory.

First, what is a 'racist society'? How do we know when we may legitimately characterise a society in this way? A basic premise must surely be that the concept of racial superiority of the dominant group underpins social and political policy. The state formally categorises its citizens on the basis of race and determines variable, and unequal, civil liberties accordingly. This means that the dominant group controls educational and vocational opportunities so as to preserve the political, economic and social *status quo*. Power is retained and perpetuated through the official articulation of the theory of racial superiority. Genuine multiracial equality is prevented since the necessary liberties to allow its emergence simply do not exist.

If we look now at some examples of where this is the case we can perhaps throw light on the question of how far contemporary Britain is a 'racist society'.

The USA

Let us take, for instance, the plight of non-white groups in the southern states of America before the civil rights legislation of the 1950s and 1960s and the coming of Martin Luther King. Although the rights of citizenship and the franchise had been granted to negroes by the Fourteenth and Fifteenth Amendments to the constitution (1868 and 1870), segregation and inequality of rights and opportunities continued through the operation of a poll tax and literacy tests. Money and education were the means by which social and vocational progress (and, through them, political influence) were ensured, and these were precisely the rights denied to black people through their historically lowly status imposed through slavery and its aftermath. Segregation, denial of human rights and the ghetto condition they created guaranteed the continuance of white hegemony and the myths of racial superiority on which it was based.

This frustration of constitutional rights for the blacks was achieved by a legal device. Dominant, white Southerners could claim that their state rights were supported by Supreme Court rulings in 1833 and 1896. The racialist policies were justified formally by the questionable (but successfully argued) notion that the national constitution, which applied to all citizens regardless of colour, took second place to state rights. Thus, in places such as Alabama, Mississippi, Louisiana and Georgia blacks suffered the indignity of occupying separate and inferior places on buses, in restaurants, shops and, crucially, schools and colleges. This state of affairs was enforced formally through the courts and unofficially through the lynch mob.

Nazi Germany

Again, we should consider the condition of the Jews in pre-war Germany. In that country there had been periods of hostility towards the Jews from the Middle Ages onwards, the basic justification of persecution being the insistence on religious conformity sanctioned by the myths of the permanent responsibility of the Jews for the death of Christ. The real reason was more related to envy at the Jews' commercial and professional success—but bigots never lack rationalisations. Formal anti-Jewish prejudice, in terms of theoretical justifications, dates from the 1870s, when a group of German writers drew on Renan's distinction between 'Semitic' and 'Aryan'. This false and scientifically absurd notion was henceforth used as the basis for attacks on Jews as members of a distinct and inferior race.

Hitler and the National Socialist Party preached this doctrine in Germany in the period 1920–33, using the Jews as the scapegoats for all the nation's (and often all the world's) ills. They took over and developed the theory of the 'Aryan' master race propounded by H.S. Chamberlain, and this racial myth was formalised in the Nuremburg Laws of 1935. Jews were denied citizenship and forbidden to marry 'Aryans', and in 1938 a law confiscating Jewish property was enacted. Thus the myth of racial superiority was given pseudo-scientific and legal validity, and a false and barbarous view of a whole people led to the greatest tragedy in human history—the Holocaust.

South Africa

South Africa is perhaps the best-known contemporary example of an indubitably racialist society. Here, again, we see the operation of a master-race theory. Although the system of racial segregation had been practised in South Africa since the earliest days of colonisation, the election of Dr Malan and the Afrikaner National Party in 1948 meant that the policy of 'separate development' was to be formally and vigorously prosecuted. The apparatus of white, Afrikaner supremacy in the Transvaal was extended to the rest of the Union. There was partial disfranchisement of Cape Coloured in 1956, the prohibition of strikes by African workers in the period 1953–7, deportation from selected areas in 1952 and the segregation of education for all African children in 1953. Criticism of Apartheid was effectively quashed by the Suppression of Communism Act 1950, and the state expropriated control of sexual relationships in the name of racial purity by the prohibition of mixed marriages and the tightening of the earlier Immorality Acts. The ultimate in racial segregation was accomplished in the Bantu Self-government Act 1959. This meant the eventual creation of seven separate African areas with non-white chief ministers, the first being the Transkei, created in 1963. The denial of basic, human rights to blacks was thereby accomplished and perpetuated.[30]

What links these three instances of racist societies? I suggest that they display three characteristics. First, there is an underlying theory of racial, superiority. Second, there is a legal and educational framework which controls, expresses and helps to transmit the theory to present and future generations. Third, there are the means provided through political institutions, the police and the military for enacting, implementing and monitoring appropriate legislation. This formidable state apparatus not only ensures that existing tendencies to racial prejudice will be legitimised and reinforced, it will also help to create and nurture racial prejudice as a natural, taken-for-granted sentiment in the young. It will also, of course, effectively suppress dissent and prevent the emergence, or at least the success, of liberal, humane ideas about human rights. Racism, then, is the very basis of the relationships between white and non-white, major and minority cultures. If you believe (and the state leaves you no alternative) that blacks or Jews are inferior, then it seems part of the natural order of things for you and your family to want to exclude blacks and Jews from all your social, vocational and educational arrangements, and to accept them only when they function as a servile race. Perhaps even worse would be the natural (because enforced) acceptance of this definition of their human possibilities by blacks and Jews.

If, then, we take such avowedly racist societies as our starting point and employ civil liberties as our criterion it clearly would not be possible to describe contemporary, multi-ethnic Britain as a 'racist society'. None of the theoretical, legal and political criteria I have proposed applies in Britain nor is it a place in which relationships follow racial lines. People mix on an equal footing in schools, factories, shops, DHSS offices, hospitals and every other kind of human meeting-place. There is no hint of segregation, except the self-chosen separation characteristic of minority groups. Access to education has no reference to colour, school intakes simply reflecting local housing patterns. The benefits of the Welfare State are available to all, and civil liberties have no limits regarding race or colour. Freedom of expression, assembly and religion are available to all citizens. The vote, that symbol of full participatory citizenship in a democracy, goes to all adults, even those first-generation immigrants who cannot speak a word of English.

Of course, it might be objected that here I am failing to make a sufficient distinction between society and the state, and the two are, indeed, separate concepts. However, civil liberties and the Welfare State are not simply the products of government action but of a distinctive national mentality evolved over time. We have such enviable levels of personal liberty and such a highly developed official compassion for the sick, poor and needy in Britain because the British people as a whole are the kind of people they are. These civil liberties could only flourish in a society where high levels of tolerance are the traditional norm. Moreover, when anti-racists speak of Britain as a 'racist society', they are not simply referring to the private domain of complex relationships among people in society but constantly to institutional and political discrimination.

Ethnicity and the Law

As we have seen, the law plays an important role in the creation and maintenance of a racist society. Without legal sanction, discriminatory practices would have no official support and the rules of the marketplace—both social and economic—would tend, over time, to reduce initial defensiveness or hostility to minorities, as would that reservoir of compassion and concern for the despised and rejected that marks all developed societies. The law can enshrine racial discrimination or it can forbid it. Equality before the law prevents distinctions according to skin colour.

Where does Britain stand in this respect? The answer must be unequivocal: official, legal support for the principle of ethnic equality is expressed in the Race Relations Act 1976. Far from underpinning a 'racist society', the law not only guarantees racial equality: it could be argued that it positively favours the ethnic minorities in Britain. The Act embodies the concept of 'special needs', thereby promoting and sanctifying the principle that the ethnic minorities may gain access to public funds denied to other citizens, and, in certain areas, to favoured treatment (see Chapter 3). Whether this is justified on grounds of 'historic disadvantage' or disparate ethnic outcomes in the labour market and education, or whether such special legal treatment is likely to create resentment in the majority population is the subject of debate. What cannot be doubted is that the ethnic minorities in Britain occupy a distinctive place under the law, and that certain privileges are attached thereto.

Secton 35 of the Race Relations Act 1976 makes this explicit:

Nothing in parts II and IV should render unlawful any act done in affording persons of a particular racial group access to facilities and services to meet the special needs of that group in regard to their education, training or welfare, or any ancillary benefits.

Both 'special needs' and 'welfare' are subjective terms, which leave open the widest possible interpretations. 'Welfare', in particular, would be very difficult to locate within legal limits. Any public authority or private organisation could rely on this term to justify virtually any expenditure or special measure directed at ethnic minorities. It has, for instance, been employed to support the use of public money to provide visits to the Caribbean for British/West Indian delinquents, as well as justifying the provision of official information and forms in a variety of ethnic-minority languages.

Moreover, section 37 of the Act empowers any training body to reserve training exclusively for members of a particular racial group, provided only that ' . . . there were no persons of that group doing that work in Great Britain; or the proportion to persons of that group among those doing that work in Great Britain was small in proportion of persons of that group among the population of Great Britain'. Since it is so wide-ranging and since precise information about the proportion of minority and majority doing a particular job nation-wide would be virtually impossible to ascertain, this clause effectively sanctions reverse discrimination which, according to other statutes, is illegal in Britain. Moreover, it permits a level of official interference in the free labour market unheard of except in time of war. A commentary published the year the Act was promulgated says this: 'The pendulum of discrimination is given a

substantial push in the opposite direction . . . [it] positively encourages discriminatory training for ethnic minority groups.'[31]
There is no doubt that this now occurs, as anyone familiar with the
employment practices of certain official bodies will confirm. (Just
how far this principle can be pushed is made evident from a recent
appointment made by the Manchester City Council. An immigrant
from Sri Lanka who has been served with a deportation order, has
been appointed 'Immigratiion and Nationality Officer' at a salary of
£10,000. The trade unions are reported to be furious about this.)

Again, section 11 of the Local Government Act 1966 supports the
principle of special needs and increased public funding for the ethnic
minorities:

> Subject to the provisions of this section the Secretary of State may pay
> to local authorities who in his opinion are required to make special
> provision in the exercise of any of their functions in consequence of the
> presence within their areas of substantial numbers of immigrants from
> the Commonwealth whose languages or customs differ from those of the
> community, grants of such amounts as he may with the consent of the
> Treasury determine on account of expenditure of such descriptions
> (being expenditure in respect of the employment of staff) as he may so
> determine.

('Commonwealth' here includes Pakistan, which is not, of course,
a member of the Commonwealth.) In essence, this enables the
government to pay certain authorities 75 per cent of the cost of staff
employed to make 'special provision' for immigrants whose
languages or 'customs' differ from those of the indigenous community. 'Immigrant' here is interpreted to mean the children of
immigrants born in Britain (i.e. in practice the test is not immigrant
status but ethnicity). All public bodies may make use of section 11,
those most affected being the education, social services and health
authorities. The proportion of 'immigrants' necessary to qualify is
only 2 per cent of the total population in the area (i.e. the state
interprets the need of public bodies with regard to ethnic minorities
very generously). Money paid under this clause has risen rapidly, in
real terms, since the inception of the Act in 1966, and the following
are the yearly figures:

	£
1967–8	1,409,290
1968–9	1,817,328
1969–70	3,691,743
1970–1	4,399,619
1971–2	5,499,586
1972–3	7,009,991
1973–4	9,353,806
1974–5	10,242,464
1975–6	13,801,366
1976–7	20,420,443
1977–8	24,583,847
1978–9	31,083,131
1979–80	33,104,848
1980–1	46,027,171
1981–2	52,228,353
1982–3	60,807,081
1983–4	76,232,656
1984–5	76,297,824
1985–6	63,410,226
1986–7	102,247,946

In addition to this, more recent legislation emphasises the unique provision made for ethnic minorities in Britain. The Education (Grants and Awards) Act 1984 allows the government to pay 'education support grants (ESGs) to LEAs for education, innovation and improvement.' In June 1984 the DES announced that during 1985/6 £1 million would be allocated to 'pilot projects to meet the educational needs of people from ethnic minorities', and this figure, under the pressure of sectional interests, is bound to increase. Just how widely the term 'needs' can be interpreted here is made clear from the fact that the City of Bradford obtained a substantial grant to promote the teaching of Asian folk music in its schools at a time when musical provision in Bradford schools was far from generous.

If the reader will pause here for a moment and compare this legal support for black and coloured immigrants and their descendants with the picture we drew above of the legal position of ethnic citizens in avowedly racist societies he will surely recognize how far Britain has come in disavowing any suggestion of its being, in any legal sense, a 'racist society'. One further point needs to be made here. The term 'racial group' is defined in very broad terms in the 1976 Act. Section 3(1) defines such a group as ' . . . a group of persons defined by reference to colour, race, nationality or ethnic or national origins . . .'. This very wide definition (which goes far beyond any use of the term 'race' in any dictionary, in scientific or in common usage) has been emphasised in the courts. In *Mandla v Dowell-Lee* (1983) the Law Lords decided that Sikhism referred to 'a racial group'. Until this time the term had always been understood to refer specifically to a religion, an interpretation confirmed in both the High Court and the Court of Appeal. (Just how widely the term 'racial group' is legally interpreted can be seen from Lord Fraser's judgment quoted in *Review of the Race Relations Act 1976*[32])

The effect of this, of course, is to extend the benefits of a unique and privileged legal status to a much wider group of people than would have been the case with a more precise definition of what constitutes a 'racial minority'. Again, this is not the kind of development likely to be found in a 'racist society'. Racist societies, insofar as they ever do make positive provision for racial minority groups, would have a built-in tendency to restrict definitions so as to limit the number of people receiving benefits paid for by the state.

Britain's Popularity

Another and obvious (though rarely noted) way of looking at this issue is to ask the simple question: How much do ethnic minorities actually want to settle in Britain and how far do they tend to remain, have families and create communities with a permanent character? By examining this question we can see how far such immigrants perceive Britain as being, broadly speaking, hostile or welcoming.

A key influence here will be the reports of immigrants to relatives and friends in the homeland regarding the kind of country they feel Britain to be. Although annual inflow has varied and immigration from the Caribbean has declined (which has to be set against the Caribbean's very small total population and necessarily smaller population of potential immigrants), in terms of proportions of ethnic minority immigrants and total numbers there is little doubt that people of every race, creed and colour have a continuing desire to come and settle in Britain. Indeed, there is a very strong demand from non-white groups to come and simply *visit* the country. There was a considerable increase in this group when the British government introduced a visa system for visits in 1986. The latest available figures show that Britain has world-wide appeal as a centre for immigrant settlement, and those for acceptance for settlement by nationality for 1985 are as follows:

European Community	2,830
Other Western Europe	2,900
EasternEurope	540
Americas	7,130
Africa	4,710
Indian Subcontinent	17,510
Middle East	3,580
Remainder of Asia	5,000
Australasia	6,660
British Overseas Citizens	2,180
Other countries	900
Stateless	1,420
All nationalities	55,360

(*Control of Immigration: Statistics UK, 1985*, Cmnd 9863, HMSO)

The total figure represents an increase over the previous year of 9 per cent (4,410) and 1,990 more than in 1983. The Indian Subcontinent provided almost one third, 18 per cent up on 1984. These figures have to be set against a country with over 3 million people on the dole and the fact that immigrants, as in all societies, have a greater risk of unemployment than members of the indigenous population. Even that bleak prospect fails to deter folk from all over the globe, and of every race, colour and creed, settling in Britain.

It is significant here that a very high proportion (32 per cent overall) of immigrants in 1985 were the wives of people already settled in Britain and 21 per cent were children. This suggests that first-generation immigrants have a strong tendency to put down roots, create families and commit themselves to permanent residence. Futher evidence of this can be detected in two factors: birth rates and the quality of life of those who started in Britain as ethnic-minority immigrants.

Precise details of comparative birth rates are difficult to obtain, but there are three sources which suggest that ethnic minorities in Britain have comparatively large and, with regard to Pakistan and

Bangladeshi households, very large families. First, six years of working in a neighbourhood and school where the great majority were of Asian origin suggested to me that Pakistani couples have a birth rate between two and three times the national average. Second, official statistics issued by Bradford City Council in 1984 indicate that although the Asian population accounts for about 13 per cent of the city's total population, one third of all live births are to Asian mothers. Third, statistics issued by the office of Population Censuses and Surveys, based on the Labour Force Survey,[33] suggest that ethnic minorities do indeed produce larger families than the majority population. For instance, whereas only 4 per cent of white households have four or more dependent children under nineteen, the corresponding figures for West Indians and Guyanese is 7 per cent, for Indians 14 per cent and for Pakistanis and Bangladeshis 40 per cent. The comparative percentage figures for couples with no children are whites 27, West Indians and Guyanese 14, Indians 10 and Pakistanis and Bangladeshis 4; whereas the figures for couples with dependent children are whites 30, West Indians and Guyanese 30, Indians 58 and Pakistanis and Bangladeshis 71.

Clearly, the reasons why particular communities vary in their respective birth rates are many and complex. Not least will be the effect of history, religion and recent experience of living in communities where large families are traditional and where the notion of planned parenthood in the Western sense has not taken root. However, it has long been recognised that high reproductive rates are unlikely to be the norm when a community feels the insecurity of living in a generally threatening or hostile environment.

The quality of life is a much vaguer and less easily measured variable than family size and birth rates. How do we measure the extent to which a particular group of people, who define themselves as a community, enjoy a quality of life they regard as adequate or appropriate to their needs? Crucial in this context, how do we assess the quality of life across communities? How do we enable comparative judgements based on objective statements about socio-economic advantage and disadvantage to be made? Since subjective factors determine *for the individual and his community* what life is like and how far expectations are being met, then objective assessment is very difficult. Also, measured comparative data are beset with a further crucial problem; within the framework of equal opportunities, communities make systematically different choices. Social and cultural values and history operate to produce very different patterns of material outcomes. (The distinguished black authority on this issue says: 'The great mindless idea of our time is that all groups would be equally "represented" everywhere if it were not for discrimination or other sins of "society"'[34]) This question is further complicated by variations across communities in age levels, fertility rates, geographical location and length of residence. Moreover, subjective estimates of the quality of life will vary with the generations. Would a first-generation Pakistani from a poor, underdeveloped part of, say, Mirpur, who now finds himself the heir to a womb-to-tomb Welfare State, to education for his children and reasonable expectations of a longer life perceive the improvements in his material existence in the same way as his British-born children, whose expectations are a function of a Western education and predominant consumerism?

I intend to look at more obvious criteria later, when I examine employment, housing and education. What I wish to stress here is the inherent complexity of an issue that suffers greatly from all kinds of logical fallacies and *a priori* thinking. A key factor in the public's perception is that most of the material bearing on this subject is produced and disseminated by people who have already made up their minds in a pessimistic direction. (Anyone who cares to read, for example, the material produced by the Runnymede Trust or the CRE cannot fail to be struck by the essentially selective nature of their enquiries and conclusions. They *never* concede the possibility that Britain has had any multi-ethnic successes, despite the fact that it is surrounded by them.) In truth, the linking of quality of life with racial discrimination is a far from simple matter. Perception may well owe more to ideology than to the facts. Those who begin with presuppositions about history, class, economics and a deterministic, view of the nature of man will produce a very different picture from that evinced by the less ideologically committed. Since I am neither a Marxist nor a pessimist about human possibilities, I am inclined to doubt the validity of the anti-racist picture of black or Asian life-chances in Britain. The stereotype of the ethnic minorities as exploited unsuccessful victims is undermined by the following data culled from readily available sources:

(1) East African Indians have a lower level of unemployment than any other group, including whites.

(2) A higher proportion of Pakistani/Bangladeshis (and a much greater number of Indians) own their own businesses than do white.
(3) Significantly more Asians own their own homes than any other group, including whites.
(4) The majority of Britain's ethnic minorities are satisfied with their jobs and with the education their children are receiving.
(5) In the 16–24 age group the ethnic minorities produce a higher proportion of students—an indication of hope rather than pessimism.
(6) Immigrants from India, Pakistan and Uganda have been very successful in business. In 1986 the Asian business community in Britain had a combined annual turnover of £2 billion.
(7) Eastern religions, particularly Islam, have taken root in Britain and are growing rapidly. Moreover, Britain now has more than 70 ethnic newspapers and magazines (over 40 in Asian languages) provided on a regular basis.

'Britain is a racist society' is the battle cry of the whole anti-racist movement. However, although racial prejudice and discrimination undoubtedly exist in Britain as they do in every other multi-ethnic society, to characterise the country in such a way is a largely mindless, not to say extremely damaging, allegation which owes more to ideology and self-interest than to the truth.

Racism: A White Man's Problem

The notion that racism is specific to white people is a key proposition of the anti-racist lobby. Moreover, white people have no choice in the matter. To be white is, *per se*, to be a 'racist', and there is no escape route from this. The notion of 'unconscious racism', nicely arising from the Marxist concept of 'false consciousness', is wrenched into the argument to seal off any escape route the morally impeccable might have discovered. Here are two quotations which encapsulate this standpoint:

> Even those of us who have made every effort to rid ourselves of racism may fail to see how deep rooted racist attitudes . . . affect our treatment of minorities'.

However well meaning an anti-racist I am, I am still racist because I am white. However much I try to rid myself of the straitjacket of monoculture, some of it will surely remain tied to me.[36]

Not only are white people necessarily racist but this genetic condition is extended to include the institutional apparatus and the power structure. Basing the concept of prejudice on the doctrines of the neo-Marxists outlined above, the anti-racist intelligentsia intone as follows:

In structural terms racism is represented by the formula racism = power + prejudice and discrimination. Accordingly power and resources in the education service, as in other institutes of our society, are in the hands of white people.[37]

Therefore, it is alleged, racism is a uniquely white problem. This is not always so sweepingly asserted. It may be that the tradition of academic rigour imposed a certain tentative disinclination to engage in the totalist thinking the allegation implies on the work of those academics the Open University chose to include in its standard book on the subject, *Race in Britain*.[38] There, an attempt is made to give the issue the degree of complexity academics usually demand: ' . . . Ninety per cent of the English are racialists.' The remaining 10 per cent stand as evidence, no doubt, of the protagonist's genuflection to intellectual seriousness. However, as David Dale[39] has pointed out, ILEA, the nation's largest education body, a leader in the anti-racist movement and an organisation unconstrained by the niceties of academic discourse, go for the satisfying and sweeping sounds of total unanimity: ' . . . All whites are racists.'

These twin propositions, that all whites and only whites are racists, are so manifestly questionable that it might be considered a redundant enterprise to seek to undermine them. Again, this would be to underestimate the power of false myths to determine policy-making. All those LEAs dedicated to anti-racism would accept this allegation, and it is quoted uncritically in the Swann Report; indeed, the anti-racist policy of ILEA is a theme running through large sections of Swann (see Chapter 6). In short, this particular allegation is one that the authorities responsible are seeking to implant as a self-evident truth in the minds of the large numbers of schoolchildren in their areas. Before going on, though, it is perhaps useful to refer to what has become the classic expression of the mentality that preaches this anti-white doctrine. The following took place at a meeting of the Home Policy Committee of the House of Commons. Alf Dubbs, MP, was discussing the idea of racism with the chairman of the Haringey Black Parents' Pressure Group:

> *Mr Dubbs*: 'Are you saying that being white automatically makes you a racist?'
> *Mr Virgo*: 'Of course. It is my definition of a racist.'

It is necessary, therefore, to make our objectives explicit. Implicit in the allegation is the notion that people with white skins have a monopoly of the positions of power and influence in Britain. This is true. In government (at both local and national levels) the civil service, the police, the Church, education, the professions and the media there is a manifest tendency for power to concentrate in the hands of people who happen to be white. However, the assumption that this is a conspiracy against black people, and the result of a dominant class deliberately seeking to prevent power-sharing with an exploited underclass, suffers from a number of defects. First, as we have pointed out, there are good grounds for believing that the ethnic minorities enjoy a disproportionate amount of public funding and legal priority aimed at furthering their progress. Second, an ethnic-minority middle and professional class is emerging in our 'white' society. Here, for instance, is a view expressed as early as 1982, and included in a report from the Home Affairs Committee of the House of Commons on Racial Disadvantage:

> The government response stated that a study of trends over the previous fifteen years showed that whilst ethnic minorities continue to experience disadvantage . . . over that period there had, according to most indicators, been important absolute advances in the fields of housing and employment. The West Indian and Asian minorities do not constitute a coherent group barred from all awareness of social progress in our society.

Third, the allegation ignores history. This is relevant in two respects. In the first place, there were no significant groups of blacks or Asians in Britain before the mass immigrations of the 1950s and 1960s. It is not, therefore, suprising that there is, so far, little institutional leadership in the hands of what are, historically speaking, very recent immigrant communities. Gaining a foothold in the power structure of any established nation takes time. The fact that time may be the relevant variable here, rather than white conspiracy, is evidenced from the extraordinary success in Britain of an ethnic, and originally immigrant, community—the Jews. Despite predictable hostility, particularly in the early days of settlement, Jews now occupy a very disproportionate position of power and influence in British society. Their success does not suggest implacable, institutional opposition to the progress of minorities in Britain but the very opposite. Second, Britain owes its origins, in terms of its emergence as a nation-state and the establishment of its political, legal and social institutions, to the people of Western Europe—the ancient Britons, Celts, Romans, Anglo-Saxons, Normans—all of whom happen to have been more or less white-skinned. It is no exaggeration to say that the whole of Britain's status as a civil society is due to people who happen to have been white. It does not seem odd, therefore, to anyone with a modicum of historical knowledge and imagination that, in this very early stage of non-white settlement, whites largely control Britain's institutional life. It would be very surprising if this were not the case.

The allegation also holds that only whites can be racist. Of course, if one starts by defining the word 'racism' in such a way that the ethnic minorities are necessarily excluded from this particular human failing; by proposing a definition, that is, characterised by circular logic and the ignoring of history, then it is possible on this dishonest basis to erect a case. That is what happened, of course, with the standard definition of racism proposed by ILEA, Brent, Bradford and many other LEAs, as quoted above. However, if one assumes that the way we define words, the meanings with which we invest them, requires a conscious attempt to pursue the truth rather than the deliberate use of language to confirm *a priori* ideology and win over the unsuspecting, then it is a proposition which only the gullible or the politically committed can begin to entertain. It is instructive here to look at the discussion of this question of definition provided by Thomas Sowell,[40] himself a member of an ethnic minority group:

> 'Racism' is a term used to cover so many different kinds of behaviour that it is difficult to pin down a specific meaning. 'Racism' can be used legitimately as a term of moral denunciation of racially discriminatory

behaviour and no confusion results so long as that is understood to be its purpose and significance. Confusion and illogic results when this general usage alternates with a more specific designation of racism as a belief in the genetic inferiority of various peoples . . . The question is not about the 'right' or 'wrong' or 'best' definition of the word 'racism'. Words are servants not masters. The real problem is to avoid *shifting* definitions which play havoc with reasoning.

It is by playing 'havoc with reasoning' that those who construct meaning to suit the argument do so much damage. I wish to make clear, therefore, how I am using the term 'racism' here. I take it, in this context, to refer to hostile, rejecting behaviour by a dominant ethnic group towards a minority ethnic group which may or may not be numerically smaller. The reasons justifying this behaviour may differ from time to time and place to place. However, the intention, although not necessarily the consequence, is the same—the attempt by the more powerful to reject and despise the less powerful and to impose their will and view of society on the minority. I wish to argue on this basis that 'racism' is far from being the exclusive property of white people. It is, in reality, an international phenomenon discernible throughout history and in virtually every group on Earth. It requires no more than a perfunctory glance at the plight of various minority groups to grasp this, and any doubts will be quickly dismissed by the information supplied by the Minority Rights Group.

In Japan, for instance, there is a group consisting of 2 million people known as the Burakumin, and these are regarded as unclean and outcast. In the same country the aboriginal Japanese—the Ainu—are despised by the modern majority; the Korean immigrants and their descendants are likewise rejected. Indeed, in Japan, a manifestly non-white country, the very notion of foreignness is a token of rejection. In Sri Lanka, thanks to the caste system, a fierce hierarchy ensures that the concept of group inferiority is a central fact of social and political life. The Tamils, 30 per cent of the population, are designated as inferior by the Sinhalese—a rejection currently creating violence and bloodshed. Africa is a continent excoriated by ethnic and racial divisions. The Kikuyu tribe of Kenya, for instance, constantly seeks to impose its will on the Luo, while there is communal conflict in Zambia between the Bemba and the Lozi. In Ruanda and Burundi the historic conflict between the Hutu and the Tutsi tribes has resulted in great suffering. In 1972 the aristocratic Tutsi ruthlessly suppressed a Hutu revolt and 100,000 literate Hutu were massacred. The genocide practised by the dominant Hausa during the Biafran war called into question the very existence of the minority Ibo people of Eastern Nigeria. In the Middle East the ancient Assyrian peoples are systematically exploited in Iraq and Syria. In Pakistan the Pathans are the constant butt of the kind of rejecting and unkind humour experienced by the Poles in the USA or the Irish in Britain. In South-east Asia the Chinese immigrants and their descendants have been persecuted for centuries, sometimes to the point of genocide. After the departure of the European powers and the achievement of independence following the Second World War the countries of South-east Asia began officially sponsored campaigns of discrimination against the Chinese; for example:[41]

(1) In Malaysia quota systems aimed at restricting Chinese access to government, business opportunities and education.
(2) In Indonesia a law of 1959 forbade Chinese retailing in the villages; there was anti-Chinese preferential business licensing and Chinese-owned rice mills were confiscated.
(3) In Thailand employment quotas favoured the indigenous people.
(4) In the Philippines it was decreed that no new Chinese businesses could be created and Chinese shops were closed down. In some areas Chinese private schools were strictly regulated by the government, which stipulated languages and curricula and forbad certain Chinese books.

In short, it requires no more than a cursory glance at the history of minorities in various parts of the world to realise that the proposition that only white people discriminate against ethnic-minority groups is essentially false. I would go further. Given the Western nations' commitment to the concept of human rights and their exposure to world opinion through the presence of a media system, we are far less likely to find officially supported racism in the white than in the non-white world—with the bizarre exception of South Africa.

The 'Black Underclass' Thesis

Implicit in this belief are two assumptions: (1) that Britain's ethnic minorities define themselves in terms of skin colour; and (2) that they are a uniformly depressed and exploited proletariat. This claim has received widespread support. It is difficult, for instance, to read the pages of the CRE's *Education Journal* or its annual report (both of which are marked by a consistent and depressing tendency to highlight ethnic failure as a symbol of a common cause) without sensing this assumption. Again, those academics identified with the ideology of anti-racism appear to give more or less uniform assent to this notion. Rex, Moore, Tomlinson, Cashmore, Troyna, Sivanandan, Mullard and Sarup—all, in their different ways, seem to perceive the ethnic minorities in this light. All the LEAs committed to anti-racism subscribe to this same view, and the many anti-racist pressure groups—notably the very influential National Anti-racist Movement in Education—make great play with the idea. How far, though, are these two assumptions true?

The Black Community

It is certainly true that blacks and Asians in Britain have one thing in common—they originate in countries that once formed part of the British Empire, and they both have colonialism as an essential feature in the history of their mother-counties. However, how far this is experienced as a binding force either within or between the different ethnic communities is very difficult to assess. Politically aware black and Asian intellectuals often give voice to this view, but it is doubtful if thoughts about the Empire play much part in the actual daily experiences of the ethnic minorities in Britain. In six years of interacting daily with black and Asian folk I never once heard mention made of the British Empire—although one thoughtful Pakistani parent once pointed out to me an obvious, but overlooked, truth: that the only reason he and his compatriots now enjoyed the benefits of British citizenship was that his mother-country had once formed part of the Empire. Moreover, we need to bear in mind that, for a growing proportion of blacks and Asians, Empire is a diminishing memory, since increasingly more were born and have been raised in Britain.

It is clearly the case that, if we look dispassionately at Britain's ethnic minorities and without the distorting influences of political ideology, what is striking is not the notion of a single, unified identity but of an immense diversity. All the major concepts men employ to define both social and individual identity—race, nationality, colour, language, religion, caste—can be seen operating, as it were, at the very heart of Britain's ethnic minorities. To illustrate this, let us think of two contemporary British citizens living in the inner-city area of any one of a dozen or more major British cities. Think of the Jamaican bus driver who speaks Patois at home and lives a life mapped out by his fervent commitment to his evangelical Christian tradition; then think of an elderly, orthodox Moslem from Pakistan's rural Mirpur region, whose mother- language is Urdu, who speaks little or no English and who has no particular desire to learn it. It would be difficult to contrast two more significantly different people, divided as they are by origin, religion, language, race, colour and experience of urban life. Neither would be inclined to think of the modest social position he occupies in similar ways, since their backgrounds may well have created a very different set of expectations.

In more general terms, let us consider the economic and historical backgrounds of black people in Britain, compared with, say, East African Asians. One looks back to an experience of slavery, followed by poor pay and poverty in insecure agricultural employment; the other is the product of a Western missionary education and the imperatives of self-improvement conveyed by European capitalism. Attitudes in the two broad groups to, say, family life, private property and the role of the state are likely to be very different. Again, let us consider further variations within the black and Asian groups. Among West Indians, for instance, island of origin is an important defining characteristic: a Trinidadian does not want to be confused with a Jamaican, nor a Barbadian with someone from the Leeward or Windward Islands. Among groups from the Indian subcontinent, again, there are differences that can amount to positive animosities. No Indian would thank us for regarding him as a Pakistani, nor would a Pakistani want to be confused with, say, a Bengali from secessionist Bangladesh, though both would probably share the same religion.

Quite apart from these obvious historical tendencies towards minority differences there are, as Professor Peach[42] has pointed out, powerful cultural impulses towards segregation *within* particular groups:

Punjabi Sikhs [are] different from Punjabi Muslims, and they, in turn from Punjabi Hindus. And so on. And this extends beyond religious practices. Economic activities, too, provide a further dividing line. Punjabi Muslims, for instance, tend to confine their market appeal to their own cultural group, whilst the Gujerati Hindus of East Africa employ techniques aimed at larger scale and much wider marketing.

Further evidence of intra-ethnic differences can be found in marriage statistics that cross ethnic boundaries. Figures issued in 1984 by the Office of Population Censuses and Surveys make clear the following facts. No West Indian or Guyanese husband had an Indian, Pakistani or Bangladeshi wife, and no Indian, Pakistani or Bangladeshi husband had a West Indian or Guyanese wife. Indeed, these figures reveal a far greater—though by no means large —tendency for white husbands to have black or brown wives than for marriages to cross ethnic boundaries *within* the minority communities.

For instance, 11,000 white men had West Indian or Guyanese wives, 4,000 had Indian and 1,000 Pakistani or Bangladeshi wives and 11,000 had wives of mixed social background.[43] If we take intermarriage as an index of attraction between the races, there would be a stronger case for arguing black and white solidarity than black and brown.

Perhaps the most telling rejection of the 'black' solidarity thesis has come from a member of the British/Asian Community. Samir Shah was a producer of *Eastern Eye*, a Channel 4 television programme catering specifically for Asians. As such, he would be likely to have, as it were, inside knowledge and awareness of relationships between black and brown British citizens and their organisations. He emphatically rejects the notion of West Indians and Asians having some sort of common cause or identity. Shah[44] expressed himself in strong terms:

> But the myth, epitomized by the use of the term 'black' to describe anyone from a Jamaican Rastafarian to a Bangladeshi Muslim is supported by a formidable body of opinion . . . They believe the myth because of their vulnerablility to the ideological boot boys of the race relation industry . . . Yet the notion of West Indian–Asian solidarity is based on an inversion of historical truth. Wherever the two communities have lived together, for example in Uganda, they have been locked in an antagonistic relationship . . . it is meaningless to talk of a joint struggle.

Shah points to a national survey carried out in 1984 by the Harris Research Organisation. This found that Asians consistently singled out blacks as the least desirable neighbours, employers, employees and those with the least respect for authority: 'just as in white culture, there is an anti-black feeling among many Asians.'

It is clear from these simple and obvious instances that there are profound differences *within* and *between* the ethnic minority communities in Britain. Only the most vigorous and convoluted intellectual gymnastics, it seems, could succeed in imposing group solidarity on such a disparate collection of peoples. The use of the word 'black' with this intention must raise questions about the motives of those who do so.

What of the second half of the black underclass thesis? How far are Britain's ethnic minorities members of a uniformly depressed and uniquely exploited proletariat? This is complicated by two problems. First, how do we define a group's success? Second, how far can we assume that the values that make for success in our kind of society are evenly distributed across the ethnic minorities? Success is defined for the individual by himself or herself, and there will be many personal definitions of the word within any group of people. However, for the sake of argument I shall adopt the method adopted by the anti-racist lobby itself and look at group performance in housing, employment and educational achievement. 'Group values' refers to such aspects as the work ethic, respect for law and order, self-improvement, thrift and attitude to education, i.e. those things that both define the group's public identity and help to decide its progress in society. Attempts to compare the socio-economic performance of different groups always assumes that groups are identical with regard to such matters, and to attribute variations to the major influence of 'racism'. However, we now know for certain that groups *do* vary in their values, and sorting out how far variations in outcome are due to this and how far to discrimination is a far from simple matter. One further point needs to be made. We know that in the areas of employment, housing and, particularly, education Asians consistently do better than West Indians, so we need to look at differences *between* those two groups. Producing average results by combining the two communities' performances would not be legitimate—although that is precisely what those who suggest the 'black underclass' thesis always do, the consistently lower West Indian levels always thereby depressing the average.

My sources here are as follows: (1) the Runnymede Trust's summary of the social and economic position of the ethnic minorities, published as *Black and White Britain 1984: the Third PSI Survey 1984*; (2) the article entitled 'Labour Force Survey: Preliminary Results for 1984', *Department of the Environment Gazette*, May, 1985; and (3) the interim report of the Committee of Enquiry into Ethnic Minority Children—known as the Rampton Report, 1982. It is worth noting that the Runnymede Trust is essentially an ethnic minority defence organisation which, to judge from its literature, is in the vanguard of the anti-racist lobby, while the Rampton Report is widely regarded as providing the anti-racist movement in education with much of its justification (see Chapter 6).

Housing

This is a complex phenomenon. According to the Runnymede Trust: 'The relationship between class and housing tenure which exists among the white population is quite different from black people, and Asians and West Indians live in different kinds of housing from each other.' So we should be wary of sweeping generalisations that presuppose a white-versus-black distinction in housing. For instance, since Asians favour the extended family, they had, until very recently, a more marked disinclination to take council property than either whites or West Indians. Moreover, since 1974 the proportion of West Indian council tenants has continued to rise from 26 to 44 per cent in 1982, compared with corresponding figures of 30 per cent for whites and 19 per cent for Asians. There is little variation in the ethnic proportions in renting from housing associations, while 6 per cent of West Indians and Asians compared with 9 per cent of whites are in private rented accommodation. Perhaps most interesting of all are the comparative figures for owner-occupation: 72 per cent for Asians, 59 per cent for whites and 41 per cent for West Indians. This pattern of housing is constant across different types of household, region, city and neighbourhood. The only sign of convergence lies in the gradually increasing tendency for Asians to accept council-house tenancies.

Although these are nationally based figures that might well mask a degree of local variation and personal preference, the following observations appear justified. The fact that a far higher proportion of West Indians are in council accommodation belies the most frequent allegation that municipalities discriminate in their housing allocation policies, unless we assume that discrimination is directed against white and Asian applicants. In the intense competition for council housing, overall outcomes suggest that blacks are actually being favoured.

The fact that the ethnic variation in housing patterns is consistent and cuts across any suggested white-versus-black distinction suggests that personal habits and cultural values play a significant part in housing outcomes. For instance, the far greater tendency for West Indians to create single-parent families and for young West Indians to leave home may be related to variations in the size of council property allocated, and the tendency for Asians to buy large properties may simply reflect the phenomenon of the extended family.

If we assume that a sign of socio-economic progress in our 'property-owning democracy' is one's own home then there is nothing in the available figures to suggest that the ethnic minorities are losing out in a market dominated by whites; rather the reverse, in fact: 'When the 1974 survey was conducted, nearly three quarters of Asian households owned or were buying their homes and, although not as marked, the proportion of West Indian households which were owner occupiers was still larger than that of white households from equivalent occupational classes' (Runnymede Trust, p. 9). It is reasonable to assume that a significant proportion of the heads of ethnic-minority households would require mortgages. That being so, it would appear that any tendency to prejudice has been overcome by the colourblind imperatives of the capitalist marketplace. The only colour in which the building societies and local councils appear to have been interested was that of people's money.

If we turn now to housing conditions there is no doubt that people from the ethnic minorities are more likely to live in older housing and to experience overcrowding. For instance, West Indian council tenants are much more likely to live in flats than are white people, and in terraced as opposed to detached or semi-detached houses. Again, this is bound to be related, at least to some extent, to the far higher proportion of single-parent families among West Indians. (I am, of course, assuming that single-parent families tend to be smaller.)

Greater clarity about what is actually happening is provided by looking at the improvement in housing conditions among the ethnic minorities over the recent past, as well as by examining poor housing facilities across ethnic barriers. For instance, the proportions of households lacking exclusive use of both hot water or inside lavatory is as follows: white 5 per cent, West Indian 5 per cent, Asian 7 per cent. This is how the Runnymede Trust sums up housing conditions:

> There have, however, been considerable improvements in the housing standards of black people between 1974 and 1982. The proportion of black families sharing facilities with other households, or lacking the use of basic amenities fell considerably in the period from 26% to 5%, and 37% to 7% respectively as did the proportion living in properties built before the end of the First World War from 46% to 35%.

We should not underestimate the importance here of taking a constructive and optimistic view of ethnic-housing progress. Housing is an obvious source of inter-communal comparisons (not to say conflict) based on appearances. Attitudes based on ideological assumptions rather than the facts can be readily sustained where a very complex issue such as housing is considered. Selective perception and tendentious interpretation are natural concomitants of ideological commitment.

This is well seen in the controversy that surfaced in 1970 involving two groups of academics, Rex and Moore and Davies and Taylor. Rex and Moore had published *Race, Community and Conflict* in 1967.[45] They alleged that discrimination forced immigrants into neighbourhoods and certain kinds of housing. However, Davies and Taylor[46] found the very reverse, and maintained that housing outcomes were the consequences not of 'racism' but of personal preference and choice. This, however, is not simply an academic matter. Beliefs condition race relations and result in actual policy and practice. Parkins,[47] in an essay refreshingly free from any preconceptions, has drawn attention to the inherent dangers. The CRE, for instance, in a survey of housing in Hackney, assumed that ethnic variations in housing outcome was good evidence of racial discrimination, and indicated that it would use its statutory powers to compel changes in policy to ensure equality of outcome—and this despite the fact that, in the same area, only 12 per cent of whites own their own homes, while the figures for Asians, West Indians and Africans are 48, 35 and 26 per cent, respectively. Moreover, 82 per cent of West Indians and Asians were satisfied with their housing accommodation, with 45 per cent very satisfied.

Although the CRE admit that their argument is not perfect they insist that statistical variation in outcome and the elimination of a number of alternative explanations not only prove anti-black discrimination but is sufficient to force the council to change existing policies. Parkins quotes Thomas Sowell on the inadequacies of this kind of mentality:

> Once having waved aside all differences between people, many social analysts are then left with no real explanation of inter-group differences of income, occupation, residential pattern or other socio-economic outcomes. Only evil intentions—discrimination, racism, exploitation—are left as possible explanations

It is a sad fact that in this, as in so many other areas of Britain's national life, we now have a publicly funded and extremely powerful organisation—the CRE—which so often engages in this kind of deterministic demonology. A more constructive approach would show that, while inequalities do exist, they are not simply the outcome of white-versus-black conflict or of failed minorities being exploited. The general picture is of a situation which is improving. There is very little to support the ethnic depressed underclass thesis in Britain's housing conditions.

Employment

I have quoted figures above that suggest that we should be cautious in assuming that Britain's ethnic minorities are uniformly failing in the job market. It is undoubtedly true that, if we consider economically active people, then blacks or Asians are more likely to be unemployed than whites. Again, we need to realise that the job market, like housing, is far from simple—sweeping assertions about cause and effects are unlikely to reflect the truth. For instance, it is interesting to note that according to the Runnymede Trust[48] the rise of unemployment *generally* is associated with higher unemployment in the ethnic minorities:

One of the major changes between 1974 and 1982 has been the massive rise in unemployment, and the disproportionate effect this has had on black workers. In 1974, the unemployment rate for both black and white people was about 4%.

That is, the tendency for those in management positions to choose their own kind is sharpened in an increasingly competitive labour market. Whether this constitutes 'racism' and a desire to produce an ethnic underclass or whether it reflects a normal human tendency which operates in all multi-ethnic societies is a matter of opinion. Moreover, those who lack the necessary qualifications—which a seller's market in labour can afford to raise—are likely to suffer most. Two factors in particular are likely to emphasise minority disadvantage here—the West Indians' comparatively poor educational performance and the reputation of young West Indians for an adversarial rather than co-operative stance towards authority; and the poor command of English among first-generation Asian immigrants.

Moreover, even where qualifications are equal, the ethnic variations in outcome cannot be too readily attached to racial discrimination. A reluctance on the part of employers to take on blacks or Asians may well be related to a fear of what might happen if a new recruit is found to be unsatisfactory. Sacking anyone in these days of voluminous labour-protecting regulations and trade union support for members is very difficult. Getting rid of, or even disciplining, anyone who happens to be non-white is virtually impossible. The knowledge that the CRE—with its considerable statutory powers and public funding—will almost certainly support anyone from the ethnic minorities in a labour dispute may well deter prospective employers, who can pick and choose from an over-abundant supply of potential workers. Lengthy and costly tribunal cases, with the possibility of damaging allegations of 'racism' and embarrassing publicity, is enough to deter anyone from taking on non-white labour.

The result of the state actively seeking to equalise job outcomes has been well stated by Sowell in his examination of quota systems:[49]

Quotas often create new injustices and breed new animosities to plague us in future years. On what grounds can the government [of the USA] legitimately show preference for the Chinese over, say, the Irish? The

Chinese have higher incomes and more education than the Irish. Of course the government does not single out the Irish for discrimination. It singles out various other groups for preference. But all the various groups, including women, add up to about two-thirds of the population of the United States. What this means is that affirmative action authorises discrimination against one-third of the population of the country . . . No one planned it this way. That is just the way things often work out when everyone hops on a bandwaggon.

Although quotas are, strictly speaking, illegal in Britain, the wording of section 37 of the Race Relations Act 1976 enables the CRE to pursue the principle of equality of outcome in the labour market. Simple correlation disparities are constantly used by the CRE to support allegations of discrimination, i.e. the effect is very similar to that of a quota system. Demonstrated ethnic inequalities can always be used to support allegations of 'racism' in any individual labour dispute. If employers do take on blacks or Asians, they take the risk of being landed with unsatisfactory workers they cannot effectively get rid of; if they do not, they risk allegations of 'racism'. The uncertainty this dilemma creates has not, as far as I know, been empirically demonstrated, but it does not seem unreasonable to assume that it is a factor affecting the labour market for the ethnic minorities.

The point I wish to emphasise here is that the progress of the ethnic minorities in the job market is not as uniformly depressing as is often alleged. Examination of the evidence suggests that, in some areas, certain groups actually do better than whites. Moreover, disparities of outcome cannot always be attributed to the desire of white society to produce a 'black underclass'. The malign effect of discrimination may well have been operating since the sharp rise in unemployment, but we should beware of sweeping allegations of 'racism'. There are far too many other factors involved. Radical political propaganda and professional rhetoric and image-making effectively create the public's perception of this subject, and these are not objective guides.

Educational Achievement

In all the allegations concerning the creation of a 'black underclass' educational achievement has received most attention. The comparatively poor academic performance of black (i.e. West Indian) children's performance in English schools has received widespread publicity. It was, essentially, the *raison-d'être* of the Swann Committee of Enquiry, and it is invariably explained by the anti-racist lobby as the product of white teachers' 'racism' and an inappropriate 'white, Anglo-Saxon' curriculum. I considered this issue in some detail in Chapter 4. Here I simply wish to refer to evidence that does not support the thesis of a 'black underclass' in education.

First, I wish to look at evidence quoted in Swann.[50] This gives details of statistics gathered with reference to educational results in 1978/9 and 1981/2. The performance of Asian, West Indian and All Other School Leavers, first in six relevant LEAs (for 1978/9) and then for five of these same LEAs (for 1981/2), is compared. The criteria of performance are the results obtained in O level, CSE and A level, and a selection of the results is shown in Table 5.1.

Table 5.1

	ASIAN		WEST INDIANS		OTHERS	
	1979	1982	1979	1982	1979	1982
	%	%	%	%	%	%
O level CSE						
5 or more higher –						
grade results	17	17	3	6	16	19
English Languages						
—higher grades	22	21	9	15	29	29
Mathematics						
—higher grades	21	21	5	8	19	21
At least 1 A						
level pass	12	13	2	5	12	13

The following observations appear justified:

(1) West Indian pupils do much worse than other groups.
(2) In overall O level and CSE performance Asians did nearly as well as other groups, and slightly better in 1979.
(3) In A levels West Indians do much worse than other groups, but Asians are the equal of other groups.

(4) In English Language both Asians and West Indians did less well than other groups, although Asians did much better than West Indians.
(5) In Mathematics Asians are equal to, or better than, other groups over the two years, and West Indians are considerably worse than either of the other two groups.
(6) On all these measures the West Indian pupils improved their performance and to a statistically significant extent.

This same source reveals that Asian children stay on longer at school than others. They have a greater tendency to follow some kind of full-time further education and are only slightly less likely to go to university or sit a degree course. West Indian children, particularly girls, also tend to stay on longer at school—except for Asian children. They also tend to go more frequently than the average child from school to some form of full-time education course but not to university or to pursue a degree course.

Second, I wish to refer to research reported in 1982 by Professor Michael Rutter,[51] who looked at the educational performance of youngsters attending twelve inner-city non-selective schools. He showed that where pupils stay on at school (after sixteen) blacks did significantly better than whites. The following are the most interesting findings:

(1) Twenty-nine per cent of all blacks had one to four O levels compared with 24 per cent of whites, and a further 19 per cent had five or more O levels compared with 11 per cent of whites, taking into account exams passed in both fifth and sixth forms.
(2) Eighteen per cent of blacks left school without any graded exam passes in CSE or O level compared with 34 per cent of whites.
(3) Ten per cent of blacks gained at least one A level compared with 6 per cent of whites.
(4) Seventeen per cent of blacks went on to tertiary education compared with 3 per cent of whites.
(5) Of those who found jobs, blacks were just as likely to be in skilled work as whites.

In the context of the case I am attempting to make, Professor Rutter's conclusions are worth quoting:

These findings on black children are a testimony to what can be achieved with educational persistence and application. The story is an interesting and important one. In its emphasis on the value and rewards of individual initiative, it provides a complement to earlier findings which pointed to what schools can achieve and what education authorities can do.

Third, I wish to refer to the findings of Dr Christopher Murray,[52] who studied educational attainment, self-concept and attitudes among the first-, third- and fourth-year children attending ten multiracial comprehensive schools in Manchester in 1981. Attainment in the basic school subjects and a measure of non-verbal reasoning were obtained for each child and a measure of twelve pupil attitudes was also established. After examining the detailed results, Murray concluded thus:

> Using standard statistical techniques to adjust for these effects [i.e. social status and IQ] we find that, though there is a significant difference between ethnic groups, it is not particularly meaningful in actual performance terms . . . The result is most encouraging and suggests a rough comparability in attainment between ethnic groups when allowance is made for factors known to be related to them . . . In particular the results offer little support for suppositions made about racism in schools, negative teacher attitudes, inappropriate curriculum or low expectations of career teachers/officers as these relate to ethnic minority group pupils' attitudes and attainments (p. IV).

None of this research is decisive. For one thing, it is concerned with different samples of ethnic-minority children and uses somewhat different measures of attainment. It was carried out in different areas and at somewhat different times. Like all such research, it is subject to sampling errors. However, it is fairly recent and authoritative. Taken collectively, it is optimistic about the educational progress of ethnic-minority children in British schools. Even the performance of West Indian children—which is undoubtedly a cause for concern—appears to be improving and, taken alongside children of comparable ability, it is clear that black children can significantly improve their academic performance when they have supportive parents who allow them to stay on at school. The performance of Asian children is little different from that of whites, while entry rates to further education suggest that ethnic- minority youngsters are *more* ambitious than their white counterparts.

None of the research I have quoted throws light on why, overall, black children do less well than other groups. No doubt there are many different factors interacting in complex ways, but the notion that they are the victims of some kind of anti-minority conspiracy established by a malign 'system' and racist teachers and curricula receives no support whatever. Moreover, the significantly better performance of Asian children could not be explained in these terms.

To sum up: the three basic contentions of the anti-racist lobby — that Britain is a racist society, that all white people (and only whites) are racists and that Britain has a uniformly depressed and exploited 'black' underclass—are descriptions of contemporary multi-ethnic Britain that are highly dubious, and can be sustained only by manipulating language and perceiving reality through ideological spectacles.

References

1. S. Tomlinson, *Ethnic Minorities in British Schools*, Heinemann Educational, London (1983)
2. F. Taylor, *Race, School and Community*, NFER (1974)
3. C. Husband (ed.), *Race in Britain: Community and Change*, Hutchinson, London (1982)
4. M. Sarup, *The Politics of Multiracial Education*, Routledge and Kegan Paul, London (1986)
5. *Race Relations in Britain: A Register of Current Researches*, 2nd edn, Commission for Racial Equality, London (1983)
6. *West Indian Children in Our Schools* (The Rampton Report), Cmnd. 8273, HMSO, London (1981)
7. F. Fanon, *Black Skin, White Masks*, Pluto Press, London (1986)
8. J. Marks, *Education, Race and Ethnic Differences*, Unpublished paper (1986)
9. C. Mullard, *Black Britain*, Allen and Unwin, London (1973)
10. S. Hall, 'Introduction' to A. Sivanandan, *A Different Hunger: Writings on Black Resistance*, Pluto Press, London (1982)
11. D. Dale, 'Racial Mischief: the Case of Dr Sivanandan', in F. Palmer (ed.), *Anti-racism—An Assault on Education and Value*, The Sherwood Press, London (1986)
12. A. Sivanandan, *How Racism Came to Britain*, Institute of Race Relations, London (1985)
13. Sivanandan, *A Different Hunger*
14. *Anti-racist Strategies Team Progress Report*, September 1983–August 1984, Inner London Education Authority Centre for Anti-racist Education
15. J. E. Lane, 'Childcare Shapes the Future—the Need for an Anti-racist Strategy', *Education Journal*, Commission for Racial Equality, September (1984)

16. H. Ashley, 'Education, Institutional Racism and Black Youth', *Headteachers' Review*, Winter (1983)
17. *Britain 1986: An Official Handbook*, HMSO, London
18. M. Stone, *The Education of the Black Child in Britain: The Myth of Multiracial Education*, Fontana, London (1981)
19. M. Durham, 'Anti-Racist Overkill', *The Times Educational Supplement*, 5 April 1985
20. *Education for Equality*, Advisory Committee for Multicultural Education, Berkshire County Council (1983)
21. A. Flew, *Education, Race and Revolution*, Centre for Policy Studies, London (1984)
22. M. Shipman, *The Limitations of Social Research*, 2nd edn, Longman, Harlow (1981)
23. G. Parkins, 'Positive Racism in Britain', in *Reversing Racism*, The Social Affairs Unit, London (1984)
24. E. J. B. Rose and N. Deakins, *Colour, Citizenship and British Society*, Panther Books, London (1970)
25. T. Hastie, 'History, Race and Propaganda', in F. Palmer (ed.), *Anti-racism*
26. Shipman, *op. cit.*
27. E. J. B. Rose, *Colour and Citizenship*, Oxford University Press, Oxford (1969)
28. R. Radford and E. Govier (eds), *A Textbook of Psychology*, Sheldon Press, London (1980)
29. C. Cox, *Encouraging Hostility to the Police*, Unpublished paper (1986)
30. A. Palmer, *The Penguin Dictionary of Twentieth Century History—1900–1978*, Allen Lane, London (1979)
31. D. J. Walker and M. J. Redman, *Racial Discrimination*, Shaw, London (1977)
32. *Review of the Race Relations Act 1976*, Commission for Racial Equality, London (1985), pp. 6–7
33. *Labour Force Survey, 1984*, Ref. L.F.S. 85/1, PPI 85/3
34. T. Sowell, *Pink and Brown People*, Hoover Institute Press, Stanford, CT (1981)
35. ILEA, 'Race, Sex and Class', *Multi-ethnic Education in Schools*, No. 2 (1983), p. 23
36. A. Redgrave, Letter to *The Times Educational Supplement*, 3 May 1985
37. ILEA, *op. cit.*
38. Husband (ed.), *op. cit.*
39. Dale, in F. Palmer (ed.), *Anti-racism*
40. T. Sowell, *The Economics and Politics of Race*, William Morrow, New York (1983)
41. *Ibid.*
42. C. Peach, 'Stranded in the Inner City', *The Times Educational Supplement*, 22 February 1985
43. *Labour Force Survey, 1984, op. cit.*
44. S. Shah, 'Hard Facts about Black–Brown "Solidarity"', *The Times*, 19 September 1985
45. J. Rex and R. Moore, *Race, Community and Conflict*, Oxford University Press, Oxford (1967)
46. J. G. Davies and J. Taylor, 'Race, Community and No Conflict', *New Society*, 9 July 1970
47. Parkins, *op. cit.*
48. 'Race and Immigration', *Runnymede Trust Bulletin*, No. 169, July (1984)
49. Sowell, *Pink and Brown People*

50. Lord Swann, *Education for All*, Report of the Committee of Enquiry into the Education of Ethnic Minority Children, HMSO, London, March (1985), pp. 110–16
51. Reported in D. Spencer, 'Staying on Helps Blacks to Exam Success', *The Times Educational Supplement*, 8 October 1982
52. C. Murray and A. Dawson, *Five Thousand Adolescents*, Manchester University Press (1983)

CHAPTER 6

The Swann Enterprise: A Critical Commentary

Background

In response to a report by the Parliamentary Select Committee on Race Relations and Immigration, in 1979 Mrs Shirley Williams set up a Committee of Enquiry into the education of ethnic-minority children. This produced an interim report on West Indian children in 1981 (the Rampton Report[1]) and its final report in 1985 (the Swann Report[2]). The Select Committee Report, *The West Indian Community*, had drawn attention to the comparatively poor academic performance of British West Indian children. The terms of reference of the Committee of Enquiry were as follows:

> Review in relation to schools the educational needs and attainments of children from the ethnic minority groups taking account, as necessary, of factors outside the formal education system relevant to school performance, including influences in early childhood and prospects for school leavers; consider the potential value of instituting arrangements for keeping under review the educational performance of different ethnic minority groups, and what those arrangements might be; consider the most effective use of resources for these purposes; and to make recommendations.

The Committee was urged to give 'early and particular attention' to West Indian pupils and its work was confined to England.

Context

Two broad aspects are relevant in considering the work of the Committee: the Committee itself and how it operated; and the intellectual climate within which it did its thinking. Relevant factors are as follows:

(1) The Committee was large—31 members over its lifetime.
(2) A very high proportion of members were from the ethnic minorities—30 per cent, compared with 4 per cent in the general population.
(3) A high proportion of the members were committed to the doctrines of anti-racism from the outset.
(4) The enquiry took a very long time to produce its final Report (five and a half years).
(5) The Report is very long and was very costly (807 pages, together with a 13-page summary—£692,618).
(6) There were serious divisions within the Committee, many of them along ethnic lines.
(7) Eleven members resigned, including the first Chairman.
(8) Six members signed a dissenting report about separate schools.
(9) The Committee defined 'ethnic minority' in astonishingly wide terms. In addition to Asian and West Indian children they looked at Chinese, Cypriot, Italian, Vietnamese, 'Liverpool Blacks' and 'Travellers' children', but they ignored Jewish and white English children, who form the ethnic minority in a growing number of inner-city schools.

The intellectual climate can be characterised in immediate and implicit terms. Specifically, the Committee could not escape the fact that any issue touching on race is, by its very nature, likely to generate strong feelings and controversy. Moreover, there were events occurring during its sittings that had wide publicity and were bound to affect its perceptions and inclinations: ethnic conflicts in various parts of the world; the issue of sporting links with and sanctions against South Africa; race riots in British inner cities; the re-surfacing of the nature versus nurture controversy in relation to variations in ethnic-minority progress; and the growing tendency for anti-racism to be given institutional expression, notably by left-wing municipalities. Less obvious, but perhaps more influential, would be the values that have dominated the system within which the issues concerning the Committee were located—the state education service. These are chiefly three.

First, there is a strong tendency to assume that deterministic explanations of pupil behaviour and attainment, and group performance, are self-evident. The child is perceived as the more or less passive victim of large impersonal forces such as history, the economic system and class, the Freudian unconscious, and, latterly, 'sexism' and 'racism'. Second, cultural relativism is taken as read. The notion that qualitative judgements can be made *across* cultures, that one culture may be intrinsically and morally superior to another, has been anathema in state schools for many years. This mentality is neatly encapsulated in the famous remark by D.F. Swift, an Open University Professor of Sociology: 'We cannot accept quality distinctions between cultures.' (One wonders, if all cultures are equal, how the transparently unjust and immoral Apartheid culture of South Africa can be logically condemned.)Third, there is the dominating influence of egalitarianism. The concept of equality has, at least for the past 40 years or so, been the key assumption to which everyone employed in the state system of education has been expected to subscribe. The power of this assumption, and its ability to effect radical change, can be seen in the success of the comprehensive school mentality. There is a very influential school of thought—and one which is dominant in an organisation that had a powerful influence on Swann, the CRE — which argues that egalitarianism means not simply equality of opportunity but equality of outcome. A corrollary of this is that unequal performance is assumed to be conclusive evidence of discrimination against those groups achieving less. The mechanism producing differential outcomes is always assumed to be 'the system', a mode of explanation that lifts the burden of responsibility from the shoulders of the individual and the group to which he belongs.

Less apparent than these implicit values would be what might be called the contemporary *angst* surrounding English intellectual life. This is brought out in a brilliant essay on Swann by Dr D.J. O'Keeffe in *Encounter* (December 1985). Misanthropy is fashionable. Self- denigration and an urge to underestimate the British achievement in establishing the rule of law, affluence, long life and the dominant mood of tolerance, as well as the supreme achievement of Parliamentary democracy, all these the British can lay claim to having crucially influenced, and yet the propensity to sneer at patriotism has been a major factor in Britain's intellectual life for generations, and remains so. Moreover, since the loss of

Empire, a sense of guilt about colonialism and a lack of certainty about Britain's role in the world have exacerbated this mood. This sense of spiritual decline has occurred at a time of considerable material advancement, and this paradox has resulted in a feeling of bitterness.

O'Keeffe has little doubt that this crucially affected the whole Swann enterprise:

> Nowhere, alas, is the contradiction more bitter than in Great Britain: nowhere is it more savage and unjustified than in contemporary British writings on race relations; and nowhere are the self-inflicted wounds of publicly-financed *angst* more evident than in Lord Swann's report *Education for All*.

As someone who worked in the state education service for 25 years—including a spell as part-time tutor with the Open University—I have to say that this observation has the ring of truth.

In evaluating the Swann Report, then, we need to remember the specific conditions of its production—clear evidence of much internal wrangling, its interminable progress, its anti-racist bias and its tendentious assumptions about what constitutes an ethnic minority. Also, we need to bear in mind its implicit values and the pessimistic mood surrounding its deliberations.

Specific Aspects

The Coard Influence

Having outlined the context it is now necessary to examine specifics. A key influence running throughout the Swann Report is what can be called the 'Bernard Coard thesis'. In order to explain this it is necessary to outline the background.

In 1972 Bernard Coard, a West Indian teacher, working in London, published a book entitled *How the West Indian Child is Made Educationally Sub-normal in the British Schools System* (New Beacon Books). Coard also collaborated with Bagley in research published in 1975. In this the authors sought to show that West Indian children were being deprived of their parent culture in

British schools, and asserted that this had a harmful effect on their sense of identity and caused them to behave badly.

Although each of these works has been severely criticised, their influence has been seminal. Their two basic allegations that the school system actually produces a disproportionate number of black educationally sub-normal pupils and that schools are damagingly dismissive of Caribbean culture have exerted great influence on the debate about the education of black children in English schools. For instance, the much-quoted NFER study *Race, School and Community*, published in 1974, implicitly accepts the Coard ESN theory:

> The factors he outlines are those already mentioned in other studies, biases in assessment by teachers or tests, due to differences in culture, social class, and to cases where children are emotionally disturbed. Children's academic achievements are also influenced by low teacher expectations, lack of motivation and a negative self image due to negative social attitudes (pp. 102–3).

In 1983 Professor Tomlinson's review of the literature, *Ethnic Minorities in British Schools*, which brings the evidence up to 1982 (the centre point of the Swann Committee sittings) also refers to Coard's work, although the author rightly avers that on the black/ ESN issue 'There is however, very little actual research' (p. 42). However, this does not prevent the same author in *Home and School in Multiracial Britain* (1984) from uncritically quoting Coard's work:

> In Britain Coard's (1972) influential polemical booklet on the 'ESN issue' specifically used Rosenthal and Jacobson's work to contend that attitudes towards and expectations of West Indian children caused them to underestimate the children's ability . . . Coard suggested that the children built up resentment and emotional blocks as a result of such treatment (p. 42).

Tomlinson's uncritical reference to Coard's theoretical framework is unfortunate. The work of Rosenthal and Jacobson had resulted in a book, *Pygmalion in the Classroom*, published in 1961, which became a best-seller. Its sociological explanation of variations in pupil performance chimed perfectly with the dominant environmentalist climate, and it exerted considerable influence on education, particularly teacher-training. Its power to influence opinion is still a significant factor in educational debate, especially among the dominant lobby that perennially seeks deterministic explanations of educational outcomes. Shipman[3] says: 'It remains one of the most widely quoted books on education, and Pygmalion effects became the basis of much pedagogical work in teacher training.' It was this 'Pygmalion' assumption that formed the basis of Coard's allegations, yet the original research on which the booklet was based had been savaged in the professional press.

Essentially, Rosenthal and Jacobson claimed that the teacher's expectations were decisive in determining pupil performance. The less the teacher expected of the child, the less he got; the more he expected, the more the pupil achieved. There is a grain of truth in this. It has been reliably shown that the self-image depends to some extent on what others think about one's strengths and weaknesses; we tend to accept others' judgements and incorporate them into our view of ourselves and of what we can do and achieve. However, the processes involved are complex. We do not know, for instance, just *how* powerful the expectation effect is, how it relates to other factors or how the individual child reacts to its influence. Some sociologists have argued that children do not necessarily accept the teacher's judgements; rather, they scan the whole of their social environment, in and out of school, to select information tending to reflect credit on them. In other words, children are not necessarily passive observers but active participants in developing a self-image they find acceptable (see Chapter 5).

However, Rosenthal and Jacobson ignored or were not aware of these complexities. They claimed decisive, significant expectation effects. Pupils, they claimed, responded in a direct, uncomplicated way to the teacher's original judgement of them, but the popular welcome the book received was balanced by highly critical responses from professional doubters. Shipman says:

> But the psychologists who reviewed the book were mainly critical. It seemed out of line with other work and the experimental design looked sloppy. Once Rosenthal and Jacobson had provided their data for analysis, and their methods were scrutinised, a thorough demolition job was published, confirming the doubts of earlier reviewers. Work on the expectation effect continues, but this episode on *Pygmalion in the Classroom* is a reason for caution and scepticism . . . nine attempts to replicate R & J's work failed . . . Indeed public confidence in psychological research could have been undermined by this episode.

Rarely can influential research have been so devastatingly criticised. Yet, as Shipman points out, 'R & J's work remains on the menu in teacher education and in the folklore of teaching'.

As I have said, Coard's work—and his joint work with Bagley—have been similarly criticised, and yet remained similarly influential. The latter work has been exposed by Maureen Stone as naive, incoherent and worthless: 'The case for poor cultural knowledge and rejection of ethnic identity has not been sub-stantiated by the author's own research'. Moreover, Coard's tendency to extreme ways of perceiving the world has been emphasised by his involvement in the violent *coup d'état* in Grenada in 1983.However, the allegations about British teachers causing black pupils' failure have remained remarkably tenacious. They are, perhaps, a good example of how ideology can sustain itself by a selective view of the world—however bogus the sources. The Coard thesis appealed to those twin intellectual strands 'which run through the Swann Report—the guilt-laden, liberal conscience of the many British academics who inhabit the world of race relations, and the dogmatic certainty of those neo-Marxist agitators and professional race experts who constitute the anti-racist movement. If black children were achieving less than white, then the attitudes of white teachers must be the reason.

When reading Swann one is repeatedly struck by this kind of crude determinism, not least when support is given to racism-awareness courses to free white teachers from their assumed hostility—real or 'unconscious'—towards West Indian pupils. (The only point in Swann where awareness of the insufficiency of the teacher-expectation effect is shown is in a critical reference to Rosenthal and Jacobson by Mackintosh and Mascie-Taylor in their discussion of race and IQ. However, this had no effect on Swann's deliberations or recommendations.)

Attitudes to Research

It is a truism that sound information is a prerequisite of policy-making; but although Swann contains several reviews of existing research, the Committee completed no original research of its own to guide it in making policy recommendations. In this it appears to violate one of its own terms of reference, which requires the Committee to take account ' . . . as necessary of factors outside the formal education system relevant to school performance, including influences in early childhood.' How this could be achieved without discovering what these factors actually are is difficult to see. After all, the Committee had the time, money and personnel available to institute the necessary enquiries.

This curious attitude to research is first apparent in the interim Rampton Report, which was concerned exclusively with West Indian pupils. A brief Guide was sent to schools and was likely, therefore, to have been more influential than the original Report—and it is this which is my source here. At several points the Guide makes statements and allegations which appear to have no foundation in valid and reliable research. For instance, on the question of language (a vital one when considering pupil progress) the Guide quotes the following from the original Report: 'For the majority of West Indian children in our schools, who were born and brought up in this country, linguistic factors play no part in underachievement'—a view Tomlinson dismisses as 'rather simplistic'. The Guide goes on: 'The attitudes towards West Indian children's language held by some teachers . . . may have an important bearing on the motivation and achievement.'

Now whether West Indian children are adversely affected by using Creole, Pidgin or Patois at home in their efforts to master the standard English that is the daily discourse of the school is, to judge from the literature, still an open question, and a very complex one. However, the question of teachers' attitudes to the West Indian vernacular could be readily assessed by a simple survey, one which, it seems, Rampton did not commission. Yet in the absence of such evidence it is difficult to see how any kind of valid observation can be made. The very loose nature of the Report's language here also puzzles. What, for instance, is one to make of the formula ' . . . some teachers'? Was it a majority, about half, very few? Again, consider the collocation ' . . . may have an important bearing on their motivation and achievement'. How can the tentative 'may' stand validly beside the emphatic 'important' without raising questions about the coherence of the meaning? One might legitimately aver that factor X (which has not been measured) may have an influence on outcome Y (which has been), but how can we logically presuppose an 'important' influence in this context? The conflicting nature of the two words makes nonsense of the allegation. Only controlled research could resolve this dilemma.

A similar kind of attitude is present in the Report's references to disciplinary measures involving West Indian children. In referring to the possibility that an unjustified proportion of West Indian pupils are suspended or excluded from school, it says: 'Again the absence of statistics meant that it was not possible for the Committee to establish whether West Indians were over-represented, although in the units the members visited this did not seem to be the case.' (The units are commonly called 'sin-bins', and they are for pupils who behave so badly that they have to be excluded from normal classrooms.) However, this absence of evidence, and their failure to confirm their belief from observations, does not prevent the Committee from recommending changes which ensure that the belief *has* been borne out: 'It therefore recommends that procedures after a pupil is suspended or excluded should be tightened up' (i.e. the proportion of West Indians in sin-bins must be reduced). The only basis for this is that 'West Indians believe that their children are often wrongly referred to these units'. How many of the parents took this view, one wonders? Do West Indian parents whose children do not behave badly, i.e. the great majority, also believe this?

However, the most alarming consequence of this cavalier attitude to research, and the part it ought to play in the making of allegations and recommendations, appears in the Report's comments on 'racism':

Many West Indians who gave evidence to the Committee saw racism as the major reason for their children's underachievement, and other people mentioned this as a contributory factor. The Committee believes that only a very small minority of teachers could be said to be racist in the commonly accepted sense.

However, the Committee claims that a teacher's attitude towards and expectations of West Indian pupils may be subconsciously influenced by stereotyped, negative or patronising views of their abilities and potential, which may prove a self-fulfilling prophecy, and can be seen as a form of 'unconscious racism'. The Committee concludes that: 'Whilst racism, whether intentional or unintentional, cannot be said *alone* to account for the underachievement of West Indian children, it can and does have an important bearing on their performance at school.'

This clearly is a very serious allegation, which the supporters of the anti-racist movement could seize upon to belabour both schools and teachers. Yet the Committee commissioned no specific research to substantiate its view on this matter. Hearsay is the basis of its findings. Moreover, the authors give no evidence to support the theoretical validity of the notion of 'unintentional racism', nor do they appear aware of the severe criticism to which the self-fulfilling prophecy, and its power to influence pupil progress, has been subjected. They do not seem to be conscious of the difficulty raised for their 'racist teachers' thesis by the good academic performance of Asian children, who, like West Indians, presumably suffer from the alleged disadvantage of minority skin colour. At no point in this whole enterprise is the influence of Coard and his discredited polemic more apparent, and at no point was rigorous intellectual honesty more desperately needed.

The Work of P.A. Green

Further evidence of the Committee's commitment to the Coard thesis is to be found in its selection of research for inclusion in this Report. The central part of the Report in terms of research is given over to a long (about 6,500 words) summary of a PhD thesis by Peter A. Green. Green, like Coard, but at a much more distinguished level, was working in the Rosenthal and Jacobson tradition as refined by Rabovits and Maehr. Now I have touched on the genesis and mechanics of the self-fulfilling prophecy as applied to teacher-behaviour, but I now wish to be rather more specific about its assumptions, which are as follows. As considered in detail in Chapter 5, there is something called the self-concept, which every person possesses; this can be thought of as a mental image or object, which can be located, analysed and measured in its various dimensions. The self-concept develops as a result of information conveyed to the growing child about its strengths and weaknesses, and it can be modified through learning and experience; the self-concept—crucially that part connected with self-esteem—significantly affects behaviour. Within the classroom it is held that the teacher plays a major part in creating and sustaining the child's self-concept, and this, in turn, helps to determine the child's educational performance and behaviour.

Although this paradigm of the concept of self has a certain logical persuasiveness it is based on large assumptions. Both philosophers and some sociologists have questioned its coherence, and attempts to provide supportive empirical evidence have encountered considerable difficulties. A key criticism is of the theory's assumption of the all-pervasive effect of psychological process generated by the social context. It may be that other factors are equally, or even more, influential—social structure, the economic system or the group's history, for instance. At a more fundamental level the deterministic explanation for human conduct, on which this whole theoretical edifice is based, is by no means generally accepted. I suspect that the view of the child as a passive object of outside influences, impassive in the process of creating and sustaining its own reality, is one that most parents and teachers would want to resist.

However, leaving aside the theoretical objections, we need to look carefully at Green's work, since it met not only with acceptance by the Committee but was perceived by the anti-racist lobby as evidence to support allegations of teacher-prejudice acting to the disadvantage of West Indian children—the unsupported assumption made in the interim Rampton Report. Indeed it was not unreasonable to assume that Green's work may well have been selected for priority treatment in the Swann Report precisely because it appeared to lend support to this assumption. Even before it had appeared in Swann, Green's work had been widely published, not least by those academics associated with the anti-racist cause, notably in two books by Tomlinson,[4,5] who said this of it:

> Green's study demonstrates powerfully that, on the whole, white and Asian children benefit substantially more from teacher attention in the classroom, whatever the tolerance level of the teacher, than children of West Indian origin. His research adds substantial empirical weight to previous research which had suggested logical, rather than empirical connections between teacher attitudes to and expectations of West Indian pupil's, *and their subsequent academic performance.* (My emphasis. In fact, Green made no attempt to relate his findings to academic performance.)

Green operationalised his theoretical position by rating a group of teachers on a scale of ethnocentricity, which he defined as 'the tendency to consider the characteristics and attributes of ethnic groups other than one's own to be inferior'; established their attributes to education in terms of the three dimensions of tough-minded/tender-minded, idealistic/naturalistic, and conservative/-radical, and related these to the sex of the teachers. These variables were then linked to different modes of teaching-questioning, informing, explaining, reproving, etc. An attempt was then made to establish whether the teaching thereby characterised was related to the child's self-concept. In short, were there significant correlations between teacher-attitudes, modes of teaching and pupil self-concepts?

The results were complex. It was established that those West Indian children taught by highly intolerant teachers had the lowest self-concepts, and this could, especially if it confirms one's expectations, be read as lending support to the theory that black children do less well than other children because of teacher-'racism'. However, such a glib interpretation would need to be balanced by some attempt to explain the following, perhaps unexpected, results:

The teacher question ratio shows that all teachers, irrespective of whether they hold tough or tender-minded attitudes towards their task, spent a higher proportion of time asking questions of children of Asian and West Indian origins than they did with children of European origin.

Within those classes taught by tender-minded teachers there was no significant difference in the levels of self-concept of boys and girls in each ethnic group.

Turning to the conservative-radical dimensions, no significant differences were found between the self-concept levels of children taught by either group of teachers.

Teachers inclined towards naturalism recorded a significantly higher response ratio than those inclined towards idealism . . . those teachers inclined towards naturalism had a tendency to respond more positively to pupils of Asian origin than to those of European or West Indian origin.

Boys of European origin taught by highly tolerant teachers received less attention than their numbers warranted in respect of nine of the ten modes of teaching.

These boys [i.e. European] taught by highly tolerant teachers have a significantly lower level of self-concept than those taught by highly intolerant teachers.

Boys of West Indian origin are given more individual teaching time by highly tolerant teachers than their numbers would justify in respect of every teaching mode except for the even balance achieved when responding to the boys' feelings.

Despite their exceptionally high level of ethnocentrism, highly intolerant teachers give considerable excess time to the responses (+50%) and initiatives (+49%) made by boys of Asian origin.

Clearly, then, any conclusion based on this research would have to be heavily conditional. It would have to bear in mind not only that the self-concept of West Indian children may be adversely affected by highly intolerant teachers but that the attitudes of highly tolerant teachers may depress the self-concept of white boys—a decidedly new element in the debate. To be fair, Green himself sounds a scholarly caution about the interpretation of his research:

> That there is no all-embracing explanation of, or solution to, under-achievement in the multiethnic classroom seems to be axiomatic especially since the range of influential factors is unknown and makes elusive any simple aetiology of the problem. Bearing in mind that . . . correlation is not causality, the findings should be interpreted with caution, assessed with discretion and ascribed with prudence.

(It is enlightening to compare this kind of proper tentativeness with the sweeping generalisation of Tomlinson quoted above.)

What, however, of specific limitations? How far are. Green's conclusions applicable to teachers and pupils in general? How far do they throw light on the Swann Committee's key concern—the academic performance of West Indian children? The following are relevant factors here:

(1) The sample was very small—just six schools, (three juniors and three middle schools), involving 1,814 pupils and 70 teachers, drawn from two LEAs. The most recent information (1985) indicates that there are 36,500 schools, 9.9 million children, 520,000 teachers and 121 LEAs. In no sense, then, can the sample be considered representative.
(2) The number of highly intolerant teachers, i.e. those teachers associated with low levels of self-concept in West Indian children, was twelve, and there is no means of knowing whether the proportion of such teachers in the sample, i.e. 17 per cent, is true of the whole teaching service.
(3) This research suggests that concern about the effect of the highly intolerant teachers on the self-concept of West Indian pupils needs to be extended to that of highly tolerant teachers on the self-concept of white children.

(4) There is no attempt here to relate either teacher-attitude or pupil self-concept to actual attainment or progress among the children of different ethnic groups.

It is by no means self-evident that ethnocentricity in the teacher causes or sustains poor academic performance. Some of the most spectacular victims of racism have exceptionally high levels of scholastic achievement (for example, the Jews, Japanese Americans and the Chinese of South-east Asia). The view of Maureen Stone,[6] is particularly apposite here since she is herself of West Indian origin: 'The assumption, however, that actions and behaviour follow from the individual's sense of his own worth, is quite illogical.' I am not, of course, arguing that intolerance is not deplorable, especially when children are its victims. I am simply suggesting that Green's work does not touch on the central question—why do West Indian children, on average, do comparatively badly in English schools? Academic achievement as related to ethnic origin was not part of his remit. However, it is not difficult to read Green's work as providing support for the 'racist teacher' thesis, especially if we are predisposed to do so. Nor is it difficult to see why it earned its central place in the Swann Report.

The Work of Murray and Dawson

However, if we approach the question of West Indian school performance with a rather more open mind than the Swann Committee appears to have done we are able perhaps to achieve a more balanced assessment of the issues. The key research here is the work of Murray and Dawson.[7] They, too, published their findings during the sittings of the Swann Committee. Unfortunately, Swann totally ignored them.

As mentioned earlier, essentially what Murray and his collaborator did was to take 5,219 pupils attending ten comprehensive schools in Manchester—638 Asians, 626 West Indians and 3,790 white children—and examine a range of factors, including pupils' attitudes, self-esteem and attainment in basic school subjects and performance on non-verbal reasoning tests. They then made comparisons across the different ethnic groups. The pupils were drawn from first- (11+), third- (13+) and fourth- (14+)year classes.

It is important to stress that this research—insofar as it touched upon attitudes and self-concept—was based on the young persons' own perceptions. It was the children who completed the necessary protocols. I can do no better than quote Murray's conclusions:

> It follows that we must be sceptical about some of the assumptions underlying the debate on 'multicultural education' as presented in chapter two. In particular, there is little support for the suppositions made about 'racism' in schools, negative teacher attitudes, inappropriate curriculum or low expectations of career teachers/career officers in the school sampled for this research. Any 'underachievement' of ethnic minority group pupils, measured objectively in terms of attainment is associated with individual characteristics, rather than social influences.

Murray also says:

> In addition the idiom of the multi-cultural–racial–ethnic debate characterised by such vague phrases as 'positive discrimination' and 'racism' has done little to enhance clear thinking about some of the issues involved.

It is, of course, precisely this idiom that we find in Swann and even more so in Rampton. Moreover, in contrast to the interpretation often made of Green's research (not, of course, the same as what Green actually said) Murray found that 'there is no significant difference between the groups on self esteem', a finding that will surprise no-one who has actually taught ethnic-minority children.

The following observations emphasise the contrasts between the work of Green and that of Murray:

(1) Murray's sample was much larger than Green's—both in terms of schools and pupils.
(2) Murray, unlike Green, included reliable assessments of the pupils' attainment in maths, reading, and also their non-verbal IQs.
(3) In Murray's work information about self-concepts was provided by the pupils themselves.
(4) Murray's findings were optimistic and encouraging regarding the school progress and self-concepts of ethnic-minority children.

Why, one wonders, did Swann ignore Murray's research? Although Green's work was completed before Murray's, the latter's was copyrighted in 1983 and issued in May 1984, as far as can be ascertained; and included in the Swann bibliographies is work published as late as June 1984. Why did the Committee not commission Murray to make a summary of his findings for inclusion in the report, as they had with Green? This would have enabled the reader to form the kind of balanced view of the issue that only a range of research perspectives can provide. Could it be that the compilers of the Report chose to highlight Green's work and ignore that of Murray because the former can be read as providing support for the anti-racist stand that Swann endorsed, whereas Murray's work challenges the anti-racist assumptions about 'racism' in British schools?

Stereotyping

Whereas we can detect a certain ambivalence towards research running throughout the whole Rampton/Swann enterprise there is no hesitation to call upon research when the Committee focuses on the question of teachers' attitudes towards ethnic-minority children. That teachers stereotype such children is taken as read. For instance, the NFER's summary of research commissioned by Swann, insofar as it touches upon teachers' attitudes towards their minority pupils, is given considerable emphasis and space. A work by Brittan[8] is summarised as follows: '[The] study revealed a high degree of consensus of opinion concerning the academic and social behaviour of pupils of West Indian origin, with more than two- thirds of the teachers in the sample indicating unfavourable opinions of West Indians.' Stewart[9] is summarised as: '[The] study showed the teachers interviewed as having a positive stereotype of the Asian pupil as industrious, responsible, keen to learn and having none of the behaviour problems associated with West Indian pupils.'

Although the authors of the Report concede that, 'comparatively little research has, in fact, been carried out on teachers' attitudes towards ethnic minority pupils . . .' the allegation that teachers stereotype ethnic-minority pupils is treated as though it had been decisively demonstrated. The Committee's support for 'racism-awareness training' for teachers is a direct consequence of this assumption.

Now stereotyping is the tendency to generalise about an individual or the group to which he or she belongs on the basis of very limited information. It is the tendency to prejudge, in the absence of the necessary knowledge, to substantiate an invalid perception. Certain conclusions about a person may be drawn, for instance, simply because of his appearance, the role he is occupying or the ethnic group to which he belongs. The term 'bank manager' for example, is likely to evoke a stereotype image of someone who is cautious, conscientious, hard-working, responsible, ambitious and money-minded. However, if one has met a large number of bank managers over a period of time then the generalised view one holds is legitimate in that it is based not on prejudice or on limited information but on full and confirmatory experience. It would be reasonable, at least initially, to allow that experience to influence one's view of a new and unknown bank manager as an aid to social awareness and successful interaction.

Therefore it does not seem unreasonable to assume that teachers' perceptions of children from different ethnic groups are similarly created. After all, teachers' experiences of their pupils are particularly rich, and include the process of spending many hours in their company in close proximity as well as such powerful forms of information as the pupils' attitude towards work, authority, peer group and self; their personalities, levels of aggression, interactional style, response to teachers' questions, directions and admonishments; their work—both oral performance and written expression; observation of them in social settings—in the school playground, at school dinners and in dressing rooms; and objective information such as performance in public examinations and rates of referral for anti-social behaviour. In short, teachers are particularly well informed about their pupils. Their data are varied, being based on lengthy, direct observation and experience and sustained by objective criteria.

It may well be that teachers, on the whole, *do* have a tendency to perceive different ethnic groups in distinctive ways. Equally, it is true that teacher-judgement arises not from the limited, fleeting perceptions that form the basis of stereotyping (as the researchers in this area tend to assume) but from actual, daily experiences over a period of time.

Why, then, do the authors of the Swann Report so readily and uncritically accept research here, and so thereby readily discredit the validity of teacher opinion while maintaining an ambivalent and inconsistent response elsewhere—as in the Green/Murray episode? Could it be that, in so doing, Swann is better able to sustain the 'racist teachers' thesis so mindlessly propounded in the interim Rampton Report? Could it be that such an attitude provides support for the highly dubious thesis that the comparatively poor average performance of West Indian children is the fault of their teachers?

The Mortimer Factor

However, nothing of what has been said so far is so revealing of the deeply ambivalent attitude of the Swann Committee towards research as the fate of the one piece of original research that they did attempt to commission.

We need to put this in context. The Swann terms of reference included the following injunction: 'Review in relation to schools the educational needs and attainments of children from ethnic minority groups, *taking account, as necessary, of factors outside the formal education system relevant to school performance, including influences in early childhood* and prospects for employment' (my emphasis). This is in keeping with what is known about factors affecting school performance, which are many and varied. There is now a consensus that educability, the ability of the child to develop its intellectual and creative potential, is crucially influenced by the kind of home he or she comes from, the attitude of parents to education and their own level of formal education, family cohesion and stability and so on. Second, the Rampton Report made a specific plea for research into the home background and parental attitude of West Indian children:

> Schools can, however, only go so far in this respect; parents must also appreciate and understand the role that they must play in supporting teachers. The NFER review of research drew attention to the concern, which has been frequently expressed to us by teachers and others whom we have met on our visits, that West Indian parents need particular help in recognising their responsibility in this respect . . . At the pre-school stage, as the NFER review states, 'Many writers have suggested that, although West Indian parents are evidently concerned about their children's development, they often do seem to lack understanding of the developmental importance of stimulation by conversation or use of toys

as part of the function of the baby minder, as she does not appreciate the significance herself'.

The way forward in this respect, according to Rampton, was to commission original research:

The question of home and parents in relation to the education, and particularly the educational progress of West Indian children, is clearly a sensitive and complex issue, and is one we do not feel we have been able to deal with in sufficient detail to enable us to offer guidance. We intend to look at this whole question of home background in respect of all ethnic minority pupils in our main report.

More specifically, Rampton took the view that there was a need for information relating to those West Indian youngsters who had done well in school, and to obtain this there was clearly a need for research which looked at 'The particular factors which have led some West Indians to succeed and the obstacles which they have had to overcome'. This need to look at the general culture and family environment of West Indian pupils was reinforced in Swann:

The reasons for the very different performances of Asian and West Indians seem likely to be deep in their respective cultures . . . the tight-knit nature of the Asian community and family—more so than whites and West Indians—could explain the differences [in achievement rates] since parental influences on educational success have long been recognised (p. 86).

This, then, was the context from within which the need for research into the West Indian child's background was recognised. Both the consensus among educationists on the crucial importance of home, family and the cultural values they embody and transmit and the specific concerns of Rampton and Swann pointed to this particular kind of research. Moreover, Swann's emphasis on successful West Indian pupils and their backgrounds was essentially constructive. If we could discover what it was about the children's backgrounds that enabled them to succeed, despite prejudice and discrimination, then there would be a solid basis of information and advice from which all West Indian parents could benefit.

With this in mind the Committee commissioned a well-known educational researcher, Dr Peter Mortimer, Director of Research with the ILEA. According to *The Times Educational Supplement* (30 July 1982) a contract was signed, a teacher seconded as a research assistant and a grant of £78,000 allocated for the research, the proposals of which were to include investigations into 'the factors in school, in the community, and in the home that led to success or failure of ethnic minority pupils'.[10]

However, when the proposals were submitted the Committee, it seems, was subjected to sustained objections from certain West Indian organisations and an anti-racist pressure group very active in the state education service calling itself the 'Anti-Racist Movement in Education'. As a result, the research was suppressed. In commenting on this episode Lord Swann said: 'Unfortunately, however, the project aroused hostility in various circles, and it had to be abandoned, leaving the Committee with little chance of deciding with certainty the relative importance of the many factors in the educational system and outside it, that might be, or are held to be crucial.' *The Times Educational Supplement (TES)* put it this way: 'Conflict within the Committee itself prevented it pursuing its proposed factual survey into the social circumstances of successful and unsuccessful pupils in each major ethnic group.'

In other words, the central purpose for which Swann had been formed was frustrated because of pressure against disinterested and honest research. The possible consequences of this are well captured in this comment of one of the instigators of the notion of a committee of enquiry, Professor Alan Little: 'If, however, the study is prevented by threat of veto, then this can only undermine the credibility of the whole Swann Report, which could well be rejected out of hand by the Government and professional groups it hopes to influence, on the grounds that it was loaded' (*TES*, 23 July 1982). The research, as we have seen, was vetoed, and few now doubt that the whole enterprise was indeed discredited as a result.

In view of the vital questions with which Swann was concerned, not to mention the legitimate right of the public to know why over £600,000 was invested in a project from which relevant, original research was excluded, it is clearly important to examine the motives of those who succeeded in suppressing the research. It is not possible to obtain direct information, but a clue is provided in two letters to the *TES* (6 August 1982). These also point to one of the crucial influences which shaped the whole ethos within which the Committee operated—the reluctance of the anti-racist lobby to allow any factor other than 'racism' to be examined. The *TES* had published two letters (one from me) and the piece by Professor Little from which I have quoted above, that regretted the suppression of research. The first of the letters in reply is from Marti Francis, Press Officer of a group calling itself 'All-London Teachers Against Racism and Fascism'. (I shall not comment on this portentous title except to wonder how many people realise what a miniscule proportion of London teachers this organisation actually represents.) The second is from a group called 'The Haringey Black Pressure Group on Education'—it is not signed. It is clear from the content of the letters that these groups regard themselves as being representative of British West Indian opinion on education. Whether this is illusory or valid is difficult to say, but there is no doubt that they express a view of Mortimer's research which the Committee clearly accepted.

The first letter accuses the 'teaching profession' (there is no formally recognised teaching profession in Britain so it is difficult to know to which organisation this is referring) of suppressing research into teacher-racism carried out by the NUT and the National Association for Multiracial Education (NAME). Mortimer is condemned for his 'traditional assumptions' and for proposing to use CSE and O level results as the criteria of academic success, although this was precisely what the Committee had done in its interim Report in order to demonstrate West Indian 'underachievement'. Also, the research is implicitly accused of being deliberately designed so as to confirm *a priori* assumptions: 'By choosing these areas the research seemed to be prefiguring its own results.' The writers of the letter claim to be able to predict the result of research which had not then been (and was not subsequently to be) carried out. The Research and Statistics Branch of ILEA (of which Mortimer was then the Head) is accused of deliberately delaying the publication of research into the number of black pupils in disruptive units, so that they 'got lost in the heady days of the first weeks of the summer holidays'. I am taken to task for referring, in a previous letter, to 'highly trained and disinterested researchers', the implication being that Mortimer is neither of these. In short, this first letter is little more than a sustained attack on the integrity of the researcher and the organisation he worked for, although there is guarded support for a revised version of Mortimer's original research, which was to have included material on 'anti-racist policy, number of black teachers, staff attitudes on race and multiethnic education, black parental involvement . . .', i.e. they were in favour of an approach which, they hoped, would be likely to confirm their own *a priori* assumptions about teacher racism. The notion that family background, parental attitudes and cultural values might be implicated in the question of black pupil success or failure is fiercely rejected.

The second letter accuses those of us who had regretted the suppression of Mortimer's research of being 'white, middle-class people', and therefore incapable of understanding the matter (one wonders whether this offensive remark also applies to the same reported regret of Dr Gajendra Verma—a British/Asian academic (*TES*, 6 August 1982)). Because Mortimer had wanted to examine family characteristics he is accused of adopting 'a eugenic structure of academic research', which is not only patently incorrect but, in its implications, offensive. As in the first letter, only research that omits any reference to the structure and dynamics of West Indian family life would be acceptable: 'It follows that it is the system which needs to be investigated and not the individuals and their families.'

Although these two letters may appear to provide little in the way of evidence, when they are linked to the kind of material issued by the various anti-racist organisations described in Chapter 5, they provide an insight into the mentality that suppressed Mortimer's research, and which exercised such a profound influence on the Swann Committee. These observations help to illuminate this mentality. First, anyone who proposes objective research which includes information about West Indian family life and dynamics will be pilloried, yet research that omits this will be manifestly worthless. Second, the notion that comparative West Indian school failure is due entirely to defects in 'the system' is taken as being beyond question—'the system' to be conceptualised in such a way as to include only those factors external to the West Indian community. Third, blacks must be regarded as the victims of a 'white middle-class' conspiracy, whose object is to deny West Indians a place in the sun—despite the fact that Asian pupils (also alleged victims of this conspiracy) do significantly better educationally than West Indian ones.

Moreover, evidence from ILEA indicates that black, African children in London schools do significantly better than West Indian children at O level. A large-scale analysis of examination results in

1985 (published in June 1987) shows that whereas 4.6 per cent of Caribbean children obtained five or more O levels, the African children did more than twice as well, with 10.3 per cent obtaining this level of success.

How far, one wonders, should those of us who believe that there ought to be a disinterested search for truth into this important question allow ourselves to be bullied into silence by this manifestly ideological and anti-intellectual mentality? And how seriously can one take a government-appointed committee with huge resources that allowed itself to be so intimidated?

I have tried to indicate some of the ways in which Swann's deliberations were influenced by the intellectual climate within which the Committee laboured. I have also pointed to the decisive influence of the Coard thesis, to an ambivalent attitude to research and to the fatal decision to suppress a vital original enquiry. The next task is to look at the Swann recommendations.

The Swann Recommendations

Only a selective view can be attempted here; a comprehensive critique would require far more space than is available. The recommendations make two basic assumptions: that institutional and bureaucratic processes can effect fundamental changes in pupil's attitudes, even in something as subtle and irrational as ethnic prejudice; and that the proposed changes need to be total. There would have to be a considerable increase in officialdom, in red tape and in the presence and the powers of racial 'experts' for the Swann proposals to be implemented. Considerable injections of public money would also be required, although Swann, predictably, made no attempt to cost its sweeping reforms. This obvious deficiency in no way lessens the passion of the Committee's demands on the government of the day: 'Although it has not been possible to propose any detailed costings for our recommendations, it is clear that a number will carry resource implications, and we would urge the government to demonstrate its commitment to the development of *Education for All* by ensuring that the necessary additional resources are made available.' (There are *no* costings in Swann, detailed or otherwise.)

The extent of the bureaucratic initiatives necessary to effect changes in Swann's direction can be gauged from the areas of national life which will have to be reformed: '[It is] a matter for the law, the Government, Housing Authorities, Employers, Unions, the Commission for Racial Equality, and many others.' This is in addition, of course, to the educational changes, which will be almost total: 'All LEAs should declare their commitment to the principle of *Education for All.*' The extent of the organisational and bureaucratic demands to be made on the education service is evident from the Report's policy outline, *A Strategy for Change* (summarised, pp. 769–70): 'Every department of the education service is to be involved. LEAs should appoint additional advisors and officers. They must also expect their schools to produce clear policy statements on *Education for All* and monitor their practical implications.' All schools 'should adopt policies to combat racism' and 'should review their work in the light of the principles we have put forward. In secondary schools it may be necessary to establish departmental working parties to appraise provision in different subject areas.' Her Majesty's Inspectors are urged to check school curricula to ensure that they are following the Swann philosophy, and 'issue clear guidelines'. The School Curriculum Development Committee, the Secondary Examinations Council and the Examining Boards must all carry out work, which means additional money and organisational change. The DES is enjoined to convene conferences, prepare reports and start to collate ethnic statistics. The government 'should revise the provision of section 11 of the Local Government Act 1966 to make it more appropriate to the needs of the ethnic minority communities'. The Secretary of State should include more 'initiatives and pilot projects' which espouse the Swann doctrine in the grants system.

It is no exaggeration to say that if any government were to take the Swann recommendations at face value the effect would be little short of revolutionary.

'Education for All'

This is the core of the Swann recommendations. The phrase itself contains an assumption that not all children *are* enjoying the benefits of education (if only a type or style of education were being referred to the phrase would require the initial word 'an' to make this clear). Some children, it is implied, are being excluded or 'denied access'. The only evidence quoted to support this takes the form of statistics showing differential outcomes, i.e. some children do better educationally than others. How this can be linked to the concept of access is nowhere made clear. It is about as convincing as arguing that if someone wins a 100 metres dash this proves that the other competitors must have been prevented from entering the race. In reality, of course, 'access' in this context carried notions not of results or consequences but of availability.

If the allegation is to have any weight it must rest on a demonstration that some children have been excluded from certain kinds of experience. For instance, if West Indian children were prevented from entering particular schools then it would be legitimate to assert denial of access. Again, if, having entered school, such children were not permitted to study certain subjects or participate in certain activities then it would be correct to say that they are not enjoying equality of opportunity in school. The same applies to entry to public examinations.

However, none of these things is true. In reality *all* primary and middle schools are comprehensive in character, as are the great majority of secondary schools. As such, they are entirely non-selective in their pupil intakes. They take children as they come, and ethnic origin plays no part in the process. Schools are now necessarily neighbourhood schools, and simply reflect in their pupil populations surrounding housing patterns. Insofar as such schools restrict cross-class and (since the end of bussing) cross-racial friendships and tend to trap their pupils in a social and cultural ghetto, then that applies to *all* the children involved. It is a function of society's commitment to the theory of comprehensive education in the 1960s, and has nothing to do with denying opportunity to ethnic-minority children. Once in the school, all children study a curriculum according to their age, ability, aptitudes and needs; entry to public examinations rests essentially on academic criteria. Since none of this is questioned in Swann, one wonders where the phrase 'Education for All' comes from.

One suspects that it owes more to the fashionable habit of encapsulating the demands of this or that interest group in a snappy catch-phrase than it does to substantive argument. Certainly, it has a fine egalitarian ring—one that the myriad anti-racist pressure groups can seize upon as their rallying cry. It has just the right degree of conciseness and vagueness to make it a winner.

Racism

Recommendations on racism indicate clearly one of the major sources of Swann's rationale: the 'anti-racism checklist' provided is taken, word for word, from ILEA's *Race, Sex and Class*, Booklet 4, issued to all London schools in 1983. There have been several cogent criticisms of this document, but Swann appears unaware of these; schools are simply enjoined 'to develop explicit policies to combat racism'. This recommendation is based on the assumption that they have an endemic racial bigotry or what is called 'the overall climate of racism' (p. 354). This depiction of schools' attitudes to race is not based on direct observation or empirical research but arises from hearsay and anecdote. It is directly rejected by many of the people who work in British schools and who gave evidence to the Committee. Moreover, evidence provided by the Community Relations Council[11] suggests that ethnic-minority parents have little anxiety about their children suffering from racial bullying in school: 'Only a small minority of parents believed this constituted a problem for the child'. In addition, the interim Rampton Report said of teachers assumed to have explicitly racist views 'Such teachers are very much in the minority'—although, again, even this is mere conjecture, since Rampton failed to carry out research into teachers' racial views. Moreover, it seems extremely doubtful if racist schools, as depicted by Swann, could produce the kind of academic results being obtained by the Asian children attending them, nor indeed, by the very encouraging results obtained by those West Indian groups researched by Rutter (see p. 157). Most telling of all, of course, is the work of Murray, quoted above, in which ethnic-minority adolescents themselves explicitly reject the 'racist schools and teachers' thesis.

It is very difficult to read what Swann has to say about racism in schools without feeling that the authors are simply engaged in *a priori* thinking—racism in schools is a precondition of the whole Swann enterprise, its very *raison-d'être*. No matter how many are the contrary instances, the charge is made to stick, and the recommendations regarding racism reflect this. They are all-embracing, and include not only curriculum matters but also institutional practices, individual behaviour and ethos. 'Unconscious racism', as well as the overt variety, must also be considered and tackled. At no point in the recommendation is there any suggestion that an institution which is concerned about racial bigotry might logically begin by discovering whether the offending phenomenon actually exists. Institutions must *begin* by 'considering how racism can and *does* [my emphasis] operate in the school/college's particular circumstances' (p. 355).

It is, of course, impossible to engage in rational discourse with the mentality that produces this kind of categorical imperative, the product of a closed mind. The possibility of alternative formulations, of challenging assumptions, of demanding evidence, of suggesting the presence of obsessional thinking—none of these methods of furthering the argument and the search for truths is available when the reader is confronted with this mode of conceptualising the issue. Fanaticism is not amenable to reason.

The difficulty Swann has in demonstrating overt racism is offset, at least to the Committee's satisfaction, by the introduction of two further notions—institutional and unconscious (sometimes confusingly described as unintentional) racism. I have considered the first in Chapter 7, and will do no more here than quote the judgement of Lord Scarman[12] after his enquiry into the Brixton riots: 'If an institutionally racist society means that it is a society which knowingly, as a matter of policy, discriminates against black people, then I reject that allegation.' 'Unconscious racism' deserves closer attention.

Unconscious Racism

The Swann recommendations lend support to those who, like ILEA, maintain that there should be anti-racist censorship in schools and that there should also be a curriculum which is 'permeated' with an anti-racist perspective. The grounds for this are as follows. The ethnic minorities are 'underrepresented' in British culture; where they do appear, they are depicted in lowly roles which confer little status and esteem; the legacy of Empire has left indigenous, white people with a built-in tendency to downgrade ethnic minorities whose forebears were the subject peoples of the colonies. This background creates negative, unconscious stereotypes of black and brown people, poisons Britain's multiracial atmosphere and generates a hostile anti-minorities culture. As far as teachers and white people are concerned, this causes them, albeit without conscious intent, to act in negative ways to Asian and West Indian pupils.

The basis of Swann's position here is the work carried out over the past ten years or so by a number of academics and teachers with committed anti-racist views. Notable among these is Gillian Klein.[13,14] an employee of ILEA. She has systematically set out to establish that schools contain and transmit a racist culture, claims to have discovered quantities of material which stereotype and demean black and brown people and has ardently advocated anti-racist purges and censorship of libraries. She has also brought pressure to bear on publishers to withdraw certain books and to reject manuscripts which do not accord with anti-racist directives. Her views have become very influential and she is regarded as an expert in this field.

Now there is a grain of truth in the Klein contention. Britain did produce a literature of jingoism that consistently portrayed whites as the master race and black and brown people as dependent, immature and generally inferior. The Biggles books, and some of Arthur Ransome, Rider Haggard and Rudyard Kipling are examples of the genre. Children's comics, story books and annuals also reflect this way of regarding colonial peoples. However, to argue that this same tendency still forms an influential part of today's children's cultural diet is a very doubtful proposition. Such books are still read, of course, but they are read within a totally different cultural and political climate from the age of imperialism.

First, there is now no British Empire. People under 40 scarcely remember it, and it is as remote to today's children as the Norman Conquest. Children are now more likely to base their perception of black and brown people on television pictures of the Queen surrounded by multiracial Commonwealth leaders than on Kipling's *Mowgli* stories. Second, children and young people have grown up in a world where anti-colonialism has been a major theme in current affairs; rejoicing in colonial possessions and the superiority of the white man has formed no part of the cultural experiences of children in school or of the great majority of their teachers. The very reverse is true. Since the Second World War, white liberal guilt, rather than imperialist triumphalism, has been a major theme in the political and cultural life of the West. Third, present-day white children in Britain are increasingly aware of racial minorities as classmates, not as stereotyped images. Fourth, despite the claims of the anti-racist censors (which Swann quotes with approval) it is difficult to see how the notion of a racist culture connects with children's actual out-of-school experiences.

Three cultural forms dominate the life of today's children and adolescents: television (including advertising); the products of the pop industry; and professional sport. The ubiquitous presence of these influences is doubted by no-one. The power of television can be gauged from the amount of time young people spend watching it (on average, as much time as they spend in school); pop is everywhere that young (and not so young) people congregate—its exponents are the major source of hero-worship; and professional sport draws large audiences, running into millions for television events, and receives huge press coverage in both the quality and the popular press. How do the ethnic minorities fare in this cultural milieu? It would be very difficult to show that they are in any way demeaned.

Television companies are acutely sensitive to any suggestion of racism, unconscious or otherwise, in their programmes. (There has been an almost total failure to look critically at the anti-racist cause and at least six transmissions have so far sympathised with it.) Moreover, since pop and sport provide youngsters' heroes and heroines, and since blacks are probably 'over-represented' in both, it is difficult to see how the ethnic minorities' view of themselves, or others' views of them, can be adversely affected. For example, the successes of Daley Thompson, Fatima Whitbread, Tessa Sanderson, Frank Bruno and Imram Khan has meant that many youngsters — not least white ones—now have black and brown heroes and heroines. Also, an examination of children's comics, teenage magazines and pop papers does not sustain the notion of anti-black bias. Nor, indeed, does present-day advertising; my impression is that firms like Marks and Spencer often display images in which the ethnic minorities are over-represented. A recent advertisement for children's clothing showed six youngsters, two of whom were non-white, whereas a photograph of 20 would need to be produced before one non-white image could be justified by the kind of 'representative' argument constantly displayed by anti-racists.

The picture in schools is more difficult to discern. There are about 36,000 schools, and no two are the same. Between them they must contain millions of print-based and visual items, in a very wide range of subjects and spread over countless rooms and libraries. It would be surprising if, out of this mountain of material, there were none that might conceivably offend someone. Unfortunately, the evidence which so impressed Swann is a miniscule sample, and all of it gathered by anti-racist activists determined to sniff out and publicise racial heresy. Moreover, the assumption that such material has a decisive effect on children's perceptions, attitudes and behaviour (forming, as it must, a tiny fraction of the child's total cultural experiences) has never been remotely confirmed by any research or theory. There is, in fact, considerable controversy about how children are affected by literature. The wrongheadedness of anti-racists here can be illustrated by their attempts to suppress or bowdlerise Mark Twain's *Huckleberry Finn*, on the grounds that it contains the word 'nigger' and is offensive to black people. In reality the book is a work of great subtlety and irony, both qualities which require open minds in order to be perceived and appreciated; and the hero of the book is Jim, the runaway slave. In their travels Huck and Jim encounter a collection of drunkards, murderers, bullies, cheats, liars, thickheads, hypocrites and child abusers—and all are white.

The Swann Committee shows no awareness of how the kind of crude censorship favoured by anti-racists threatens both literature and the academic freedom of the teacher, nor do they understand how writers producing work to fit anti-racist perceptions will create not literature but propaganda.

Lack of space prevents development of this theme, but two further points need briefly to be made. The notion that one human failure, racial bigotry, should be allowed to dominate the whole curriculum shows a defective understanding of moral education, through which a properly trained moral sensitivity will condemn not only racial bigotry but *all* human wickedness. If we allow that education should be exclusively concerned with the evils of 'racism', what place can we find for the condemnation of political and religious persecution? It must indeed be appalling to suffer rejection because of one's skin colour, but no worse, presumably, than being tortured or killed for one's political beliefs. Would anyone take seriously the notion that schools should base their whole curriculum on a study of, say, political persecution in the USSR or perhaps the history of anti-semitism in Britain?

The 'unconscious racism' thesis, then, cannot be sustained by reference to the actual cultural experiences of today's children or their teachers, nor does censorship, and the moral obsession that appears to underlie the 'anti-racist' permeation of the curriculum, offer constructive solutions to the issue of racial bias. (It is perhaps worth mentioning *sotto voce* that Swann totally ignores what might well be a phenomenon that *has* tended to form an adverse public response to black people, i.e. the series of inner-city riots in which 'over-represented' young blacks performing criminal acts were shown on British television screens.)

English as a Second Language

The idea of providing English as a second language on a withdrawal basis is condemned in Swann: 'We believe the needs of second language learners should be met through integrated provision within the mainstream school as part of a comprehensive programme of language education for *all* children.' There are sound arguments in favour of this policy. Separation involves a restriction of curriculum, loss of social contact with fluent-English children, a sense of being marginalised and loss of good models in the child's minority own peer group. However, the recommendation suffers, as do so many others, from lack of contact with practicalities.

For instance, how can children having no English at all (or even those with minimal English) be integrated into a class that might well contain, say, 30 children? What effect will the presence of such children have on the general academic standard, particularly if they form a substantial proportion of the class? Will not the teacher have to give a disproportionate amount of time to such children? Would not the whole-class teaching involve a slowing down of the pace and complexity of instruction? How could the confidence of parents be sustained in such circumstances? Would not intensive English as a second language teaching on a withdrawal basis, on the same campus, be wiser—at least initially?

The burden on the teacher in this context is, indeed, great. He is enjoined 'to cater for the linguistic needs of pupils'. What those 'needs' are is never addressed in Swann. It is clear, however, that the very diversity of languages now found in Britain's schools make it somewhat unlikely that there is, or ever could be, a comprehensive pedagogical theory that would enable the teacher even to conceptualise the child's linguistic 'needs', let alone create corresponding teaching approaches. How, for instance, do the language needs of Vietnamese children compare with those of Urdu-speaking Pakistani children, or a West Indian child's Patois with an Indian child's Gujerati? The notion that there is some overarching theory which ties together these profoundly different language communities and provides guidelines for the teacher is surely pie in the sky.

Even weirder than this is Swann's reference here to teacher-training. LEAs and individual schools, we are told, should seek to provide *all* teachers 'with a knowledge and understanding of the languages of the ethnic minority communities they serve'. This despite quoting a report from the Linguistic Minorities Project,[15] which showed that in Bradford no fewer than 64 foreign languages were spoken at home, 87 in Haringey, 50 in Coventry, 42 in Peterborough and 65 in Waltham Forest. ILEA discovered 146 different languages among its pupils, and the phenomenon is growing. It is quite possible that an inner-city teacher today could find himself in a school with 20 or more foreign languages involved, and Swann demands that he be granted access to all of them! It is not just the number of languages that makes an absurdity of this; it is the astonishing diversity. Here, to make the point, is a list of the most common community languages found in schools in the London borough of Haringey: Greek, Turkish, Creole, Gujerati, Italian, Bengali, Urdu, Punjabi, Spanish, Chinese and French. Clearly, the LEAs involved will need to recruit some formidable polyglots—not to speak of their need to impose punitive rates and demands on central government to implement this Utopian policy!

Mother-tongue Provision

Swann uses the term 'mother-tongue' to refer to the traditional language of the ethnic-minority child. This is misleading, since an increasing number of such children are born and bred in Britain, and *their* mother-tongue is, presumably, English. A better term would perhaps be 'community language'.

However, it is not only this which makes this section a deeply contradictory one. While accepting that there is no place for bilingual education, i.e. instruction in the 'mother-tongue', Swann argues 'We are "for" mother-tongue teaching in the sense that we regard linguistic diversity in Britain today as a positive asset to our national life . . . in just the same way as everyone welcomes the many dialects and two indigenous languages (Welsh and Gaelic)'. In what sense, one wonders, is Welsh for Welsh children in Welsh schools the same as Gujerati for a British/Indian child attending school in England? This could only be convincingly argued if we assume that England is now part of the Indian mainland. (Would a Welsh-speaking parent expect instruction in Welsh for his child attending an *English* school?)

This illustrates a fallacy that runs throughout the whole Swann recommendations—there is a constant tendency to regard ethnic-minority children, first and foremost, as children with foreign rather than British identities but as having calls on British privileges. This ambivalence is never resolved. The relationship between the concept of national coherence and the language of the school is never seriously considered.

There is yet another contradiction. While Swann accepts that schools should not 'seek to assume the role of community providers for maintaining ethnic minority languages', and that the task belongs to the communities themselves, this is immediately followed by an assertion that schools should put such languages on their timetable, examining boards should seek to examine them, the DES should take special measures to train teachers of such languages and grants should be given to community groups for this purpose. In short, the state *should* maintain foreign community languages—the contradictions here are palpable. Anyone seeking support for *any* approach to this issue could find comfort in the pages of the Swann Report. (A fuller discussion of the language issue can be found in Chapter 7.)

The Separate Schools Debate

In general, the Swann Report comes down firmly against separate schools for the ethnic minorities. It also rejects the notion of 'black' schools. The ideal is an integrated school catering for children on a neighbourhood basis. The demand for separate schools would, according to Swann, be 'much diminished' if the principles of *Education for All* were implemented. This assertion would be more convincing if the concept of *Education for All* were either intellectually coherent or practicable. Since it appears to be neither, the demand for separate schools cannot be assumed to be over.

There is a key issue that Swann fails to address, and which makes its discussion of this issue superficial, i.e. its failure to grasp the spiritual/secular dichotomy as seen through the eyes of, say, a devout Moslem. We in the West, at least since the Renaissance and more particularly since the Enlightenment, have accepted the essential distinction between the things of the mind and those of the spirit. This development in Western psychology occurred only after considerable conflict between the custodians of the totalist medieval world view and the apostles of rationalism, of whom Bacon and Galileo stand as outstanding examples. The compromise effected resulted in a new Western outlook, one which enabled science and religion to live together, as it were. This ability to allow the spiritual and the secular to co-exist in the one society, so that an essentially secular order could encapsulate both strict religious institutions and freedom of conscience – this peculiarly Western arrangement cannot be assumed to be acceptable to devout British Moslems seeking an appropriate education for their children. The voluntary-aided system of schools in Britian bears witness to an age and a world view which pre-date the growth of Eastern religions, and the mentality that accompanies them, in Britain. The contemporary resurgence of Islam worldwide and the difficulties Moslem countries have in coming to terms with essentially Western notions about individual human rights, sexual equality, the humane treatment of criminals and secular democracy (as in Iran, for instance) bears witness to this dilemma. Voluntary schools subsist on the principle that a compromise between religion and science, Church and State, can be successfully effected. The child's religious formation can go hand in hand with his secular education.

However, this has little meaning for the strict Moslem parent, and this is made clear in the Report. Commenting on representations from Moslem organisations the Report says: 'There is a growing tendency to take the view that no accommodation is in fact feasible or indeed desirable within the existing system, and in order to provide a true Islamic education for their children, it is necessary to provide Moslem aided schools.' This is spelt out in evidence from a Moslem to the Committee:

Islam is not something which can be learnt and adhered to overnight. It must be lived, breathed and fostered until it cannot be separated from life itself. It requires constant practice . . . it is hard to judge how possible it is to live as a Moslem within society as a whole.

This refreshingly honest statement sums up the problem—what would satisfy a Moslem parent we would probably regard not as education but as religious indoctrination, so total and uncompromising is the approach to the formation of the young in Islam. To assume that such a mentality could be accommodated within the fatuities of *Education for All* is absurd. To assume that it could be brought within the framework of voluntary schools is a misunderstanding. Voluntary schools, be they aided, controlled or special agreement, while retaining full control of the religious aspect, all entrust oversight of the secular part of the curriculum to secular society, embodied in the powers of the LEA and the DES. Would a Moslem parent, for whom this separation of powers is meaningless, be able to subscribe to the voluntary schools principle? Those Moslem organisations that advocate voluntary-school status appear not to have grasped the essential spiritual and secular dichotomy which underlies such schools. Nor would this dilemma be resolved by current proposals to allow parents to opt out of LEA control in the running of schools. The fact that the state would still supply the funding would mean a continuing, legitimate interest by society. Nor, indeed, would full independence exclude the state—even independent schools are, rightly, subject to inspection to ensure certain standards of provision. The inability of Islam to compromise is a fundamental problem Swann never addresses.*

I have tried to touch on those aspects of the Swann recommendations that are likely to be influential and which, I believe, are obviously flawed, ill thought out and unconvincing. It is time now to assess the reception provided by public opinion.

The Response to Swann

If the circumstances surrounding Swann's creation were highly charged and controversial, the response that its publication evoked was predictably diverse, not to say acrimonious. The official response was polite but mooted. In a press notice notable for its very

* Addressing the Association of Metropolitan Authorities in 1988, Professor Sayed Ali Ashraf said that, for Moslems, knowledge could not be divided between secular and religious: it was all one. Teaching could only be done properly by those with a commitment to religious values (*Municipal Reviews*, No. 687, May 1988).

carefully chosen words, the Secretary of State, Sir Keith Joseph, gave the Report a guarded welcome. While accepting that many ethnic-minority pupils are achieving less than their potential, the Minister placed their problem firmly within the issue of under-achievement as a whole:

> Under-achievement is not confined to the ethnic minorities. Many in the majority community could be doing far better, and I am determined that they, too, should be helped, wherever they are at school.

Second, in referring to the obstacles to achievement in ethnic-minority children he made it clear what the central problem was: 'We are tackling the obstacles to opportunity, notably by promoting good practice in teaching of English as a second language.' Third, while respecting the need for schools to promote understanding of and respect for the ethnic minorities, the Minister asserted that this was to be placed firmly within a national context: 'We want schools to present and transmit our national values.' Specifically, account of ethnic diversity was to be taken in initial teacher-training, the new GCSE and the new objectives for relevant subject areas being currently formulated. A small sum of money (£1 million in 1985/6) was to be devoted to this aspect for in-service training. Money for Section 11 of the Local Government Act 1966 was to be spent on teaching English and the 'mother-tongue'; ethnically based statistics would be gathered and an increase in ethnic-minority teachers sought—'without positive discrimination and without any reduction in the required level of qualification'.

Four recommendations in the Swann Report were rejected: the statutory requirement for daily worship and RE would not be abolished; the voluntary school system was to remain; there would be no grant for sixth formers; and Section 11 of the Local Government Act 1966 would not be amended.

The most interesting, not to say ironic, of the Minister's comments concerned research:

> We badly need hard information about the effect on achievement of factors in and out of school. I intend to commission research which will look at these factors, and at the extent to which they contribute to under-achievement among pupils of all backgrounds; ethnic minority pupils would be one part of such a study.

This was a virtual re-run of the Swann Committee's terms of reference. One wonders how the Minister and his successors were proposing to overcome the obstacles to research which the Committee had so signally failed to surmount. In view of the attitude to research displayed in Swann and described above one cannot help feeling that in the absence of a change of heart in those who suppressed research in Swann the Minister was being optimistic and naive—at least as far as researching the West Indian pupils' performance was concerned.

The Opposition spokesman on education, Giles Radice, said 'Generally I want to see specialised help for particular black and Asian groups who are underachieving. That's the point at which the report is at its blandest'; while Frances Morrell, the leader of ILEA, Britain's largest education authority, used the occasion to attack the government: 'The report calls for action at a time when the government is cutting money for education authorities.'

The teachers' associations gave the report a mixed reception. The NUT spokesman is quoted as endorsing the Report's message and as believing that there must be a change of attitude to educating children in a multi-ethnic society 'in a way which combats racist assumptions and stereotypes'. The National Association of Schoolmasters and Union of Women Teachers (NAS/UWT) said: 'We welcome the more balanced approach compared with the earlier findings of the Rampton Report which unfairly accused teachers of being racists.' The National Association of Head Teachers (NAHT) appeared to be the only organisation to spot and honestly expose one of the report's basic flaws. While welcoming 'a number of recommendations' the NAHT spokesman correctly asserted that the Committee had ducked two crucial issues—that attitudes among the ethnic minorities themselves must change and that full account must be taken of the role parents play in encouraging children to do well at school. The Afro-Caribbean Teachers Association was favourable to Swann, but it regretted that the interim Rampton Report appeared to have been shelved.

The press showed a varied but, on the whole, critical response to the Swann Report. *The Times Educational Supplement*'s leading article was bland, while broadly welcoming the Report. However, echoing the NAHT, it pointed to the unfortunate suppression of research:

It is a pity that the excessive sensitivity of some leaders of minority groups frustrated attempts to discover more about the conditions which promote success (and therefore, by contrast, which inhibit it also). There are important lessons to be learnt; it is not enough to counter all attempts to investigate the differences with blanket accusations of racism.

The *Daily Telegraph* praised teachers for their efforts in coping with the tremendous challenges to the schools consequent upon significant changes in the pupil population, and blamed successive governments for failing to give teachers the necessary recognition and support. It was guarded about the Report's views, but pointed to one issue that Swann failed to examine with the critical honesty it deserved: ' . . . A reluctance by first generation Asian parents to be assimilated into our culture.' The *Guardian* mentioned the hostility evoked by Swann in some of the West Indian leadership, and said that the Report meandered through the extremes of individualism and determinism: 'The result, though, is a failure to spell out an agenda for teachers that means, in turn, that the Swann Report will live on as a much-thumbed reference book, not as a manifesto for change.'

Perhaps the most critical response in the quality press came from *The Times*. It pinpointed one of the crucial problems for Swann — the determination of the West Indian members of the Committee to make the racism charge against teachers stick—by quoting the shouted comment at the press conference of Mr Ernie Harris, Chairman of the National Anti-Racist Movement in Education, directed at Lord Swann: 'You have let teachers off the hook, and you have let the government off the hook with this racist rubbish.' *The Times* also referred to the Committee's 'long and chequered history . . . dogged by controversy, internal disagreement and press leaks'. Its leading article mentioned the large number of members of the Committee who had resigned: ' . . . Fewer than half the total crew lasted the whole course . . . How far the voyage was worth it is another matter.' The conditions under which the Committee laboured were also referred to:

The Report, born out of much acrimony and special pleading shows visible signs of despair. In organisation and typography it is the strangest dog's breakfast ever to emerge from HMSO, a huge rag-bag of semi-digested material, some bland, some truculent, some impenetrable.

The suppresion of research was also deplored: 'But what should probably have been the most relevant piece of research is absent.'

The spirit of the popular response to Swann was to be found in the tabloid newspapers. A leading article in the *Sun* headed 'Dump it, Keith!' referred to the recommendations as ' . . . quite frankly, crazy', and totally rejected the notions of both 'mother-tongue' teaching and the use of an Asian language as the medium of instruction: 'This approach is totally unacceptable.' It rejected separatism and the creation of ghetto mentalities while welcoming the presence of ethnic minorities in Britain: 'But down the ages the most successful immigrants to Britain have learned our language and our customs—not stayed locked away in their own communities.' Its judgement had a typical candour: 'Shove the whole thing —all 1,000 pages of it—in the Whitehall incinerator.' The *Daily Express* took a similar line. Referring to the 'multicultural perspective' proposed by Swann, the leader writer said:

> The best way for ethnic minorities to be integrated into British society —the best hope of multicultural harmony—is through their absorbing our historic and traditional culture. Those who hanker after the language and culture of other societies can do so in their own time and at their own expense.

Swann's conclusions are given very short shrift: 'They are appalling and dangerous where they are not simply worthless.' Its advice was correspondingly robust: 'The government must have no truck with the Report.' My hunch is that the majority of the 95 per cent whose children were not the concern of the Swann Committee would probably agree with these sentiments.

How did the anti-racist activists respond to the Swann Report? A clue is to be found in a report in the *TES* of 19 April 1985, about a month after the report was published. This concerned a conference of the National Association for Multiracial Education (NAME), which, perhaps significantly, had changed its name during the conference to the National Anti-Racist Movement in Education. By all accounts, the proceedings were marked by very strong feelings. Mr Carlton Duncan, a West Indian member of the Swann Committee, attacked Lord Swann for issuing his brief Guide to the report. He accused the committee's chairman of 'playing a trick', and said that the writing of the Guide should be 'condemned as an exercise in dishonesty'. Duncan also regretted not having resigned from the Committee: 'With hindsight, I made an error of judgement.' Together with the other three West Indians on the Committee he had considered going, but had decided 'to stay to fight for our black brothers and sisters'. Duncan, nevertheless, gave some support to the Report: 'The Report is not a document for the waste-paper basket, as there are a lot of sensible recommendations in there.'

However, this view was not shared by all those present. Mrs Greta Akinpeyna, deputy head of a school in Southwark, asserted that the Report ' . . . insults black people . . . it repeats every stereotype and adds some of its own. Tell everyone to burn it'. Mr David Lake, treasurer of NAME, was scarcely less emphatic in his condemnation. He said that black people had hoped Swann would improve the 'miseducation of our children', but they now realised they could not depend on 'the establishment'. (This is a curious view of 'the establishment', since a disproportionately large number of members of the Swann Committee came from the ethnic minorities.)

It is perhaps worth commenting on the above-mentioned NAME conference since it illustrates one of the key problems of the debate over the education of black children—the attitudes and rhetoric of those who would regard themselves as the West Indian leadership. The intemperate responses of Mr Duncan and Mrs Akinpeyna are not untypical. The literature of British/West Indian protest is marked by a strident condemnation of intellectual opponents, and by an unwillingness to accept self-criticism as a necessary function of any mature community's intelligentsia. As someone who has suffered the offensive and hysterical rhetoric in which the *Caribbean Times* specialises, I can speak with some knowledge about this. Duncan's offensive attack on Lord Swann appears to arise from the latter's refusal to ascribe the comparative academic failure of West Indian pupils to 'racism'—a conclusion the West Indian leadership had ardently hoped the Committee's chairman would have endorsed. However, Lord Swann, a distinguished scientist, had refused to take refuge in that kind of oversimplified and irrational response to what is a very complex issue. It is significant that, when asked at the press conference why he had failed to use the terms 'racism' and 'racist', he had replied that it was because he was a scientist, i.e. someone who insists that his statements arise from a dispassionate consideration of convincing evidence and not from *a priori* thinking and confrontational attitudes.

On the whole, then, the response of both press and anti-racist activism might be said to be critical. The conditions under which the Committee laboured, the interminable delay in producing the Report, the evidence of internal disputes, its lack of coherence and, above all, the suppression of research all combined effectively to undermine the credibility of the Swann enterprise. It might, therefore, be imagined that the Swann doctrine would have little influence, but that would be a mistake. Self-interest is a powerful force in the huge national bureaucracy we call the state education service. Like all bureaucracies, the state service generates and sustains its own inward-looking imperatives. The various interest groups, professional, political and bureaucratic, which gather round the process of a supply-based industry are bound to regard reforms, however ill advised, as a godsend. The Swann recommendations could be implemented only by an increased supply of money and personnel, more bureaucracy and the creation of new areas of career development—all manna to 'educationalists' eager for increased power and influence. The anti-racist/multicultural education initiatives already set in motion by many LEAs would be given a considerable boost by the presence of a weighty report which could be used to provide the necessary justifications for policy-making. Likewise, the academic establishment surrounding anti-racism and multiculturalism—and which links with the state education service via teacher-training and the provision of in-service work—would welcome a report that promised rich pickings for researchers and lecturers. (Within months of the publication of the Report Bradford had introduced in its schools a document entitled *Education for All*—the same title as the Swann Report.)

The early signs of this boost to professional self-interest was the emergence of what might be called the Swann circus, which continues to wind its way round colleges and universities, dispersing the official doctrines to those teachers, academics, LEA officers and whoever else feels the need for anti-racist enlightenment. One such was held in July 1985—just four months after the Report appeared —at Bradford University. This was convened by Dr Gajendra K. Verma, a Reader at the 'International Centre for Inter-Cultural Studies'. In announcing the event Dr Verma described the appearance of the Swann Report as 'the most significant event of 1985'. He went on to announce that he was writing to 'all chief Education Officers, Chairmen of Education Committees,

Vice-Chancellors of Universities, Principals of Colleges and Polytechnics, leading academics in the field of intercultural relationships, and others operating at high levels of policy-making and implementation' to draw attention to his conference.

This ardent enthusiasm, this assumption that everyone at 'a high level' in the field of education was at long last to have his keen desire to be inculcated into the Swann doctrine fulfilled—this passionate commitment illustrates strikingly the enormous gulf between those who control the supply-side of education and the consumers. The contrast with public opinion about Swann as reflected in the press could scarcely be greater.

It is not entirely surprising that at Dr Verma's conference the five 'keynote speakers' included four members of the Swann Committee—as well as Dr Verma himself, who was a member from May 1982. The fifth star turn was Chris Mullard, of inflammatory 'Black Britain' fame. This movement to disseminate the Swann gospel is now actively seeking converts wherever supply-side educationists gather—colleges, polytechnics, universities, LEA offices and council chambers.

I hope that the reader will forgive my relapse into a somewhat satirical style. This arises not only from my scepticism about the whole Swann enterprise but from a well-founded anxiety that, despite its obvious and fatal flaws, the Swann philosophy, thanks to the enormous influence of the leaders of the state education industry, may well come to have a decisive influence in the state education service. Satire is a measure of my anxiety.

Evidence for this can be found in the response to Swann by the Schools Council. This was a kind of official, publicly funded watchdog in matters relating to the curriculum, values, ethos and management of state schools. In 1983 it was replaced by the Schools Curriculum Development Committee (SCDC). Now the Principal Professional officer with the SCDC is Alma Craft, and since she was in charge of the School Council's project on multicultural education, and was a well-known and ardent advocate of the anti-racism cause, it is not surprising to find her rhapsodising somewhat lyrical about Swann:

The message of Swann relates to issues of justice and equality, to individual rights and responsibilities, to relationships between individuals and groups. It is this unique moral dimension of the Swann

Report which separates it from the avalanche of recent government consultative papers and policy documents on the content and organisation of education.

This totally uncritical, not to say gushing, response to a document which had had, at best, a very mixed public reception is precisely the kind of rhetoric we have come to expect of educational bureaucrats. For Craft, Swann is a valuable document, whose function is to support those multicultural and anti-racist assumptions she had already made clear at the Schools Council. Her enthusiasm for the Swann policy was expressed in the form of an AGENDA (original capitals) for schools, which will transmit the new anti-racist orthodoxy to teachers and future generations, as well as helping to transform 'society' in the direction of greater equality. It should be borne in mind that Craft, like Verma, is employed by a high-status and influential institution—the kind which inevitably impresses teachers, not least the young ones with a career to build in a service notorious for its commitment to intellectual fashion.

Conclusions

The Report of the Committee of Enquiry into the Education of Ethnic Minority Children was the response of a liberal-minded state to a problem causing widespread humanitarian concern: Why were ethnic-minority children 'underachieving' in British state schools? There was, at the time the inquiry was set up, a general conviction that all ethnic-minority children were missing out educationally, although the performance of West Indian children, both in terms of academic achievement and behaviour, was causing particular concern.

However, this perspective had to undergo modification during the course of the Committee's work. Accumulating evidence, published in the interim Rampton Report, indicated that the relationship between ethnic group and academic achievement was far more complex than originally supposed. While the fact of comparatively poor Caribbean performance was confirmed, the showing of other ethnic groups was encouraging. Asian youngsters, with the exception of Bangladeshis, were shown to be achieving results at O and A level that were comparable with the white majority group. Viewed collectively, Asians were not underperforming. On the contrary, statistics gathered in 1985, the year the Committee reported, and published in June 1987 confirmed the interim Report's findings that most Asian pupils not only do considerably better than Caribbeans they appear now to be doing significantly better even then indigenous white children, at least at O level. Of eleven ethnic groups in London schools the top four performers were all of Asian origin, and black African children did as well as their white English counterparts. Clearly, this kind of evidence makes the attributing of black failure in the schools to teacher and curriculum 'racism' difficult to maintain.

It was this difficulty, and the intrinsically controversial nature of the issues involved, which had caused the Committee to meet in a highly charged atmosphere. A disproportionate number of members came from that ethnic-minority intelligentsia that has always espoused the ideology of anti-racism, an ideology determined to depict Britain as a 'racist society' systematically attempting to prevent ethnic-minority progress, not least in the schools. Since the evidence stubbornly, and increasingly, declined to confirm this, the Committee had a turbulent time. There was internal wrangling, often along ethnic lines. The first chairman resigned, as did ten members. Six members wrote a dissenting report about the separate schools debate—a key issue. There was 'leaking' to the press and interminable delay. Also, in its desperate attempts to appear objective the Committee adopted a highly eccentric view of what consitutes an 'ethnic minority': while 'travellers' children', Italians and Ukranians are included, Hungarians and Poles are ignored, as are, inexplicably, perhaps Britain's oldest and best-established minority group—the Jews. Indigenous British children, who constitute the ethnic minority in an increasing number of inner-city schools in the country, are also ignored.

The climate of opinion which dominates the state school system played a decisive influence in shaping the Committee's perceptions and determining areas of interest. The notion that educational improvements rely on political and bureaucratic intervention is taken as read—a belief in the power of the state that would find little favour in the independent sector of education. That triumvirate of philosophical concepts which dominates the state system— determinism, cultural relativism and egalitarianism—provides the basic intellectual framework. These *a priori* commitments not only conditioned the whole idiom in which the Report was written, they also crucially affected the Committee's view of research.

The crude determinism of Bernard Coard, who had maintained that teacher-racism and the Anglo-Saxon curriculum functioned to ensure black failure, and the largely discredited social psychology of Rosenthal and Jacobson, which ascribed pupil performance to teacher-expectation, are two influences underlying the Committee's research perspective. This is most clearly seen in the decision of the Committee to highlight the work of Green. A careless reading of this (although not the considered response that Green himself urges) can give support to the 'racist teachers' thesis, particularly, of course, if one is already committed to anti-racist explanations and the crude determinism on which they are based. The fact that Green's research makes no mention of the central issue with which the Committee was concerned, i.e. the *achievement* of the ethnic minority, did not prevent it gaining pride of place in the Report. However, the work of Murray, which does concern itself with the achievement of ethnic-minority children and is therefore of direct relevance, was ignored. It was difficult to avoid the conclusion that the fate of Green's research was the result of its optimism regarding the apparent absence of teacher-racism in schools, and the supposed debilitating influence of the established curriculum on Asian and West Indian children.

The fact that this view of research fails to cast light on why, if the teacher-prejudice thesis is correct, Asian children do consistently and significantly better than Caribbean children does not appear to have troubled the Committee, although one member (Bikuh Parekh, a vice-chairman of the CRE) does rather feebly suggest that certain ethnic groups may have a better capacity for resisting the effects of racial prejudice than others. Why this might be so was not pursued. If it had been, this would, of course, have involved the making of value judgements across cultures, a stance the Committee's commitment to cultural relativism forbade.

However, the greatest weakness in research terms was the Committee's failure to carry out crucially important research which it itself had commissioned. Mortimer's proposed research was suppressed because it involved an enquiry into the family backgrounds of West Indian pupils. This could not be permitted; yet failure to consider this aspect would have meant the exclusion of a factor universally acknowledged to be central to educational progress. It is quite clear that two influences caused this. First, the Committee was reluctant to consider the cultural values of particular ethnic groups, except where these are manifestly laudable—open and courageous assessment of West Indian domestic values might well have involved the making of critical comments. Second, there is clear evidence that the Committee capitulated to sectarian pressures. The central issue for which the Committee had been formed —and which the public, in good faith, had invested over £600,000 to have illuminated—was thereby abandoned.

There could be no more compelling evidence of the power of the anti-racist mentality than this unprecedented failure of a high-powered official committee to carry out critical research. The great English tradition of appointing well-meaning committees to enquire openly, honestly and fearlessly into difficult educational issues was clearly subverted. The pursuit of truth, which can proceed only on the basis of disinterested research, was clearly less important to the Committee than the confirming of ideological presuppositions. Why the very distinguished scientist who was the Committee's chairman did not resign over the issue of the suppression of Mortimer's research will forever remain a mystery. What is certain is that the whole Swann enterprise was effectively discredited. We know no more about why West Indian children, on average, do comparatively badly in schools than we did before the Committee had its first sitting.

The Swann recommendations, not surprisingly, are marked by muddled thinking, a lack of grasp on practicalities and a Utopian vision of imposed 'cultural pluralism'. There is no understanding of the dangers of committing schools to a cultural view of society which public opinion has shown no signs of supporting. The notion that imported foreign cultures, which are properly the exclusive concern of those attached to them, should be financed and transmitted by the state via the eductional system is a central theme in the Swann recommendations. Yet there is no convincing evidence to show that either ethnic-minority or majority populations actually want this. The concept of 'multicultural' education (or 'Education for All' in the Swann terminology) appears to be largely a function of forces operating from within the state education system rather than a response to public demand.

The assumption that minority cultures will perish if they are not part of the school curriculum is belied by the evidence. Minority cultures are flourishing out of school, thanks to the efforts of those communities who require them (and in which they are, as it were, organically and historically embedded) as well as those British civil liberties which guarantee our cultural freedom. Swann shows no awareness of the fact that the imposition of an officially prescribed cultural mishmash on the schools runs the danger of offending those from the ethnic minorities who alone can determine the nature of their own culture and the appropriate means of transmitting it to the young—as well as the danger of upsetting those native British citizens who may feel that their own historic culture is thereby undermined and their identity with it. At no point in the Report is the essential distinction between society and the state in matters of culture effectively drawn.

The public reception of the Swann Report was generally lukewarm or hostile. The failure to demonstrate racism in the schools, while proposing controversial, all-embracing and costly measures to combat it, was bound to evoke charges of absurdity. Certain ethnic-minority leaders were angry at the Committee for failing to ascribe black failure to 'racism' with sufficient vigour. Public hostility has not, however, prevented a supply-side state education service from seizing on the Report to create yet another professional bandwaggon. However defective the Swann enterprise in pursuing the truth, and however unpopular it may be, there are sure signs that it is already playing an important role in policy decisions.

There could be no more convincing evidence of the need to free schools from the political and professional complex which effectively controls developments in the state service than the fortunes of the Swann Report.

References

1. *West Indian Children in Our Schools* (The Rampton Report), Cmnd. 8273, HMSO, London (1981)
2. Lord Swann, *Education for All*, Report of the Committee of Enquiry into the Education of Ethnic Minority Children, HMSO, London, March (1985)
3. M. Shipman, *The Limitations of Social Research*, 2nd edn, Longman, Harlow (1981)
4. S. Tomlinson, *Ethnic Minorities in British Schools*, Heinemann Educational, London (1983)

5. S. Tomlinson, *Home and School in Multicultural Britain*, Batsford, London (1984)
6. M. Stone, *The Education of the Black Child in Britain: the Myth of Multiracial Education*, Fontana, London (1981)
7. C. Murray and A. Dawson, *Five Thousand Adolescents*, Manchester University Press (1983)
8. E. M. Brittan, 'Multiracial Education—Teacher Opinion on Aspects of School Life', *Educational Research*, Vol. 18, No. 3 (1976)
9. O. F. Stewart, *The Role of Ethnicity in Teachers' Accounts of their Interactions with Pupils in Multicultural Classrooms*, MSc thesis, University of Aston in Birmingham (1978)
10. Lord Swann, *Education for All: A Brief Guide* (1985)
11. *The Education of Ethnic Minority Children*, Community Relations Council (1977), p. 40
12. Lord Scarman, *The Brixton Disorders*, Cmnd. 8427, HMSO, London (1981)
13. G. Klein, 'Kids, Schools and Libraries', *Education Journal*, Commission for Racial Equality, March (1981)
14. G. Klein, 'No Bandwaggon', *The Times Educational Supplement*, 6 May 1983
15. *Linguistic Minorities in England*, Linguistic Minorities Project, University of London Institute of Education (1983)

CHAPTER 7

The Language Issue

When a nation becomes multi-ethnic the question of language assumes new importance. The place of languages spoken by minority groups in the public affairs and education systems always gets onto the political agenda. Since language is central to the individual's and the group's identity, history and traditions, the debate is often fierce and sometimes acrimonious. In recent years there have been heated controversies surrounding language in many parts of the world. Canada, Belgium, Wales, Sri lanka, Israel and the USA are all examples of where contentious debates about minority languages have taken place. In a democracy, where head-counting is the determining process in elections, the size of the minority population is a crucial factor. The place of Spanish in the USA, for instance, did not become a significant issue until ethnic quotas were removed from the USA's immigration policies in 1965. New arrivals of Latinos increased from 21 to 41 per cent, and that excluded the sizeable illegal entries. This meant greatly increased electoral powers to Spanish-speaking groups, which was rapidly expressed as demands for separate language rights. This movement succeeded. An historic, Supreme Court decision in 1967 granted parents the right to have their children educated in the mother-language. This tendency to demand language rights appears to be an inevitable development in multi-ethnic societies. Such rights appear to function to reassure the minority group that it has a place in the world, that its demands are taken seriously and that its culture is respected by the world at large.

A debate about 'mother-tongue' provision is now taking place in Britain. Demands for official forms, information leaflets and notices in 'mother-languages' have been successfully made in many of the local authority areas. The sizeable and rapidly increasing Asian population in Britain represents an enormous linguistic diversity. In Bradford alone there are 14,201 schoolchildren who, between them, speak 64 different non-English languages; in Haringey the figures are 7,407 and 87.[1] As mentioned earlier, an ILEA survey recently discovered 146 different languages and dialects in its schools, and this phenomenon is growing. It is little wonder, then, that we find this comment in the Swann Report on the issue of 'mother-languages':

> We have indeed received more evidence on this issue than on any other encompassed by our overall remit, and in recent years there has been a proliferation of 'issue papers', conferences and articles devoted to this area of concern (p. 397).

The flavour of the demands being made can be judged from an article in the CRE's *Education Journal* for March 1981 by an Asian senior lecturer in a college of education:[2]

> Shouldn't they [Asian parents] as British parents, campaign for a rightful place of mother tongue in the mainstream schooling of their children: . . . If schools at Infant and Primary stage continue to function as monolingual and monocultural entities they will miserably fail in the education of bilingual children.

As we shall see, there is no convincing empirical evidence to support this assertion, but it is one frequently made by protagonists in the debates.

Although I am specifically concerned here about the minority-language debate in education it is important to stress that the issue has important consequences for our multi-ethnic identity as a nation. If rights regarding language are granted to minorities in Britain, as they have been in the USA, then a crucial decision regarding our whole character as a polyglot nation will also have been taken. The concept of integration, with all citizens loyal to one national ideal—with 'mother-culture's' maintenance and transmission being regarded as an essentially private responsibility—is undermined by the granting of separate language rights to minorities. There is increasing anxiety in the USA regarding the 'melting-pot' theory, which enables a large, diverse society to function as a stable coherent nation. There is a fear that this is being progressively undermined by the creation, for instance, of a separate and publicly funded Spanish-speaking community, unable and unwilling effectively to become part of the wider, dominant English-speaking community. Just as a national, generally accepted language can function to bind disparate communities together, so the granting of separate language rights can carry the danger of division and acrimony. We need to be aware that language and politics are inseparable.

The 'Mother-tongue' and Learning

The vital role language plays in learning is now unquestioned. A recent general text in psychology[3] says: 'It is generally accepted that language is the most powerful and flexible means we have for representing and manipulating the environment—for "thinking"'. However, there is no consensus regarding the precise relationship between language and thought. The work of psychologists and linguists suggests a number of positions on this issue. Some argue that thought is heavily conditioned by the language available (the Whorf–Sapir hypothesis): our thoughts are as complex or as simple as our words enable them to be. Those groups which have a wider linguistic vocabulary and more complex grammatical systems will produce more advanced ways of manipulating the environment, more complex technologies and more developed cultures generally. An extreme form of this belief holds that thought and language are one. The behaviourist approach produces an explanation which goes as follows. Language is acquired by a process of operant conditioning. When the child emits sounds which approximate to recognisable words, he or she is rewarded. This process gradually enables meaningful responses to be established as a recurring aspect of the child's behaviour, so that regular, rewarding speech inter-actions are features of daily experience. In learning to speak, the child also learns ways of thinking by internalising language. Thought is no more than a form of speaking to oneself.

Yet another school argues that thought is pre-eminent; language is produced as the result of thought, which relies in its genesis upon non-linguistic processes, such as imitation, symbolic games and, among others, mental imagery. This mode of explanation is associated with Piaget, and has been very influential in teaching methods in Britain's schools.

Finally, there are those, notably the Soviet psychologist Vygotsky, who assert that language and thought arise from separate origins —they develop, as it were, along different but intertwining pathways. Whereas thinking is the restructuring internally of an external situation, language comes from the gradual refining of emotive utterances and the need to communicate. This controversy is made more difficult to sort out since it involves very complex questions of definition. The concepts of language and thought are explicable only by philosphers who, unfortunately, also have their differences. However, on one issue there is a consensus, which can be stated thus. Language and educability are intimately connected. The extent to which a child can benefit from schooling and develop intellectually, creatively and socially is heavily dependent on the range and quality of the language available to it. In recent years this belief has been most actively employed in attempts to explain the relationship between social class and educational performance. A concept of 'linguistic deprivation' has been proposed by the sociologist Bernstein. Working-class children tend to use a less demanding and less complex 'restricted code', while middle-class pupils tend to use a more complex 'elaborated code'. These codes are differentially related to the demands of educational discourse, the middle-class code being better suited to the linguistic demands of the classroom. Although this concept has been less fashionable in recent years, due to attacks notably from the American linguist Labov, it continues to be influential.[4]

Now this debate about language and educability has spread to include not only social class but also national origins. The advent of an increasing number of children whose first language is not English has raised the question: How far, for instance, is the child who was born and reared in an Urdu-speaking home disadvantaged or handicapped, if at all, in his or her educational progress by attending schools where English is the medium of instruction? We are, as it were, faced with a rather special form of the debate about language and thought. It certainly appears to be the case that different languages encapsulate different ways of perceiving the world and varying modes of conceptualising experience. Whorf provides a famous instance of this. Hopi Indians employ the same word for insect, aeroplane and pilot, while Radford quotes Brown, who discovered that, compared with English, the Shona and Bassa languages had much less complex naming systems for colours.

Bloom[5] has suggested that Chinese users resist certain kinds of speculation because their language does not contain appropriate structures to carry them, while Honey[6] quotes an Oxford classicist as saying 'In studying Japanese one is forced to recognise that what one had lazily assumed to be fundamental categories of thought are merely local habits'. The same source refers to Whorf's discovery that American-Indian languages do not recognise the notion of measurable time and have no grammatical tenses like those of European languages, nor concepts of speed.

If, then, there are those intellectual and psychological differences among languages, might this not represent a difficulty for ethnic-minority children in British schools? Might it not be that in making the transition from, say, a Gujerati-speaking home to an English-speaking school the Asian child is involved in a complex and possibly disabling process of linguistic adaptation? Suppose there are the kinds of perceptual and conceptual differences between English and Gujerati that we have referred to above? Perhaps there are variations, for instance, in ways of expressing basic conceptual notions of time, speed, weight, distance, volume—all intrinsic to early eductional experience. Apart from this psychological issue, what of the extent to which such a child can feel at home in a school environment in which the prevailing language is strange to him — particularly in the early infant school stage? Might not such children not only fail to learn effectively but become alienated from school?

These are clearly important questions, but they are far from being easy to elucidate. A key problem is the absence of studies that make the appropriate comparisons between English and the other languages now spoken in Britain. There have been three major research projects in Britain on bilingual education, in Birmingham, Bedford and Bradford, but they provide no basis for supporting bilingualism in schools. The NFER review of literature for the Swann Committee produced the following response: 'Thus on the strength of the NFER review it would not seem possible for the case of any form of mother tongue provision to rest on research evidence alone.' This came as a surprise to those of us working in multilingual schools and who, for many years, had been pressured from several sources into believing that the case had, indeed, been well established. Regarding progress and achievement the NFER report states:

. . . Bilingual education of a pluralist character does not appear either to enhance or to depress the bilingual child's performance in the majority language, English, or in the non-language subjects . . . There do not appear to be particularly compelling arguments on the basis of promoting the academic achievement of the individual minority-language child for choosing between monolingual and bilingual education.

This judgement can be sustained by referring to the performance in public examinations of Asian children in Britain. According to detailed information provided in the Rampton Report, the average Asian performance in CSE, O and A levels was comparable with that of white indigenous children—and both these groups would have been taught in English. Moreover, according to a recent (1985) speech by the USA Education Secretary, William Bennet, the bilingual programme there has failed. Referring to the teaching of Spanish-speaking children in Spanish, Bennet said that this had not only failed to improve the English used by such children but had also held back some of them. The best way for such children to progress was for them to go to an ordinary English-speaking school and be forced to 'sink or swim', like millions of immigrant children before them.[7] This 'immersion' approach has had considerable success in for example, teaching French to English-speaking Canadian children.

Mother-tongue and Practicalities

If bilingual education is not justified on research grounds, then perhaps there are others which do support it. According to the NFER survey referred to above, certain additional reasons have been advanced by advocates of teaching the mother-tongue. These centre around the rights of the child to develop his or her full potential, to promote a pride in the minority culture, to facilitate links with relatives abroad and to enhance the nation's linguistic resources. I wish now to look at each of these arguments.

It is true that, according to the Education Act 1944, the providers of education are enjoined to educate the child according to his or her age, ability and aptitude. It is equally clear that an ethnic-minority child will have an aptitude for the language of his or her home and country. However, legislative edicts are always to be understood in terms of the age in which they are promulgated. In 1944 the concept of aptitudes could not have had any connection with the notion of mother-tongue preference. When the Act was put on the Statute Book Britain was essentially a monolingual society —at least in terms of there being an unquestioned national language in which the school had always taught. There could have been no way in which the authors of the Act could have predicted the incredible growth of foreign languages used as mother-tongues in Britain today. The mother-tongue issue is the product of large-scale immigration which came some years after the 1944 Act. Moreover, there has been no indication in statutory orders or other legislation or advisory documents from the DES that aptitude can be defined so as to include the propensity for, and potential in, a mother-language. Although the Plowden Report urged schools not to ignore the child's mother-language, it gave neither empirical evidence nor practical advice to support this recommendation.

Sometimes the argument is bolstered by references to the Welsh experience. It is argued that since, *de facto*, in many parts of Wales children are taught in Welsh, does this not set a precedent for mother-tongues in English schools? This point was put very strongly, for instance, at a conference organised in 1976 by the CRE and the Centre for Bilingual and Language Education at Aberystwyth. After all, if Welsh pupils are compelled to use Welsh to learn with, or take Welsh to appreciate the culture and history of Wales, why should not Urdu-speaking children in Bradford schools do the same with regard to Pakistani culture? This has a superficial plausibility, as well as touching on liberal sentiments about civil rights and the defence of the underdog. It suffers, however, from a number of false assumptions. First, it ignores the fact that rights have to do with time. There is a sense in which rights have to be earned—instant conferring of rights on immigrants (apart, of course, from those general civil rights that all British citizens automatically enjoy) is not possible. For one thing, there has to be a lengthy time lag before the indigenous community can be convinced that immigrants intend to form a permanent community, whose special demands can be considered: there is much more likelihood of Welsh people remaining in Wales than of Asians or, indeed, of West Indians staying in England. Second, Wales is the historic homeland of the Welsh. They are not an immigrant community at all in the sense that England's ethnic minorities are. If the analogy is to convince it would have to run along the lines of Welsh children living and going to school in England, having the right to be taught in Welsh in their English schools, and no-one has suggested that. Most people, including Welsh parents, would consider it bizarre. Moreover, no previous immigrant community has made such mother-tongue demands—the Jews and central Europeans, for instance, have never proposed such 'rights'. In addition, the argument ignores the sheer number of mother-languages now in Britain. If the right to one mother-language in schools is granted, then that same right must clearly be given to all mother-languages. The costs involved would, of course, be colossal, unacceptable to public opinion and almost certainly prohibitive.

Promoting a pride in the minority culture certainly appears a perfectly worthy objective for teachers to pursue. After all, the culture of the home is a decisive influence in the child's identity and his sense of personal worth. In terms of emotional and social development it is generally agreed that the culture of the home is more influential than formal schooling. However, the notion that the school either should or can be involved in this process, to the extent of actually teaching in the language of the home, is by no means established. There is little evidence to suggest that children are in any sense damaged by functioning in two languages. No-one now seriously suggests, for instance, that the West Indian child's exposure to the standard English of the classroom as opposed to the Creole spoken in his home threatens his self-concept—although some have advanced the notion that his intellectual progress might be impaired. Moreover, no-one has suggested, again, that previous immigrant communities have suffered in this respect. Are Jewish children any less proud of their Jewish heritage and culture because they are bilingual? The contrary view might be easier to support; the consciousness of living in a world foreign to one's origins often reinforces attachment to the original mother-culture. Moreover, even if it could be held that the school ought to teach in the mother-culture, there would be formidable practical problems. The following are just some of these:

(1) How would the principle apply to multi-lingual schools? Many of Britain's inner-city schools now contain children who speak many *different* mother-languages, and these children are often in the same class. How, apart from linguistic Apartheid, could

each child be taught in its mother-tongue? (Advocates of mother-tongue teaching often speak as if Britain were the linguistic equivalent of Canada, where just two major languages are fighting for supremacy.)

(2) Even within Britain's linguistic diversity there are local variations of dialect. Moreover, many minority parents, although they speak one language, will prefer for historical and status reasons to see their children taught in a different tongue. For instance, some of the sizeable Italian community in Britain speak Sicilian Italian, but the parents concerned would prefer standard Italian, since this carries more status. The Sylheti Bengali-speaking father might well follow the Italian parents in Britain, and for much the same reasons. Punjabi-speaking children would prefer perhaps to be taught in Urdu since that is the national language of learning for their parents; while East Punjabis might well prefer Hindi for religious reasons. Some Cantonese-speaking parents might choose Mandarin Chinese as the medium of instruction for their children, since this is the national language of China and Taiwan. In short, even the definition of what constitutes the 'mother-language' is problematic. Even if the problem of definition could be overcome, where would the many teachers required come from? One difficulty here is that there is some evidence that Asian parents have little desire to encourage their children to go into teaching. They, perhaps correctly, perceive it as a low-level occupation and much prefer their offspring to enter 'real' professions, such as medicine and the law. So the potential supply of, say, Asian-speaking teachers may be far too small to meet the demand. Moreover, would public opinion accept the very large costs involved?

Attempting to preserve and promote the child's 'mother-culture' may seem an attractive liberal principle but implementing it in linguistic terms could be a recipe for educational chaos.

What of linguistic links with the mother-country? Embedded in this notion is an assumption about the concept of 'mother-country'. It is as if we are here assuming that successive generations of minority people will always regard the country of family origins as the 'mother-country'. Now clearly, original first-generation immigrants will tend to do so, but is that the case for their children and grandchildren? Does a British–Asian child born in Bradford have the same relationship to Pakistan as his immigrant parents? Is there not a natural tendency for such links to be weakened over time and for future generations to come to regard Britain as their 'mother-country'? How many of Britain's Polish-speaking pupils in school now regard Poland as their mother-country? Even if this natural process were not to take place, how far is the state, through the school system, responsible for maintaining immigrants' links with their country of origin? Is that proces not a naturally and inevitably private one? If the state were to accept this line of argument, then again there would be a very large expenditure involved, since *all* immigrants and their descendants would share in the benefits. Since Britain (according to the Runnymede Trust) is never likely to have more than 6 per cent of its population from the minorities, it is very unlikely that public opinion would support this position.

This issue has been clouded by much talk about the EEC Directive on the education of children of migrant workers, issued in 1977. The advocates of bilingualism in schools have sought to use this to sustain their case, and they have been supported by certain elements in the press. An article in the *Guardian* of 21 December 1984 is typical of this viewpoint. Under the heading 'Immigrant Education May Land UK in Dock' the reporter quotes Ivor Richards, Social Affairs Commissioner of the EEC: 'Migrant workers' children, given their social status and the linguistic and cultural problems they face, run a much greater risk of educational failure and thus of unemployment, than do children of indigenous parents.' This kind of report has had considerable influence but its assumptions are essentially false.

First, the notion it carries (that bilingual education leads to higher levels of achievement) has no convicing evidence to support it. Second, ethnic-minority children in British schools are not the offspring of migrant workers. They are the children of British parents and are British citizens themselves, and an increasing number are born and bred in Britain. Third, the purpose lying behind the Directive has no connection with the education of Britain's ethnic-minority children. The Swann Report quotes the key passage regarding the promotion of mother-tongue teaching to the children of migrant workers; the mother-tongue should be promoted ' . . . with the view principally to facilitating their possible reintegration into the member state of origin'. Fourth, although the

EEC Directive refers to the 'promoting' of the mother-tongue it makes no reference to the fact that this is, in any sense, a *right*. It is interesting to note that the Swann Report is scathing in its criticism of the way the EEC Directive has been used to support the case for mother-tongue teaching and cultural maintenance. I suspect that this episode is a good illustration of how groups with an axe to grind can selectively perceive and exploit the evidence so as to promote their cause—a process for which the state system of education is now notorious.

However, increasing a nation's linguistic resources certainly seems a defensible objective. Trade, diplomacy and defence are all linked to foreign policy and multilingual negotiations. All may benefit from having a population proficient in a range of languages. In this sense, Britain can clearly benefit from its multi-ethnic character. However, this is not an argument for bilingual education but for putting minority languages on the timetable at the secondary level. Urdu, for instance, might well be set beside French and German as part of the school's foreign-language programme —always, of course, assuming that the necessary resources exist and there is a genuine parental demand. It cannot be assumed that Asian parents, for instance, necessarily want their mother-languages on the school curriculum. There is good evidence to suggest that they do not perceive it as a priority; the demand in Britain has not come from parents so much as Asian intellectuals, educators and professional race relations personnel. An HMI report in 1984 found, after looking at the mother-tongue in four LEAs, only moderate parental support. For instance, of 950 pupils speaking Punjabi only 71 (7.4 per cent) opted for Punjabi lessons; 25 per cent of the relevant community opted for Bengali; 17 per cent supported Cantonese; 10 per cent Turkish; and 22 per cent Greek. Minority parents had a no-nonsense, instrumental view of their children's educational needs. They opted for the mother-tongue only when it did not conflict with vocationally more valuable subjects or with those that had more status.[8] This same attitude was discovered by CRC researchers in 1977. They interviewed 700 parents for whom Urdu, Hindi, Gujerati, Punjabi and Greek were the mother-tongues and found an average demand of 16 per cent.[9] Moreover, if the mother-tongue is to be placed on the school timetable there are two vital conditions involved. First, the placing of, say, Gujerati on the timetable should not involve compulsion; it should, like many other school subjects, be optional. As I write, there is considerable public resentment being expressed about a school in Wolverhampton compelling its pupils to take Punjabi. That kind of approach is insensitive and will not improve race relations. Second, a school considering this move needs to liaise very carefully with its parents. If the school is multilingual there is a very real danger that the selection of, say, one Asian language (more would be impracticable) might well create objections from parents who speak one of those languages not selected. The great value of choosing the traditional European languages, of course, is that this danger is avoided. There are no sizeable French, German or Spanish groups in Britain. Putting an Asian language on the curriculum might be fully justified but, handled wrongly, the process could create inter-communal conflict. It should never be forgotten that there is historic animosity among many of Britain's minority groups, and history is a very powerful influence in pupils' behaviour and relationships.

The case, then, for using the 'mother-language' as the medium of instruction has not been made and there are obvious and important reasons why the proposal should be rejected. However, there are acceptable grounds for placing an ethnic-minority language on the timetable—subject to certain safeguards.

The Multilingual Classroom and Achievement

A question which has caused much debate is 'If a disproportionate number of pupils are using English as a second language will academic standards decline'? This is a difficult issue, not only because it raises complex empirical problems but because of the current emotional and political climate surrounding questions involving ethnicity. Any attempt even to propose a question whose resolution might reflect adversely on the ethnic minorities tends to be met with strident opposition and imputations of ill-will from the very influential anti-racist lobby. A review of the literature in 1983 makes no reference to this issue[10] nor does the Swann Report's chapter on 'Language and Language Education' or 'Achievement and Underachievement'. Nevertheless, it is an issue which does cause concern both to parents and teachers, including, in my own direct experience, some ethnic-minority parents themselves. One of the key problems here is that the term 'ethnic-minority pupil' has always been applied to children of overseas origin. However, as we now know, there are many schools where the minority children are white and indigenous. In a very real sense *they* are, within the context of the school, ethnic-minority children. Although it is not possible to provide objective information about the relationship between pro-portions of ethnic-minority children and average levels of achievement, there is little doubt that there is much intuitive belief that the relationship is problematic.

Although we find this concern dismissed in the literature of anti-racism as belonging to the 'assimilationalist' phase of race relations, that concern continues, rightly or wrongly. It was first officially acknowledged in 1963, when a group of parents in Southall protested about their anxieties regarding this problem. The then Minister of Education expressed the following view in the House of Commons: 'If possible, it is desirable on *educational grounds* [my emphasis] that no one school should have more than 30 per cent of immigrants.' This was echoed in DES Circular 7/65, which emphasised the need to reassure white parents about their children's schooling: 'It will be helpful if the parents of non-immigrant children can see that practical measures have been taken to deal with the problem in school and that the progress of their own children is not being restricted by the undue preoccupation of the teaching staff with the linguistic and other difficulties of immigrant children' (quoted in Swann, pp. 193–4). Although the label 'immigrant' applied progressively to a decreasing proportion of ethnic children, anxiety continued. According to the CRC's survey of teacher opinion in multi-ethnic schools there was widespread concern about the educational problems faced by the minority children. The following typical quotes give the source of the problems: 'Language problems with both Asians and West Indians.' 'If their mothers don't speak English and can't help with their books and reading this can be hard on the children.' 'Quite often a child born here will know a little English before it starts school.' 'Children born abroad do not necessarily have greater difficulties. A Greek Cypriot child born here to a non-English speaking mum can still enter primary school knowing no English.' It is difficult to see how a dispro-portionate number (a term which, in the present state of knowledge, must necessarily carry an intuitive definition) of such children in the classroom can fail to depress the overall academic atmosphere and average levels of achievement.

A press report in 1980 makes clear the kind of anxiety this problem can evoke in a head teacher. A small Church of England primary school in London's Tower Hamlets (an area with a very large Bengali community) had an ethnic-minority pupil population of 40 per cent. The head teacher insisted on having no more than 50 per cent of such children in any one class, for purely educational reasons:[11]

> Both the Authority and the Church have refused to grasp this nettle and we want it brought out into the open for informed debate. At present we have over 50 per cent non-English speaking children in our infant class and we simply cannot take any more and do our job properly . . . My policy is not racial in any way.

A not-dissimilar anxiety is to be found in a Schools Council pamphlet.[12] This was a survey of 94 LEAs divided into areas with high, medium and low concentrations of ethnic-minority pupils. There were 120 schools in the first category, 67 in the second and 30 in the third. These terms were defined as follows. 'high concentrations' meant areas with 10 per cent or more births to women from the New Commonwealth (including Pakistan); 'medium' referred to 2.5–10 per cent concentration; and 'low' concentration meant fewer than 2.5 per cent. There was information from 148 high and 77 medium concentration areas. In short, the sample was substantial and statistically representative.

It is worth quoting the relevant passage in full (p. 25). As we have suggested, both the most recent review of the literature and the Swann Committee left this issue as 'a neglected aspect':

> Several authorities reported concern about the situation of white children in schools with high proportions of ethnic minorities . . . in schools of very high proportions of ethnic minorities the situation of white children (usually of economically and socially depressed families) is greatly ignored and deserves further detailed research.

Fifty-four per cent of head teachers (who replied to the questionnaire) in schools with 30 per cent or more pupils from ethnic minority groups drew attention to the 'special' needs of their white pupils, many stressing that the needs of this group tended to be ignored:

We have to be careful that children with language problems who are not truly remedial, do not swamp the remedial teachers who should be coping with truly remedial problems . . . We are not acting in a positive way on this need of which we have long been aware.

Seventy-eight per cent of schools said that in-service courses on multi-ethnic education should cover the needs of white children in these schools and 60 per cent considered that present in-service courses do not do so—'this is a neglected aspect'.

However, intuitive judgements and professional opinions do not constitute empirical evidence. A complicating factor here is that in terms of performance in public examinations Asian children—on average—do surprisingly well. However, this countervailing evidence needs to take account of the following relevant factors:

(1) We do not know how far the pupils concerned have attended schools with high, medium or low concentrations of children using English as a second language. The high average Asian performance could reflect the results of a disproportionate number of Asian children from schools with low proportions of such pupils.

(2) We do know that Bangladeshi children are, by any criteria, low achievers at the moment.

(3) If we include West Indian pupils on the grounds of dialect problems (a judgement for which there is much support) then we have a further group whose average educational performance is significantly lower on a national scale than the general average—and possibly for reasons to do with language.

(4) Detailed surveys of examination results on a national scale for 1981[13] reveal that examination results are lower per pupil in LEAs with:
(a) More teachers per pupil;
(b) Higher expenditure per pupil;
(c) Higher proportions of pupils who are non-white or born abroad.

(5) Similar surveys for 1982[14] reveal that examination results are lower per pupil in LEAs with:
(a) Higher expenditure per pupil;
(b) Higher proportions of pupils who are non-white or born abroad;
(c) Higher proportions of inexperienced teachers.

Although these factors are intercorrelated—making simple judgements inadmissible—there does appear to be evidence for more detailed study of the effects of ethnic-minority proportions on levels of white achievement. It is important to stress that this issue has nothing whatsoever to do with race, genetics or colour but with competence in the English language; and if the concerns noted above are valid, then the effects are as damaging for ethnic-minority as for white children. However, it seems very unlikely that the necessary research could be carried out unless there is a considerable change in the climate surrounding race relations—the present one is far too prescriptive and narrow. Moreover, really reliable correlations between proportions of pupils using English as a second language and school achievement could not be established until national, academic benchmarks at key ages of, say, seven, eleven, fifteen and eighteen were available. However, it is important for educational planning—particularly the question of dispersal policies—and for good race relations.

The West Indian Language Issue

Language—even West Indian children don't have the same vocabulary or background knowledge that you might take for granted.
West Indian difficulties are more severe. Patois is often not recognised as being a language on its own.
A higher percentage of West Indian children fail than those of other ethnic groups—this may be a communication failure.
We also realise that the West Indian pupils who appeared to speak English in fact had difficulty with the language.

Those are the opinions of teachers experienced in teaching West Indian children in English schools and are reported in a survey carried out by the Community Relations Council.[15] My own extensive experience of teaching West Indian youngsters suggests that most teachers would support this view of the language difficulties such children experience in the classroom. In looking at the educational performance and experience of British–West Indian children one thing is immediately apparent: as a group they perform less well on average than Asians or white pupils. This is widely recognised with regard to public examinations results, as reported, for instance, in the Rampton Report. However, it also appears to be the case with other age levels, according to research reported in the British *Journal of Developmental Psychology*, based on a study of 1000 children in a Warwick town in 1981. The following were true of West Indian children:[16]

(1) By the age of ten West Indians are almost one year in arrears in reading compared with white working-class children and two years behind white middle-class children.

(2) Between eight and twelve years of age there is an average decline in the IQ of West Indian children of 4.6 while that of Indian children increases by 4.4.

(3) Only 2 per cent of West Indians go into the top stream of local secondary schools, in contrast to 75 per cent of white middle-class children.

(4) West Indian children perform less well than white and Asian children from the pre-school stage to the end of their school careers—and the gap widens with time.

This pattern is reflected in the judgement of Tomlinson,[17] who reviewed the extensive literature up to 1982:

> The conclusion reached after a study of research into the educational performance of West Indian children is that in general these pupils do underperform and underachieve in comparison with white and Asian minority groups . . . The optimistic assumption that 'immigrant' performance would improve with length of schooling in Britain and that black British children's performance would come up to or at least equal that of inner city white children does not appear to have come about.

Now in discussing the question of educational achievement we have constantly to bear in mind that the issues are complex. What causes an individual child or group of children to perform at a particular level constitutes a perennial—not to say controversial — debate among educators of all kinds. Indeed, so complex is this question that experts in the field tend not to talk about causes at all but rather about 'factors associated with' particular outcomes. We now know, for instance, that such factors as age, sex, motivation, social class, the school, the teacher, the head teacher, parental attitudes and basic ability can all be shown to be connected with achievement in school, and in recent years there has been intense interest in the role of language. Although there is general agreement about the link between language and educability, there are many unresolved and contentious questions surrounding that relationship. For instance, what is the nature of the link between language and thought? How is language acquired? How does language develop in the growing child? What is the relationship between spoken and written language? How do children best learn to read? Is there a specific language ability? Do the different school subjects generate their own distinctive discourse? How does the teacher's use of language link with pupil understanding and progress? Can we postulate a typical working-class as opposed to middle-class language—and if we can, what is the significance of the difference for educability? There is continuing debate about these and many other language issues, but if this phenomenon is in general intrinsically contentious, the particular question of how far the language of West Indian children accounts for their performance in schools is very much more so.

West Indian children form a distinctive racial group within society, and race is an explosive political issue. Extremists of both left and right have their own distinctive viewpoints, and those attached to the classical liberal traditions have theirs. There have been fierce controversies about the nature of Britain's multi-ethnic society, immigration, repatriation, inner-city riots, discrimination and prejudice in the country's institutional and social life, and the role of the government and the media in race relations. In education there has been an acrimonious debate about IQ and race. The black child in school has been at the very centre of all this, and is surrounded by controversy. This means that attempts to get at the truth are beset by presuppositions, ideology and fear of the outcome. Contending groups tend to perceive the evidence in highly selective ways, and are only too ready to impugn the goodwill of anyone who claims evidence which challenges their viewpoint. This needs to be constantly borne in mind.

The Basic Issue

At the heart of the debate lies the question: Are some forms of language superior to others? Alternatively, within this context can we say that the standard English of the classroom is superior to the non-standard variants used by West Indian families? If the answer to that question is no, then there would appear to be little reason to assume that the poorer academic achievement of West Indian pupils is associated with language. However, since there *is* among educationists and theoreticians a consensus that language and education are connected, we surely have to accept the need to examine the question. This is far from easy. A dominant theme in educational circles in Britain over the last 30 years has been cultural relativism. The notion that one culture is the equal of all others has been a virtually unquestioned assumption. Even to raise the question with which I began this paragraph would be considered improper by many intellectuals. Pointing to possible qualitative differences is forbidden, and this is as true of language as any other cultural product. I will not pause to examine the mental gyrations that this position requires for its maintenance. Suffice it to say that the climate to which it gives rise has created a major stumbling-block. However, if we capitulate to received wisdom then we may well be denying ourselves access to truths which could be of benefit to a significant group of children.

The striking feature of the debate is the contrast between the views of teachers and parents, on the one hand, and those of linguistic experts, on the other. I have already indicated the conviction of teachers that West Indian children do have specific language difficulties. Their parents, too, are emphatic about the importance of standard English to progress in schools. Tomlinson says: 'West Indian parents are also anxious that their children should become fluent in standard English as early as possible.' This does not, of course, indicate that West Indian parents regard standard English as being superior in general to the family Creole. Nor does it preclude the possibility that such parents correctly perceive the higher status accorded to standard English in our society. However, the crucial thing here is that West Indian parents accept that standard English is more *appropriate* to progress in an English school. This parent–teacher consensus finds no echo among those who generate influential theories about comparative linguistics.

Professor John Honey[18] has provided a set of questions which encapsulate the dominant egalitarian traditions among linguists. For example: 'It is an established fact that no language or dialect is superior to another . . . There is virtually unanimous recognition

among linguists that one language or dialect is as good as another.'
The strength of this tradition and the immense influence it has had
in education can be gained from this comment in the Rampton
Report on the education of black children: 'From the evidence we
have received . . . we do not accept that for the vast majority of
British-born [West Indian] children language factors play a part in
underachievement.' This view has been widely condemned by both
teachers and researchers, and its genesis has been suggested by
Bald:[19] 'Its contradiction of the evidence and the "mental
gymnastics" it involves can only be explained in terms of the political and social climate surrounding the debate about black school
achievements.'

Just how convincing is the 'all languages are equally good' school
of thought? Intuitively we suspect its validity. This is particularly so
when comparing the language of societies markedly unequal in
terms of intellectual and scientific development. In this context,
how does West Indian Creole compare with standard English?
There is no doubt that Creole is a developed language with its own
rule-governed systems and extensive vocabulary. Is it, however, as
rich, complex and powerful as the standard English in which, say,
nuclear physics, Western philosophy and literary criticism are expressed? Is it as likely to encapsulate and transmit abstract thoughts
and to tolerate irony, ambiguity and conceptual complexity? The
answer may well be yes to all these questions. In raising them I may
simply be reflecting my own parochialism. I do not know West
Indian Creole, but I do know that the cultural history of the two
languages and of the language populations concerned have been
markedly different. The people of the West Indies have a tradition
of poverty, economic exploitation and educational denial. They
have traditionally had to work all the hours God sent them to keep
body and soul together. They have not enjoyed that substantial
leisure and economic security which are the prerequisites of cultural
and technical advance. On the other hand, Britain has always had a
cultivated leisured class, with a tradition of exposure to both
abstract thought and empirical enquiry, and it is they who have
created the standard English of the classroom. Are these two groups
likely to have produced languages with equal capacities for producing the educated person in the generally accepted sense, i.e. in
the context of the culturally diverse and technically complex Britain
in which British black children now live out their lives? This seems

intrinsically unlikely. Those West Indian parents who complained to the Rampton Committee that language differences ought not to be used as an excuse for their children's educational failure were not pointing to the equality of Creole and standard English. They were complaining about those teachers who had effectively failed to convey that standard English which is the basis of progress in school.

However, is there more available than intuition to guide our response to this question? A further factor in assessing the validity of the linguistic relativity theory is the character of educational controversy. The educational establishment has a noted tendency to sustain its hegemony by using theory and research in self-interested ways. Interpretation of findings in research and their application to educational practice tends to reinforce current fashions. For example, the play way, the informal teaching methods beloved of progressive educationalists, demonstrated this in their wholehearted and oversimple reception of Piagetian psychology. Piaget's ideas appear to support the learning through discovery approach, so they were enthusiastically and uncritically endorsed. It was not until later and the emergence of thoughtful and critical work that Piagetian ideas were truly understood. One wonders how far this process has distorted the work of linguists. The dominant egalitarianism has certainly endorsed what it sees as support for its ideology, but how far is this interpretation correct? There appear to be two strands in modern linguistics. First, there are those who argue for the essential equality of all languages—what might be termed a pure form of the theory. However, there are also those who argue for the adequacy of language for the purpose of those using it. These are clearly different ideas, but they are often lumped together as one coherent body of opinion by those with an intellectual vested interest. Again I draw on Honey's work to illustrate. Consider the following:

> Every language has sufficiently rich vocabulary for the expression of all the distinctions that are important in the society using it (Lyons, *Chomsky*, 1970/77, p. 21).
>
> All varieties of a language are structured, complex, rule governed systems which are *entirely adequate* for the needs of their speakers (Trudgill, *Sociolinguistics*, 1974, p. 20).

Each of these writers has been frequently quoted as being a supporter of linguistic relativity, but are they actually saying that all languages are equally good or are they suggesting that language serves the needs of the group which exists in a distinctive context? That existing human need can be effectively discharged by using the available language? It may well be that, as Lyons says, every language is adequate for expressing relevant distinctions in a given society, but what if the inhabitants of a society choose to change their social context? Suppose they decide to live in another and more complex society. Will their original language still be adequate? Alternatively, in order to survive and then flourish in the new society, might they not require a different form of language? Again, although Trudgill asserts the essential complexity of all variety of language, he does not refer to equality but rather to adequacy to needs. A very simple example illustrates this. In Britain we have one word for snow; Eskimos have seven. We have no need to make a fine distinction of this natural phenomenon since it plays little part in our lives. However, Eskimos live in a more complex environment in this respect, and require a more discriminating language to reflect this. At least some of the linguists who are quoted by egalitarian theorists appear to accept this. Might this notion of linguistic adequacy to a given context be of significance to West Indian children struggling with the complex demand of formal education? Is it entirely fortuitous that the medium of instruction in Jamaican schools is standard English?

However, what of the concept that I have called the pure form of linguistic egalitarianism? If indeed there are no qualitative differences between languages, if they are all equally appropriate to very different cultural environments, where does this leave West Indian children in English schools? Can we ensure that they will make the transition from the home to the school without any particular linguistic difficulty? Or should we, for reasons of identity and cultural pride, teach in Creole? There are indeed those who would advocate the latter course, and there are those who, while not going that far, believe that the English school ought to devote at least part of the timetable teaching Creole (Maureen Stone gives an illuminating instance of this). Or should we, in view of the continued relative failure of West Indian children in English schools, question the whole argument? At least such an enterprise could have the merit of settling whether language plays a significant part.

The Pure Form of Linguistic Relativism

A very significant attack on this position has been produced by Honey.[20] In *The Language Trap* he has examined critically the pretentions of this school of thought, and his judgement is unequivocal: 'What is especially noteworthy about these theorists is that they offer no proofs for their rulings nor even any empirical evidence.' The basis of their position is in fact an *a priori* commitment to a naive cultural relativism. Honey supports his own view that there *are* qualitative differences between languages and within variants of the same language by showing that different cultures function at different levels of complexity, create different needs and produce languages which vary in richness and density. The notion of 'needs' is crucial here. The relativists argue that if a given language group lacks the vocabulary and grammar to handle, say, modern medicine, technology or communications this proves that they have no *need* of these things. While it could be argued that the impact of these on non-Western societies has not been an unmixed blessing, the state of their languages cannot be used as evidence to support the idea that they do not need them—that involves a value judgement on Western culture, and is not a description of a non-Western language. Moreover, the notion that languages and social development are synchronised—that words and culture advance in step, as it were—is very questionable. While language may reflect the current *general* needs of its users, this does not account for the time lag before innovations can occur and be named, nor for the fact that *individual* members of a language group may well be in advance of their community in perceiving a new phenonemon and borrowing it from another society. However, such an individual would have no means of describing this new phenomenon in the existing form of the language. In short, unless we reject the notion of cultural development, it is difficult to see how this can be facilitated without corresponding changes in the language.

This has a particular relevance for black youngsters in British schools. For many years, teachers have been led to believe in what might be termed the 'Labov factor'. Labov, an American linguist of considerable influence over the past 15 years or so, has argued that the non-standard speech of the American negro is the equal of standard English as a vehicle for complex thought. In this he has been in opposition to those psychologists (and, to some extent, the sociologist Bernstein) who have argued for a theory of linguistic deprivation to explain variations in educational performance. Honey examined the basis of Labov's theory in detail, paying particular attention to his crucial empirical work. His conclusion is emphatic:

> The widely publicised attempt to prove that one specific, non-standard variety of English (i.e. Black English Vernacular), which has hitherto been regarded as subject to limitations as a vehicle for the expression of logic or of the finer points of philosophical argument, is, in fact, entirely equal to standard English for all these intellectual tasks *and may even be superior to it* has been shown to be what we could charitably describe in scientific terms as bunk. So the fact is that the possibility that speakers of certain languages and dialects suffer a 'verbal deficit' which in turn may entail an intellectual deficit is still an open question and it has to be recognised that there is at least some evidence in support of that possibility.

In short, those of us who are teachers but not professional linguists may have been misled. What has for so long been presented as an established consensus is nothing of the kind. It is clear from Honey's work that there is considerable conflict among professionals on this issue. It may well be that in our proper attempts not to give offence to minorities and their culture we have been misled by inadequate and fashionable theory. Perhaps our fear of upsetting the egalitarian establishment (and latterly its multicultural education offshoot) has caused us to underestimate the language problems of West Indian children. It *may* be of some significance that, whereas considerable efforts have been made to teach Asian children English (and they have done surprisingly well in schools) we have tended to ignore the language problems of the West Indian children on the grounds that they have none. The English as a foreign language policies of many LEAs have been the almost exclusive preserve of Asian children. Since they initially speak a markedly different language from English, we have, in general, tended to assume that West Indian Creole is so like standard English that West Indian pupils can be more or less ignored in this respect. The Swann Report says: 'It is interesting to recall [of the 1950s and 1960s] that in view of this focus on language as the major 'problem', children from the West Indies were considered to have no particular eductional needs.'

A further problem here is the role of Caribbean dialect in establishing and maintaining group identities. Bald has claimed that West Indian pupils may deliberately engage in Creole in order to express an anti-authority stance. There is dispute about why so many West Indian youngsters adopt a confrontational attitude in schools, but that it happens is indubitable. Brook[21] has described their dialect as 'An anti-language, hidden, subversive and hostile'. Clearly, this kind of language is hardly appropriate for educational purposes.

The Empirical Evidence

If we look at the work of people who, rather than generating linguistic theory, have actually gone into the schools and considered the issue at first hand we find much to support the notion that, whatever the state of the argument about the relative qualitative merits of West Indian variants of standard English, the adequacy or appropriateness of Creole, Patois or Pidgin for formal educational purposes has been questioned. We should note, in passing, that the Rampton Report adopted an astonishingly dismissive attitude to this question and Swann virtually ignores it. I am indebted here to two extensive reviews of the literature by Taylor[22] and Tomlinson.[23] A survey conducted by Derrick in the first half of the 1960s found that Creole dialect English produced problems of learning for West Indian children, even for those born in Britain. A Schools Council project set up in 1967 established that difficulties distinctive of West Indian youngsters were related to the structure of their language. Jones[24] concluded after a conference on linguistics and language teaching held in the West Indies that the Creole dialect is 'an immature language which is clearly inadequate for expressing the complexities of present day life'.

In the 1970s there developed a debate about the notion of 'dialect interference' in the process of West Indian children acquiring standard English. Underlying this was the idea that while Creole, say, has many features in common with standard English, it also demonstrates considerable differences. This produces confusion for the learner and generates problems different in kind for those of, say, the Asian child, who has the advantage of approaching a standard English which is totally foreign to his mother-language. He can keep the two languages quite separate in his mind because they are so different, one from another, but it is much more difficult for the West Indian child to do this. Wright, who directed the Schools Council Project, *Teaching English to West Indian Children* (1970), noted 'interference' in oral comprehension, spelling and writing which could hinder progress. Sutcliffe[25] and Edwards[26] have made detailed studies of Creole dialect interference and bi-dialectalism, and both considered that dialect creates educational problems for West Indian children. Cheshire[27] believes that language difficulties cause comprehension difficulties, while Troyna[28] found that in a group of comprehensive schools he studied there was a correlation between dialect speech usage and membership of lower forms.

The West Indian sociologist Maureen Stone,[29] who actually sat in on lessons in a multi-ethnic comprehensive in London, made the following comment on the use of West Indian dialect in the classroom: 'Without saying that dialect should never be formally used in schools, I would argue that it is the job of the school to enable children to function with ease in the standard language', while Max Morris, a head teacher of a London comprehensive, has said: 'Should I create a black curriculum? Should I put Creole on the timetable? Over my dead body; and the majority of my parents would cheer me to the skies' (a high proportion of parents were West Indians).

It is difficult in view of the consensus one finds among teachers, parents and researchers on the language difficulties of West Indian children not to conclude that such difficulties actually do exist. For those of us with experience of actually teaching West Indian youngsters it is equally difficult not to see a link between this problem and their relatively poor academic performance. As Tomlinson[30] concludes: 'It does appear rather simplistic to conclude as the Rampton Committee concluded that language issues have no bearing on the school achievement of black children.'

Conclusion

Language is a central issue in multi-ethnic societies. While the mother-tongue is deeply significant for minorities, the wisdom of a state that grants separate language rights to minorities is questionable—assuming that harmonious integration is the ideal. If loyalty to a national ideal is thought to be desirable, the concept of a single national language has a crucial role to play. Apart from the political aspect, there are formidable practical problems standing in the way of granting language rights to minorities. The central arena in which the debate about language is to be held is the school.

The relationship between the mother-tongue and educational achievement is complicated by controversies surrounding the broader question: What is the link between language and thought? This uncertainty has enabled influential but questionable theories to be generated. However, we can say that there is no convincing empirical evidence to support the view that ethnic-minority children in school are helped by being taught in their mother-language. The pressure for mother-tongue teaching appears to have come not from parents or teachers but from people with distinctive ideological standpoints. Egalitarianism and cultural relativism appear to have functioned to prevent the raising of important questions, particularly the relatively poor academic achievement of West Indian children. Such children may well be linguistically handicapped in coping with demands of the standard English of the classroom and achieving less than they should as a result.

There is a need to distinguish between mother-tongue as the medium of instruction and as a subject in the curriculum. While the case for the first has not been (and probably never can be) made, there is one for the latter but only if certain conditions are met. Its introduction should be as an optional, and not a compulsory, subject. There should be strong parental demand. Its introduction should not alienate those parents whose mother-tongue is not selected, and the school should have sufficient resources. The sheer multiplicity of mother-tongues in Britain (perhaps even in the same school) makes this development hazardous. The great virtue of traditional European languages on the school curriculum is that they are not associated with distinctive minority groups in Britain. They have a neutral, non-controversial quality and are not related to race or race relations.

Perhaps the most important development concerning the theory of minority languages in educational achievement has been the questioning of the massively influential Labov viewpoint. His suggestion that non-standard English is as rich and complex and as capable as functioning as a vehicle of complex thought as standard English has been cogently challenged by Honey. The latter has drawn attention to the empirical shortcomings of Labov's views, and has also pointed to the debilitating effect of Labov's theory on the teaching of minority children. Bernstein's notion of linguistic deprivation is probably a more constructive and more valid view of the difficulties experienced by those children from the minorities who underachieve in school. There is an urgent need to supply teachers with a non-ideological language theory based on experience and the best available empirical work. Parental opinion of standard English should play an important part in determining the teacher's approach to this question.

References

1. *Linguistic Minorities in England*, Linguistic Minorities Project, University of London Institute of Education (1983)
2. R. Kaushal, 'Mother Tongue as an Issue of Importance', *Education Journal*, Commission for Racial Equality, March (1981)
3. R. Radford and E. Govier (eds), *A Textbook of Psychology*, Sheldon Press, London (1980)
4. *Ibid.*
5. A. H. Bloom, *The Linguistic Shaping of Thought*, New Jersey (1981)
6. J. Honey, *The Language Trap*, National Council for Educational Standards, London (1983)
7. *The Times*, 28 September 1985
8. *Mother Tongue Teaching in Four Local Education Authorities: An HMI Enquiry*, DES, HMSO, London (1984)
9. *The Education of Ethnic Minority Children*, Community Relations Council (1977)
10. S. Tomlinson, *Ethnic Minorities in British Schools*, Heinemann Educational, London (1983)
11. *Daily Telegraph*, 29 December 1980.
12. A. Little and R. Willey, *Multi-ethnic Education: The Way Forward*, Schools Pamphlet No. 18 (1981)
13. J. Marks, C. Cox and M. Pomian-Srzednicki, *Standards in English Schools*, Report No. 1, National Council for Educational Standards, London (1983)
14. J. Marks and M. Pomian-Srzednicki, *Standards in English Schools: Second Report*, National Council for Educational Standards, London (1985)
15. *The Education of Ethnic Minority Children, op. cit.*
16. *The Times Educational Supplement*, 11 March 1983
17. Tomlinson, *op. cit.*, p. 44
18. Honey, *op. cit.*
19. J. Bald, 'Ignoring the Evidence', *The Times Educational Supplement*, 2 October 1981
20. Honey, *op. cit.*
21. M. R. M. Brook, 'The Mother Tongue Issue in Britain', *British Journal of the Sociology of Education*, Vol. 1, No. 3 (1980)
22. R. F. Taylor, *Race, School and Community*, NFER (1970)
23. Tomlinson, *op. cit.*
24. J. Jones (ed.), *Linguistics and Language: Teaching in a Multicultural Society*, Allen and Unwin, London (1965)

25. D. Sutcliffe, *The Language of First and Second Generation West Indian Children*, MEd thesis, University of Leicester (1978)
26. V. K. Edwards, *The West Indian Language Issue in British Schools*, Routledge and Kegan Paul, London (1979)
27. J. J. Cheshire, 'Dialect Features and Linguistic Conflict in Schools', *Education Review*, Vol. 34 (1982)
28. B. Troyna, 'Race and Streaming, a Case Study', *Education Review*, Vol. 30 (1978)
29. M. Stone, *The Education of the Black Child in Britain: The Myth of Multiracial Education*, Fontana, London (1981), p. 111
30. Tomlinson, *op. cit.*, p. 111

CHAPTER 8

Multi-ethnic Education and the Schools:
A Case Study

I have stressed throughout this book that we should take what I have called 'multi-ethnic education' seriously. This is not because it is a valid or convincing concept. We should do so because its effects in the schools are real and, in some, decisive. The schools' curriculum, ethos, style and management can be crucially influenced by the ideals that make up the notion of multi-ethnic education. This is particularly so where the LEA is determined to impose upon the schools the doctrines of anti-racism. This was certainly the case in Bradford, where I was the head of a multi-ethnic school (overwhelmingly Pakistani Moslem in its pupil population) for six years. What I want to do now is to point to some of the practical effects in a particular school of the local authority's commitment to this approach.

The LEA's multi-ethnic stance and its determination to impose anti-racism on the schools created one set of problems. The presence of very large numbers of Moslem children (from 49 per cent of the school's population in 1980 to 96 per cent in 1985)—or, more precisely, the influence of the Council of the Mosques on the City Council—created another. The Council of the Mosques in Bradford claims to be the representative body of the various mosques and their adherents throughout the city. It is the expression of orthodox Islam, and its power resides in the respect and fear felt by the faithful towards its leaders, the imams. The imam is what the Christian would call a priest, although, strictly speaking, there is no priesthood in Islam.

In Pakistan the imams enjoy great power and influence. They are perceived there as leaders in the community—the easy distinction Westerners make between sacred and secular powers has no meaning in certain parts of the Islamic world. A high proportion of

Pakistanis in Bradford originate in the conservative, rural area of Mirpur, a place where Islamic orthodoxy, and with it obedience to the Moslem leadership, would be most likely to flourish. The status and respect, not to say awe, the imams inspire in Pakistan seem in no way lessened by their transition to Bradford. Their power, if not absolute, is considerable, and they appear to see their role as preservers of Islamic culture and tradition. They make few concessions to Western life and mores, which they regard as being essentially decadent—not without good reason—although, as British citizens, they do not object to the considerable material benefits their presence in Britain confers upon them.

The fear that the Moslem leadership inspired in the faithful was scarcely less than that which it created in the City Council. This had several sources. As a council which regarded itself as progressive and in the vanguard of race relations, Bradford feared any suggestion of its antagonising the leadership of what was, by far, the largest section of the ethnic-minority population (80 per cent of Asian children in Bradford schools are Moslems (*Education and Leisure*, Bradford Council, 1984)). In any dispute with the City Council, the Council of the Mosques could generate support from the CRE, a body which had asserted its will over the City Council by compelling it to abandon its bussing policy in 1980. Second, the City Council feared social conflict, an ever-present possibility in any multiracial area. The organised Asian demonstrations, with thousands of chanting, banner-waving Moslems packing the city centre, when the City Council hesitated over granting ritually slaughtered halal meat in school dinners, showed clearly the strength and extent of communal feelings, and how they might lead to violence if the Moslem leadership felt aggrieved. Third, the City Council was anxious to placate the imams because it did not want to see break-away, voluntary-aided schools established in Bradford. It wanted Moslem children to attend state schools—and there was, undoubtedly good reason for this. Fourth, Bradford's politicians were increasingly aware of the importance of the ethnic vote, of which Asian Moslems constituted by far the biggest constituency. According to official statistics issued in 1984, of 55,000 Bradford Asians, 39,500 were from Pakistan or Bangladesh, the great majority being Moslems. Moreover, the Asian birth-rate in Bradford is about three times the national average; one third of all live births in the city are to Asian mothers. Some idea of the growing political significance of the Asian presence in Bradford can be gained from school statistics. In the upper schools 16.9 per cent of the pupils are of Asian origin, while the figure for middle schools is 20.8 per cent, for first schools 22.6 per cent and for nursery schools 39.9 per cent (*Education and Leisure*, p. 37). Not surprisingly, politicians are very anxious to appease the Asian voter, particularly the adherents of Islam.

However, the price the City Council paid for this was a high one. It felt compelled to accede to the Council of the Mosque's every request regarding the ethos and practices of the schools that Moslem children attended. It is important to realise that the Council of the Mosque has a particularly powerful influence at the local CRC, whose offices were financed, in part, by the City Council; the CRC acted as a kind of bridge between Mosque and City Council. To be seen to be 'doing something' for the Asian community is now a political imperative in Bradford, and the schools are inevitably caught up in this. A policy of educational concession-making to Moslem aspirations has been established, and this policy is transmitted to the schools in two ways: through the very influential LEA 'advisers' and via mandatory Local Administrative Memoranda (LAMs) devised by a group of educational bureaucrats.

These underlying factors were rarely officially acknowledged, although they were common currency in the schools. Concession-making could very easily be projected as concern for a 'disadvantaged minority', the concepts of multi-ethnic education and anti-racism providing the necessary justifications in the field of educational policy-making. In more general terms the idea of good 'race relations' and the assumed ability of politicians and officialdom to maintain them provided the rationale. (A full expression of this latter mentality can be seen in the official statistics drawn up by Council officers and politicians in *District Trends 1984*. Here the whole of the ethnic minority community is described as 'black'—all social, religious and linguistic diversity being thereby abolished, and all information based on this mythical entity falsified.)

These factors meant not only that Bradford City Council employees approached all issues concerning Asians with some trepidation, they also resulted in a determined effort by the City Council to establish what can only be accurately described as a racial bureaucracy. A whole set of officers, one group being actually designated 'Race Trainers', was appointed. The result was an atmosphere characterised by uncertainty, insecurity and not a little resentment. The City Council officers' public pronouncements on race relations often bore little relation to what was said in private; and, to judge from the letters column in the *Bradford Telegraph and Argus*, the public was increasingly puzzled and resentful. However, the drive towards ethnic concession-making in the schools was relentless. There seemed no way of even questioning, let alone halting, the process. The notion that ethnic-minority children, particularly the Moslem majority, were a 'special case' who should be treated with unwonted care and attention became an increasingly dominant theme in the literature that the LEA imposed on the schools. Essentially, what was happening was that the established, fair and accepted conventions for ensuring the integration of immigrants and their descendants into society was breaking down under the pressure of unprecedented ethnic and political developments.

However, it did not seem to me sensible to treat any child or group of children as a special case. The important thing, I felt, was to regard children as individuals and to provide them with the best education available. In the case of all ethnic-minority children the school's role was to help to integrate them into the social order, while respecting the bi-cultural role that their parents' decision to come and live in Britain had imposed upon them. The general effect of the mandatory multi-ethnic education policy of the LEA was to encourage schools to emphasise Asian culture in their ethos and curriculum. This seemed to me the very opposite of what our Asian children actually needed. The desire of ethnic-minority parents to cherish and transmit the culture of their country of origin is surely understandable, indeed worthy. All immigrant communities wish to do that; and in a free and open society such as Britain's there is no reason why they should not do so. Indeed, we may all be enriched by the process. That was not at issue. The central conflict between the LEA and myself was the means by which this should be accomplished. The bureaucrats and 'advisers' insisted, under pressure from the forces I have described, that the responsibility lay with the schools. Whereas I felt that my duty was, as far as was practicable, to 'acknowledge' Pakistani Moslem culture—at least those parts of it which are compatible with our indigenous culture —the 'advisers' and bureaucrats insisted that I 'celebrate' the children's foreignness.

It is important to stress that the school had made certain changes. For instance, there had been considerable changes in Morning Assembly. As the proportion of Moslem children rose, we progressively dropped the Christian component and acknowledged Moslem festivals. I did not do this without a great deal of agonising, not simply because of questions of conscience but because of the law requiring Christian Assemblies. (I do not see how the 1944 Education Act can be interpreted in any other way.) We made concessions over school dress for girls, and changes in PE and games. I dropped my intention to develop modern educational dance, since Moslem fathers object to dance of any kind. I arranged single-sex swimming for nine-year-olds. All letters from school to home—and the school's information sheet—were written in both English and Urdu. If a parent visited the school, I was always willing to enlist the help of our two Asian teachers (one of whom I had appointed) in interpreting. Also, thanks to a City Council decision, ritually slaughtered halal meat was introduced into our school meals service—although this occurred, I must confess, against my wishes and advice.

However, none of this was sufficient. I was constantly urged to do more, and this seemed to me not in the children's interests. Moreover, it was based on the false assumption that unless the school preserved and sought to transmit the children's parents' culture, that culture would die out. This was manifestly false. In reality our pupils were saturated in Pakistani Islamic culture—for most of their waking day, out of school, they experienced little else. All their girls and womenfolk, and many of the males, dressed exactly as they would in the Pakistani town or village. They spoke the parental language and ate Asian food. Ideas about relationships between the sexes were identical to those of their ancestors (although a number of English-educated Asian girls are, inevitably, beginning to challenge this). They watched Asian videos and sat cross-legged at the local mosque for an average of eleven hours per week chanting the Koranic verses in Arabic. Moreover, our pupils lived in a district in which 70 per cent of the population was Asian, and this proportion was steadily rising; and since the enforced end of bussing and the rapid growth of Asian children in the school, very few now had the chance of a friendship with an English peer.

The possibility that these children would forget their Asian heritage was negated by an experience I had in Assembly. One morning I decided to establish who the children felt they were in terms of their nationality. I simply asked the assembled multitude how many children were Asian. All the Asian hands went up. I then asked how many were British. Ninety per cent of the Asian hands stayed down. The lesson of this was, I felt, not, as the 'advisers' were arguing, that these children might feel that their parental culture was threatened but rather that there was a very real danger of producing children trapped, as it were, in an Asian ghetto. Was not my duty, in this respect, to reassure them that they were, indeed, British and were able to cope with their bi-cultural identity in the wider British context? Also, would this duty be effectively discharged by making the ethos, values and curriculum increasingly Asian? This approach might well please the imams, the educational expert riding on the latest, career-enhancing bandwaggon and the politicians eager for the ethnic vote. However, would it meet the needs of those growing young people as they faced the realities of life in Britain?

There was, moreover, a curious paradox here. While the 'advisers' were busily producing mandatory rhetoric about the school's failing to 'celebrate' ethnic culture, the demand for places in the school from Asian parents showed no sign of flagging. When I arrived in 1980 there were about 420 pupils; when I left five years and two terms later, this had increased by 25 per cent, at a time when school rolls generally were falling, when schools outside the inner city were short of pupils and when, under the new Education Act 1980, parents could seek a place in *any* school they wished and not just from schools in neighbourhood zones. I do not believe that this high demand for places reflected any particular credit on the school. *All* schools in high birth-rate, Asian areas of Britain's inner cities are under pressure for places, but it is difficult to reconcile this with a school which is not, broadly speaking, meeting parents' wishes. Even after the trauma of the so-called 'Honeyford Affair', the school still received its usual quota of pupils; in September 1985, as I left in the December, a full complement of new entrants arrived —and only one was a white child out of about 120.

This led me to believe that, if only the City Council had not set up its multicultural and anti-racist enterprises, and had trusted the schools to educate children in ways they felt appropriate, and if only that trust had existed, parental confidence would have remained undisturbed. The insistent allegation by the officers and 'advisers' of the LEA that there was widespread dissatisfaction among Asian parents with the curriculum and the ethos of the school and that 'racism' was endemic bore little relation to reality. It was a belief based not on actual parental experiences and responses but on the professional, partisan and political influences I have outlined. I formed the conviction that the City Council was, perversely, systematically postulating 'problems' in order to claim goodwill towards the ethnic minorities by attempting to solve them. Despite the furious energy and money invested in multiculturalism and anti-racism, the one thing that the City Council never did was to commission an opinion poll among the parents of ethnic-minority children in the schools. Nor was its concern in any way a reflection of the work and expressed views of the school's governing bodies, among which the parents had their own elected representatives.

One of the unfortunate effects of the City Council's policy, in addition to distorting perception of multi-ethnic realities in the schools, was that it became very difficult for the school to convey to parents *its* needs as an institution educating British children. Whereas the schools had been successfully attempting to build bridges with parents, unobtrusively, over time, and via an element of give and take on both sides—a process from which a *modus vivendi* had emerged—the City Council now insisted that an officially inspired and imposed blueprint must dictate practices and solutions. This bureaucratic impulse had two principles at its base: a belief that Asian parents were an exploited underclass with untold grievances against an insensitive schools system; and a belief that concession-making would put this matter right. I believe that this analysis and prescription were essentially false, and the City Council's policy had two unfortunate effects: it made it very difficult to voice the school's legitimate demands of parents; and it provided the litigious trouble-making parent (every school has its quota of these) and the so-called community leaders who supported them with a field day. Genuine, unselfconscious communication between school and home was thereby undermined. I turn now to several specific issues which illustrate this.

Asian School Attendance

Compulsory school attendance is a legal requirement placed on any parent who registers his child in a British school. This is an unquestioned principle and arises from society's concern that all children of school age should enjoy an education consistent with their age, ability and aptitude. It also acts as a safeguard for the child who may be compelled by a parent to perform domestic duties at home or sent out to work for a wage. The educational benefits are obvious. Broken school attendance is a prescription for educational failure. No one doubts that.

After many years in the education service I arrived in Bradford with compulsory school attendance for all pupils as part of my understanding of my job. As a head teacher I would have a special responsibility for working with the Education Welfare Officer in ensuring respect for this educational and legal requirement among the parents of my pupils.

However, I had not been in the post long when I realised that the LEA appeared to have an inconsistent school-attendance policy. Although it had, quite properly, set up the necessary department to monitor school attendance and to prosecute those parents who persistently offended, the LEA was not applying the principle to Asian parents. It seemed that there was a well-developed practice among Asian parents of sending their offspring to the Indian sub-continent in term time, and they were doing so with complete impunity. Because the LEA had not, from the very outset, enforced the principle of compulsory and regular school attendance, in this regard a precedent had been set, and this was now regularly followed. I found Asian parents taking their children off for weeks, even months on end.

This caused me very considerable concern. The practice had a predictably bad effect on many children's progress, and if that had not been the case, then, obviously, making school attendance compulsory would have no educational justification. The teachers' morale suffered because the effort and skill invested in the children concerned could be virtually wasted. Average school attainment of Asian children, as measured by objective tests and public examinations, could be depressed as a result; and in the prevailing race relations climate, the school would be blamed for this, although the real responsibility, of course, lay with the parents. Occasionally, when a child returned from abroad the English he or she had previously acquired had been seriously impaired—a fact that necessitated a period of time in a special language centre. What this meant basically was that the system was functioning to subsidise absence from school.

Moreover, I found my own position as a head teacher, daily involved in matters relating to school attendance, increasingly difficult to defend. I was bound both by professional commitment and the requirements of the law to uphold the crucially important principle that regular, daily attendance in term was essential to the progress of the child. Yet, by 1983, 80 per cent of the school's parents, simply by virtue of their overseas origin (although increasingly, Asian parents will have been born in Britain) had implicit permission to violate this principle, while the other 20 per cent of the parents had not. (There was not the slightest doubt that if, say, one of my white parents had taken his child off to see grandmother in Scotland he would have been pursued by the forces of compulsory school attendance.) Although the precise legal position of Asian parents in this regard is uncertain—since there has been no test case brought by the authorities—there is little doubt that the process of reverse racial discrimination was operating here, and that process is illegal in Britain. The ethical dilemma in which this placed me can easily be imagined.

What was to be done? No-one appeared to know. There were those who argued that the practice would decline with time and the passing of the original Asian immigrant generation, but this ignored the fact that Asian immigration is a continuing process—new immigrants arrive virtually every day. Moreover, after 30 years from the first Asian arrivals in Bradford the practice continued. Children born of *indigenous* Asian parents were now involved. The LEA officers condoned the practice by insisting that schools reserve places for the absentees, so that the parents responsible would not be put to the inconvenience of seeking a place in another school on the child's return.

However, under pressure from the schools and the Education Welfare Officers the bureaucrats accepted—after years of permitting the practice—that there was, indeed, a problem. An education officer sent letters in English and Urdu pointing out the following: ' . . . Absence from school may cause difficulties in a child's educational progress at any age. It may lead to problems in requiring English and might also hinder the passing of important examinations at a later stage.' However, significantly, the letter omitted any reference to the legal requirements.

A number of meetings were convened to stress the importance of regular attendance. These were noisy, unseemly affairs dominated by vociferous Moslem extremists, who claimed that insistence on regular school attendance was racial discrimination. This latter term always creates a Pavlovian response in bureaucrats and politicians. They are terrified of the allegation, and often appear to believe that its imputation demonstrates its presence. This irrational guilt can be very successfully exploited by unscrupulous immigrants and the functionaries of the race relations lobby. Predictably, the practice continued unchecked—the bureaucrats' bluff had been called.

The failure of the LEA officers led me to seek advice from my professional association. They wrote to the DES (which does not, strictly speaking, have responsibility for school attendance) and sought advice. The DES's legal department came up with the view that since the child, when in India or Pakistan, was not resident in Britain, he or she was therefore outside the jurisdiction of the LEA. This being so, the LEA would be very unlikely to obtain judgment in a court of law. Moreover, since the parent sought a school place on return, this proved that the motive was not to keep the child off school.

This did not make sense, and the logic of it defeated me. The parents concerned were British citizens permanently resident in Britain, as were the children, most of whom were indigenous. The parents owned or rented property close to the school; many remained in Britain while the child was abroad; they were on the electoral register; and, according to information I received, they continued to draw a family allowance for the child. These parents had every intention of bringing the child back to its permanent place of residence and to take up its place in the same school. As I have said, this was more or less guaranteed by the insistence of the LEA officials that the child's name be kept on the school's register. How could it, in view of all this, possibly be argued by the DES that the child was not resident in Britain?

I had noticed from discussions with LEA officers that they, too, used the residency argument to rationalise this practice. They pointed to the children of British servicemen serving abroad and the children of parents working in the EEC. If such parents were permitted to take their children abroad, why should not Asian parents do the same? There were two reasons why this was a false analogy. First, British children residing abroad by reason of their parents' jobs are involved in *unavoidable* absence from school in Britain, which is very different from British-based parents taking or sending their children abroad in term time. Moreover, the children of British servicemen abroad attend service schools subject to the same school attendance regulations as obtained in Britain. Second, both service and EEC children are manifestly part of a family resident abroad at least for the duration of a specified contract or tour of duty.

If the residence argument defied logic, the motivation argument was even odder. If it is applied to all children, then any parent willing to send his or her child back to school after a prolonged absence would have official permission to send the child to any part of the world in term time for as long as he liked and for any reason whatever. Was the DES, I asked myself, seriously contending that if one of my English parents sent his child off on holiday to Spain with his uncle for three months during term time this would not be a violation of the school attendance regulations? The question only has to be asked for the inconsistent—and discriminatory—nature of this line of argument to be exposed.

The officials of the DES know perhaps better than anyone that it has been repeatedly made clear by Parliament that every child must attend school regularly for two sessions per day, or his parents must receive official approval for his private education. The courts have been strict in this respect. The standard test case is, it seems, *Jenkins v Howells* (1949) (King's Bench Division). There it was decided that keeping a child off school even for compelling family reasons (in this case the incapacity of the mother and the need for the child to do the family chores) did not constitute 'unavoidable causes'. The judgment of Lord Goddard is worth quoting:

> Parliament has not seen fit to provide that family responsibilities and duties can be used as an excuse for a child not attending school . . . I think that 'unavoidable causes' in this sub-section must be read as something in the nature of an emergency. If, for instance, the house where the child lived were burnt down that would be regarded, at any rate for a day or two, as an unavoidable cause.

In the light of that, how could the authorities reasonably argue that the practice I complained of was an 'emergency nature'?

I ought to say a word here about the size of this problem. This matters since there is always a case for turning a blind eye when a practice, although strictly wrong in principle, may be so small in extent and effect as to justify not making a fuss. The danger of creating a precedent may have to be balanced against the cost of moving against a miscreant. What is strictly correct may not be politic. However, this line of argument could scarcely justify this practice. According to Bradford City Council's own *District Trends 1980*, the practice was widespread: 'Last year over 650 Pakistani children of school age arrived back in Bradford after spending more than 12 months abroad.' Now most such visits, in my experience, occupy less than twelve months. In order to arrive at the figure for all visits then it would probably have to be at least doubled, i.e. about 1,300 children in that year were in transition between Pakistan and Bradford. There is no reason to suppose that the rate of children returning is less than children leaving the city, nor for assuming 1980 to be an untypical year. If these figures are extrapolated nationally, it could be that we are referring to as many as 10,000 children. So the problem is by no means numerically insignificant.

Quite apart from the educational, ethical and logical issues this practice raised, it also created in me anxieties about race relations generally. It is a truism that prejudice is the product of ignorance—indeed it is a tautology to say so. If we prejudge someone, then, by definition, we do so *before* we have the necessary information which could rationally justify our judgement. The great value of creating multiracial institutions and relationships (as bussing does, for instance) is that we undermine the tendency to prejudge and caricature those of whom we have little or no knowledge. Prejudice can rarely withstand honest information.

However, here was a situation in which resentment towards an ethnic minority arose not from prejudice and ignorance but from observed behaviour, from differential and preferential treatment. Whatever the rationalisations and mental gymnastics engaged in by the responsible authorities, the white parents who knew of this practice regarded it as discrimination against them—they knew that double standards were being applied and they resented it. Here was a group of relative newcomers who, while enjoying all the rights and benefits conferred by British citizenship, were *in their behaviour* failing to respect an established and respected custom with the force of law behind it—and they were doing so with impunity. Many techers felt the same way and that could not be good for race relations.

The responsible authorities would argue that, by indulging Asian parents in this respect, they were helping to foster good race relations. In reality, of course, they were doing the very opposite. This officially sanctioned practice was undermining the goodwill of the majority and providing racialists with ammunition. I, as the head teacher of a school in which this problem was highlighted, was placed in an impossible position. Concession-making may make hard decisions redundant, but it also exacts a price.

School Uniform

When I arrived in the school, standards of dress were very varied. Although I was not, at that time, particularly concerned about school uniform (as on most school issues, there were arguments for and against) I began to feel that a uniform might have a particular value in this context. We were, after all, a school marked by considerable diversity. The cultural origins of the pupils often lay outside Britain. Variations in school dinners, community languages and skin colour all attested to our international provenance. However, we were also an essentially English school, preparing children to live out their lives in Britain. The children were British children, not foreigners, and the great majority were not immigrants, but, as I have said, the culture of our pupils out of school was overwhelmingly Asian. In the interest of persuading them that they were British should we not perhaps seek some sort of symbol of our Englishness? And would not traditional, English school uniform serve this purpose?

That was one factor. Another was my desire to offset any suggestion that we were a 'ghetto school'. This is a danger for any inner-city school, but when the public perceives a large number of 'immigrants' in the playground this risk is increased. I was aware that, despite the disapproval of the progressive lobby, the public still regarded a smart, compulsory uniform as evidence of the school's concern for high standards in behaviour and work. Moreover, I also knew that the Moslem parent endorsed the values with which school uniform is associated. There is no equivalent in Islam of progressive notions about education: the formality of uniform might well reassure such parents that self-respect, respect for others and for authority, good discipline and hard work were key school values.

I was particularly concerned about the girls. Delightfully modest and diligent though most of them were, they often lacked a certain confidence in their own abilities. Traditional Islamic notions about the limited role of females might well be restricting the girls' belief in themselves. A school uniform, with a blazer the same as that of the boys, might help to convince them that they really were the equivalent of their male counterparts—although they would, of course, be allowed to wear trousers under the school skirt in accordance with their parents' wishes.

For all these reasons a uniform seemed a good idea, but a policy of school uniform needed careful tactics. Although there was majority support, there was, as always, a dissident minority, but I knew from experience that the refuseniks could be won over with patience and majority pressure. My hopes, however, were dashed by the bureaucrats and politicians.

One day a father of strict Moslem persuasion arrived at the school. He was not, he said, ever going to allow his two daughters to dress in uniform. They would dress exactly as if they were attending school in Pakistan. We had an interesting discussion. I pointed out that while he obviously had every right to create in his children a love of his homeland, the fact remained that his two daughters had been born in Britain and they were, presumably, going to make their future in Britain. Besides, his daughters' legs would be covered in accordance with his religious wishes—and many other Moslem parents seemed willing to comply. Why not talk over the matter with his compatriots? However, he was not for meeting me half-way. When I suggested that his daughters were indeed British he became angry. He clearly had not begun to accept the reality of raising his children in Britain. There was a sense in which he still lived in Pakistan. He was not typical of my Asian parents, but the extreme, orthodox body he represented was powerful in the city. While I felt it important to enable his girls to realise and express the British side of the cultural identity his decision to raise them in Britain had created, he felt that they must cling to his (but not their) homeland. What was I to do? I was worried because I knew that if his daughters successfully evaded the uniform policy there would be other dissidents, and this could spread, but he was adamant. He knew where the City Council's sympathies would lie. For the moment we agreed to differ. I hoped that he would go home and have second thoughts. He did not. He went straight to the Council offices to complain to an official.

Shortly afterwards I received a phone call. Would I please write in and put my side of the story? (I could not help thinking how nice it would be to be the head of an independent school, where one did not have to justify one's decisions to a bureaucrat.) However, I complied. Back came the answer, signalling my defeat. I was informed that the City Council had decided that, if a parent felt more Pakistani than British, then he could dress his child in national dress for school. I ruefully conjectured how a head teacher checks just how Pakistani a parent might feel. Perhaps I could adopt the satirist Peter Simple's prejudometer, whereby electrodes are placed on a person's skull and the extent of his prejudice registered on a calibrated dial, or maybe I could use a questionnaire with a five-point Likert scale, varying from passionately to barely Pakistani.

Reflections apart, how far, I wondered, should the head teacher of an English state school be concerned about the birthplace of his pupils' parents? That parental *religious* sentiments should, as far as practicable, be respected goes without saying, but is the same true of nationalism? Is it unreasonable to assume that the children of a Pakistani parent born and bred in Britain should be regarded as essentially and fully British? If they are not so regarded, but have to have special rules and privileges devised for them, will that be more or less likely to encourage the public at large, and their British, white peers in particular, to regard them as foreign, even alien? The City Council's decision appeared to be based on the principle, once an immigrant, always an immigrant or foreigner. How far, I wondered, would that help the children concerned?

Some time later a Scotsman resident in Bradford wrote to the *Bradford Telegraph and Argus* in connection with the row that blew up about halal meat (ritually slaughtered) in school dinners. He had children in Bradford schools. Why should he not, he asked, insist upon sending his children to school dressed in kilt and sporran, with haggis in school dinners and tossing the caber as a compulsory school sport? It was an amusing letter, but it made a serious point —that adaptation and change are inherent in the psychology of the successful immigrant and his offspring. However, I was working for a City Council which clearly failed to understand that. I was not helped in my endeavours by the school's progressivist 'adviser', who informed me that she 'hated uniform'—but she, no doubt, had additional reasons.

Inevitably, news of the recalcitrant parent's victory spread and the uniform policy began to be difficult to sustain. My hopes were dashed.

Beatings in the Mosque

From time to time I had read legends and stories from the Indian subcontinent to small groups of children. These groups always included Moslem children who, naturally, regularly attended either the local mosques or private houses to learn the *Koran*. The stories invariably had a moral theme, where the good triumphed and the evil ones got their come-uppance. They were valuable in that they conveyed important moral issues in an entertaining and digestible form. Inevitably, they led to discussions about ways in which good behaviour could be encouraged, which in turn focused minds on the question of punishment.

It was from within this context that I learnt of a practice which was to cause me a great deal of anxiety. When the talk turned to punishment, the Moslem children began to refer to ways in which they were punished by certain people who taught them the *Koran*. Beatings were the standard method and these, according to the children, were often severe. On 5 November 1983 I made a note of what one child said. According to him, a teacher at the mosque (and he had witnessed this) had hit eight boys across hands and backs eight times with the branch of a tree. Some children were made to squat for long periods of time. One boy explained that the 'teachers' concerned justified this approach by saying that, if the individual is unlucky enough to go to Hell, then the parts which have been beaten will not burn.

I was sceptical. Children have powerful imaginations. They can get excited and start to exaggerate and embroider, particularly if they sense drama or scandal. Every teacher knows that children sometimes tell tall stories. Besides, I was not, in principle, opposed to physical chastisement. Provided it is infrequent, moderate in form and amount, and properly recorded, then there is a case for the cane—although I had always found that the presence rather than the actual use of it was what deterred most children. There was, too, the question of parental rights. If a parent implicitly accepted what the children said was happening, what more was there to be said? Moreover, there is a tradition in Islam of authoritarian discipline and respect for elders.

I recalled a report in the *Guardian* (9 June 1983) about a Moslem priest being dismissed and a mosque in Sheffield being closed after the beating of two boys. The report contained a comment from Dr Karim Admani, president of Sheffield's Moslem Council:

✗ We do not really believe in soft-soaping our children. We believe in discipline, and perhaps people don't like it, but we are proud of the standards of behaviour of our children. If someone was to smack my child while receiving education at a mosque I would be quite happy, so long as the punishment was within reasonable limits.

I had to be careful not to impose my Western expectations on people from another culture whose ideas about the disciplining of children are different from those fashionable liberal notions prevalent in Britain. Islam still holds to the admirable principle that children are responsible for their behaviour, and should be held responsible when they transgress. Morality, rather than determinism, underpins the traditional Moslem view of discipline.

So I had to tread very carefully. However, the stories persisted. One particularly intelligent and responsible boy told me of disciplinary practices in the mosque that went far beyond being reasonable. I started to make discreet enquiries. I talked to an Asian friend, and he confirmed the children's stories. I wrote to the authorities responsible for monitoring children at risk from abuse. They informed me that they were very worried about what they were certain was going on, but their problem was getting hard information. No-one was prepared to come forward and act as a witness. I talked to the PE and games staff, who confirmed that they had seen bruises on children's limbs. They also informed me that some children alleged that they were beaten on the soles of the feet so the bruises would not show. I found it increasingly difficult to believe that the children's stories were false.

What was I to do? Turn a blind eye and live with my conscience, or risk obloquy from the anti-racist lobby and Islam leadership by exposing a scandal? The atmosphere in Bradford (particularly that surrounding a City Council employee, which I was) made it very difficult indeed to suggest any criticism of an ethnic-minority practice of any kind, however objectionable it might be to public opinion. To do so involved the risk of being labelled a 'racist'. The only real deterrent—since every other attempt to stop the practice had failed —was a police prosecution. That would attract publicity and create considerable shame in a community which was generally law-abiding.

It was while I was struggling with this problem that a games teacher brought me a boy whose legs, from ankle to thigh, were black and blue. He had not been simply chastised, he had been assaulted. I asked the boy who was responsible. I wrote down his reply. He had been systematically and repeatedly hit with part of a branch of a tree by a man teaching him the *Koran*. This solved the problem. It was no longer something I could hold at arm's length, or intellectualise about. I had to act.

Officially, I should have informed the appropriate social workers, but this would have caused delay, and bruises can quickly fade. Besides, the social workers would be likely to take refuge in a 'counselling' stance. Many of these people, in my experience, have great difficulty in coping with human wickedness and the notion of moral responsibility. Raised on the doctrines of social and economic determinism, they have a depressing tendency to excuse and explain away in the name of an ill-placed compassion. Elaborate systems of excuse-making on behalf of miscreants are an essential part of their stock in trade, and they sometimes have ambivalent attitudes to those in authority, such as teachers and police officers. I did not want waffle. I wanted an appropriate and honest response to an alleged case of assault on a child. So I ignored the social workers.

I ought, also, to have told the parents immediately, but I deliberately delayed. I knew that the parents would be afraid of a scandal, and of their son playing a central role. It was the fears of community disapproval that prevented concerned parents from complaining. The pressure to hush things up and not risk showing the community in a bad light was very strong. I decided that the first essential was to inform the police.

The boy and I were interviewed and the bruises noted. No-one doubted that the boy was telling the truth. I then informed the parents. They were shocked and disinclined to take the matter further. I told them of what I had learnt about the beatings in the mosque and other places. I pointed out that bringing the matter out into the open, with all the attendant publicity, might well provide children with the protection they currently lacked. They were not impressed and were for hushing the matter up. This, of course, was the stumbling-block. Parents, out of loyalty to their community, and fearful of bringing disgrace on the mosque, were not willing to act. They were concerned and caring parents, as eager to ensure the welfare of their child as any decent parent would be, but the pressures on them were too great. It was this pressure, together with the minorities-can-do-no-wrong attitude of the City Council, that allowed the practice to continue.

I was in a dilemma. The parents were unwilling to act. The police hesitated, uncertain of whether to bring charges, and mindful, no doubt, of being smeared as 'racist' if they did. What was I to do? Where did my duty lie? After several sleepless nights, I decided to press ahead. I could not stand by and do nothing to protect children who were being regularly and cruelly beaten. I wrote to the police. Would they, I asked, hesitate to prosecute if I or one of my staff had inflicted this excessive punishment on a child? Where did their duty lie? Should they apply a double standard, or were we all equal under the law? They decided to go ahead and summon the alleged offender to court.

I was not hopeful of a conviction. I knew that the boy concerned would be subjected to pressure to withdraw the allegation. I knew from an Asian friend that the community would close ranks; that many witnesses for the defence might well be called. However, I was hopeful that the case would at least signal to the people involved in this practice that they were being watched and the children in their charge monitored for physical injury. Once it was realised that head teachers were prepared to act to protect children, the practice might well decline. The case, predictably, was lost, but the attendant publicity would, I hoped, have the desired effect.

I was wrong. Some time later another, similar, case arose. This time I had the bruises photographed. Two individuals were charged. The case went to the Crown Court in Leeds, evidence that the authorities were taking the matter very seriously. However, there was a problem. It became clear that a case that might have taken a day, would, in fact, take a week of the Court's time. The defendants, I was told, had called 70 witnesses. The costs involved would be colossal. The judge suggested that the case should not proceed, nor should it be closed. The case should remain on file, and if the defendants came before the Court again it would be resurrected. The important thing, again, was that publicity had been generated. It would be harder in future for such matters to be suppressed. From that time on we saw no more bruised limbs, feet or backs. The message had got through.

However, I would not, of course, have endeared myself either to the Moslem leadership or the anti-racist lobby.

The Proposed Moslem Takeover

On Friday 25 January 1983 I received a telephone call from a high-ranking education official. He felt obliged, he said, to inform me that there was a possibility that the school would be taken over by a group of parents. A group calling itself the Moslem Parents Association was to meet him and the Chairman of the Education Committee and formally propose aided Moslem status for mine and four other schools. The meeting was that day.

I knew from the independent Moslem schools (i.e. private, not state-aided) which already existed in various parts of Britain what kind of Moslems would be making this proposal. There is a range of religious fervour and commitment amongst Moslems, as in most other religions. Many are, in the Western sense, enlightened, willing to integrate and accept the need to provide their children with adequate, broadly based secular education. However, the proposal had come from a tiny group of extremists well known for their fanatical adherence to Islamic fundamentalism. These people had, for some time, alleged that Bradford's state schools were corrupting their children with Western permissiveness, and that the City Council was failing in its duty to respect their religious beliefs.

A typical comment from a member of this group appeared in the *Bradford Telegraph and Argus* of 27 January, 1982. After alleging that Moslem children were being forced into Church of England assemblies and Religious Education lessons against parental wishes (a *very* unlikely possibility), Mr Riaz Shahid said:

> They [the Moslem children] are being systematically indoctrinated. They have to go to discos and perform Eastern dances to raise funds for schools . . . the local authority is trying to lure children away from the path of Islam into the abyss of infidelity.

The mentality that produces this kind of language can well be imagined, as can the kind of education, particularly for girls, it would be likely to demand. However, a much more reasonable tone emerged in a letter to the same newspaper from another Bradford Moslem, Mr Ashiq Hussain, on 2 February 1982:

> On January 27th you featured a news story about three Moslem parents of Bradford under a rather tendentious title. The overall impression seemed to be that the contents of the statement made by a member of

the Moslem Parent's Association reflected the sentiments of the Moslems of Bradford. Nothing could be further from the truth. The group you mentioned is a defunct outfit composed of a couple of malcontented individuals who specialise in stoking the fires of controversy. With a little bit of research you will come to the conclusion that this group or its so-called spokesman has no mandate to speak on this important subject on behalf of the Moslems of Bradford. I am not saying even for a moment, that Moslem parents have no complaints about the education department. But they are of a minor nature, and do not include anything which cannot be rectified with a little bit of mutual understanding.

No-one with any real knowledge of Bradford's multi-ethnic schools at that time would want to dissent from that essentially reasonable viewpoint. What caused us great anxiety in the school was the willingness of the LEA to take seriously the proposals for running no fewer than five voluntary-aided schools coming from 'a couple of malcontented individuals'. Although I am a strong supporter of aided schools, and the principle of religious freedom and parental choice they express, I had always imagined that a proposal to establish one had to be shown to have considerable support. Moreover, the proposers would also have to be able to indicate that they had the necessary financial backing as well as the educational and administrative expertise. It was well known that, on each of these factors, the Moslem Parents Association fell far short of what was required. However, it was made clear by the officials that the LEA was to press ahead and carry out all the official, statutory process of consultation and administration—a lengthy, costly process involving considerable labour—and by so doing to impose months of anxiety on the schools concerned.

It also created resentment. Why, we asked ourselves, had the responsible officers not done as Mr Hussain had suggested, and conducted 'a little bit of research'? Why did they not seek to check out what everybody knew to be the case—that Mr Hussain's view of the Moslem Parent's Association was correct? Why, too, were they not checking out the Association's credentials *before* the costly and anxiety-provoking consultation process that they were to carry out? Were they actually ignorant of the facts, or were they being machiavellian? Did they realise that a resounding 'no' from the Moslem community was the certain outcome of the consultation process, an outcome the LEA had always said it desired? If so, why not use its considerable array of contacts to establish this? Whatever the motives involved, the consternation in the school at this time was palpable.

The teachers were deeply unhappy. Out of a staff of 23, none was prepared to undertake to work in the kind of Islamic school being proposed—not even our Moslem teacher. Five said that they needed much more information before they could make a decision; 18 said that they definitely would not serve. I, as head teacher, would, of course, be removed. It would be unthinkable for such a school not to have an orthodox Moslem as its head. However, we were not simply worried only about our own careers but about the radical change in the curriculum and character of the school—things with which the parents, to judge from demand for places in the school, were happy.

We were able to predict the nature of the changes involved from three sources: the utterances and formal, written proposals of the Moslem Parents Association, the practices evident in existing private Moslem schools in Britain and a document by Imtiaz Karim, *Muslim Children in British Schools—their Rights and Duties*. This was undated, but it was in wide circulation in Bradford at that time. Its contents and aims had already clearly affected the officers of the LEA. The mandatory memorandum, *Education for a Multicultural Society: Provisions for Pupils of Ethnic Minorities*, followed Karim's prescriptions very closely. The spirit of the Karim document can be gauged from the following quotations:

 Dance and music are both un-Islamic activities and Moslem parents should take care to make sure that their children are excluded from such activities . . . All activities such as dance and music are geared to create physical attraction between boys and girls which lead to permissiveness. [What, we wondered, was the force of the words 'such as' here?]
Young people only need to be told what to do [about sex] when they contract a sexually transmitted disease . . .
Schools are willing to allow Moslem children to be excused from swimming lessons. [We were not, partly because their lives might one day depend on their ability to swim—besides, there are no legal grounds for allowing parents to withdraw pupils from swimming.]
For boys it is not at all objectionable to take showers after PE or swimming, provided that all boys in the shower wear something to cover their private parts.
In the case of Moslem girls the position is clear cut. Under no circum-

stances are Moslem girls allowed to shower in schools. [This latter injunction would effectively disbar girls from PE and games, and schools implementing it might well be in breach of the equal opportunities legislation.]

The Moslem Parents Association's proposals made it clear what would happen to the ethos of the school: 'All extra-academic activities conflicting with the tenets of faith and forbidden in Islam will, in no circumstances, be allowed in these schools.'

The staff and I felt that the efforts the school had been making for over 20 years to strike a balance between respecting parental religious wishes and providing a broad-based education which took account of the child's essentially bi-cultural needs would come to naught. We were particularly anxious about the prospects for girls. More generally, I was concerned at the effect on the native Bradford community and race relations in the city. I sensed a good deal of resentment. Here were five schools all provided for and built by native Bradfordians long before Asians appeared in the city, and the local authority was seriously considering disposing of them to people who, from all accounts, did not even have the support of their own community. It seemed extraordinarily crass.

Moreover, I was very concerned that a decision regarding the granting of voluntary-aided status to Moslems (a development of profound importance for the future of our multi-ethnic society) should be considered in the same way as previous moves involving Christians and Jews. I felt that this was a matter of national importance, and should be debated and decided in Parliament. The designers of the Education Act 1944, it can be safely said, had never envisaged that the voluntary-school principle would have to serve a society that had, over the past 30 years or so, undergone such profound changes in the radical, cultural and religious character of its people. The likes of Chuter Ede, Herbert Morrison and R.A. Butler, the architects of the 1944 Act, could not possibly have foreseen that the voluntary principle should be applied to Sikhs, Hindus and Moslems in Britain, nor could the Parliament of the day. Voluntary schools had been created as a response to Britain's Jewish and Christian tradition.

Moreover, the concordat between Church and society was the outcome of two vitally important principles: the willingness to compromise and accept negotiated settlements and the necessity to accept a distinction between secular and spiritual matters. Tradition and long experience has shown that these two principles could generate a balance between religious independence and a proper concern for the child's secular education expressed by a state supplying a good deal of the money. However, could these well-understood and essentially Western principles safely be assumed to apply in the case of a religion such as Islam? It seemed unlikely.

Islam, particularly in its orthodox forms (i.e. the very sects likely to demand voluntary-aided status) is not simply a religion in the modern Western sense. The Renaissance, the Reformation and the Enlightenment all helped to create a climate in which a spiritual/secular dichotomy became acceptable to the European mind, but these have no real equivalent in Islam. Islam has a strong tendency to a unitary, authoritarian world view. It encompasses both the spiritual and the secular, religion and politics are one, and the distinction between society and the state, second nature to a Westerner, leaves a Moslem distinctly puzzled and unhappy. It is much more literal and rigid in its interpretation of its scriptures than are the great majority of Christian churches and the Jews in the interpretation of theirs. The three faiths, in fact, took very different paths even before the Renaissance.

There is also the problem that the resurgence of Islamic fundamentalism in recent times has an anti-Western character. The attitude of the West to material progress—to modernisation, science and industrialisation, and education—is not mirrored in Islam, where a distinctive love–hate relationship to things secular and material exists. To many (perhaps most) Moslems Western progress appears to be a mixed blessing. The great advances in technology, medicine, the control and exploitation of the physical environment, and social welfare have all been purchased at a very heavy price. The decline in family life, alcoholism, drug addiction, urban alienation and sexual permissiveness appear, in Islamic eyes, to be the result of Western man's violation of a natural, harmonious order in which the spiritual and secular are one. This is readily linked with anti-imperialism, since imperialists were Western Christians; and with *Jihad*, or Holy War. This latter imperative in Islamic tradition is by no means dead. The conflict between the Shi'ites and Sunni Moslem sects within Islam is also a complicating factor, since both traditions have their counterparts in Britain.

I had other worries. The question of national loyalties had not been a factor when the voluntary-school principle was agreed.

Neither Christians nor Jews had any doubts about their loyalty to Britain. There was no sense in which religious independence in schools largely funded by the state could be attached to loyalty to another nation. The subsequent foundation of the state of Israel did not fundamentally alter this: British Jews are no less patriotic than British Christians. Islam, however, is a very different matter. Given the absence of a political/religious distinction in traditional Moslem thought, and given the expression of this in the theocratic state of Pakistan, then the foundation of voluntary schools by Pakistan Moslems in Britain is bound to raise problems about national loyalties. The attachment of Pakistani immigrants and their descendants to the mother-country is very strong, and is constantly reinforced by continued immigration and frequent visits, as well as by the considerable contribution made to the Pakistani economy by remittances from Britain. Would not voluntary-aided Moslem shools, peopled overwhelmingly by pupils and teachers of Pakistani origin, function to reinforce this process, delay integration and divide national loyalties?

This entirely new factor was paralleled by another—colour. Virtually all Moslems in Britain are brown-skinned, so that race and religion, as it were, function as one. Moslem voluntary-aided schools would be mono-racial, and the possibility of cross-racial friendships in childhood—the key, surely, to good race relations—would thereby be considerably reduced. Now inner-city housing patterns, and the CRE's ban on bussing, already create mono-racial schooling in some areas, but housing patterns change with time. There is already evidence of a movement into white areas, so that integrated housing patterns seem likely to develop; and, in due course, the school population will reflect this. However, Moslem schooling will counteract tendencies to unselfconscious integration and tend to emphasise the colour divide.

In short, the voluntary-school principle was being proposed for a situation it was never meant to accommodate. Was it right, one wondered, that a group of local authority officials in Bradford, acting in concert with a small group of DES civil servants in London—subject to the judgement of a minister who would be acting in accordance with legislation manifestly out of date—should be the basis of a decision setting a precedent that could have such far-reaching consequences? This proposal alone, in addition to acquiring five middle schools, would eventually inevitably involve a whole sector of the school's system in Bradford, from first school (aged 5–9) to upper schools (aged 13–18), being handed over to Islamic fundamentalists.

However, the consultation exercise was carried out by the LEA officers as if none of these new factors was operating. They proceeded as if they were dealing with a Christian or Jewish demand in accordance, as it were, with the old dispensation. There were meetings of the parents and the staffs of the schools covered. Trade unions and other interested parties had to be contacted and their views canvassed. It took many wearisome and anxious months.

On 13 June 1983 an education officer wrote to the Moslem Parents' Association asking them for their credentials. The lack of will and of substance in their proposals can be gauged from the fact that this request for necessary information was ignored. (See page 34 of the Council's report on this issue.) Why, we in the schools wondered, did this responsible officer not send his request shortly after the request for voluntary-aided status was made in January? Why was the whole costly, interminable and anxiety-provoking consultation process set in motion before the validity of the proposal and the goodwill of those behind it were established? Why did he wait five agonising months before calling the Association's bluff? How was it that 'a defunct outfit composed of a couple of malcontented individuals who specialise in stoking the fires of controversy', to quote Mr Ashiq Hussain's description of the Association, possessed the power to instigate a process that involved a considerable sum of public money, months of work, the generating of mountains of paper and consultations with the DES, and which imposed untold anxiety on the schools, as well as generating resentment among the Bradford public? Why had the LEA assumed that the proposals were a *bona fide* request submitted by a proper, representative organisation when virtually everybody in Bradford knew this was not so? Would this have happened if the source had been similar indigenous, white people? Was this yet another example of that debilitating 'cultural cringe' which now dominated the City Council's approach to the ethnic minorities?

The LEA turned down the proposal on 6 September, but it was not until 14 November that the schools were informed that the Secretary of State had rejected the Moslem Parents' Association's appeal—almost a year from the process's inception. It had been an extraordinary episode, one that did no good whatever for the relationship between the schools and the LEA established to serve them. Moreover, very probably, it did no good for race relations.

Halal Meat

Moslems traditionally will eat meat only if the beast has been ritually slaughtered, i.e. the animal's throat is cut and it bleeds to death. Since there is no pre-stunning, the animal suffers. It was to prevent this suffering that legislation banning ritual slaughter was introduced. However, the relevant Act, for reasons having much more to do with its successful passage through Parliament by appeasing the Jewish establishment than with any issue of principle, did not apply to either Jews or Mohammedans. This loophole gave rise to less debate than it might because the orthodox Jews involved were a tiny minority of the population; and there was, essentially, no Moslem population in Britain.

However, a rapid increase in the Moslem population in recent years has meant a massive increase in ritual slaughter. In Bradford in 1983, for instance, no fewer than 47,000 sheep were killed without pre-stunning. This has brought the Islamic community into conflict with the tradition of animal welfare characteristic of Britain. The Royal Society for the Prevention of Cruelty to Animals (RSPCA) is strongly opposed to the practice. A concerted campaign to have it banned has been going on for several years. Several animal rights organisations oppose it. In 1986 an independent, government-sponsored enquiry found that the practice was, indeed, cruel and should be outlawed.

However, I must confess that none of this caused me any particular disquiet. When I had it brought to my attention, I decided that it was a standard case of two admirable but, in some people's eyes, mutually exclusive principles—religious freedom and kindness to dumb animals. Given this, how should one decide? I felt, on balance, that although I personally find the whole idea of ritual slaughter primitive and repugnant, religious freedom, a precious liberty, should take precedence. Jews and Moslems should be allowed to continue with the practice, since they believe it crucial to their faith, but I would not be prepared to take to the streets and wave a banner if it were unlawful.

However, this somewhat detached attitude became a less than

adequate response when Bradford City Council decided that ritually slaughtered halal meat was to be introduced into school dinners. These dinners are subsidised from money provided by tax- and rate-payers. Permitting ritual slaughter as a purely private practice, financed by those who require it, is one thing: allowing it in school dinners is quite another. That, quite literally, meant cruelty to animals on the rates, and that, for many people, was an issue of conscience.

This created uproar in the city. Animal rights groups organised protests and petitions. One woman refused to pay her rates. The RSPCA was alarmed. The *Bradford Telegraph and Argus* carried many angry letters, and the teachers who assisted me in supervising school dinners expressed their disquiet. Many were practising Christians, and would not be happy, on grounds of conscience, to be involved in any way in a school service connected with ritual slaughter. There was considerable public opposition which transmitted itself to local councillors. The City Council, therefore, agreed to review the decision.

Thereupon the Islam leadership organised a mass protest. On the day the City Council met to discuss the issue there were 3,000 chanting, banner-waving Moslems outside the City Hall, including hundreds of children who had been kept off school. The atmosphere was threatening. Bradford, unlike several other multi-ethnic areas, has had very little in the way of street rioting, possibly because the dominant minority group is Asian rather than West Indian, but here was an issue that might well erupt into communal violence. However, although there was great disquiet amongst Bradfordians generally, their voice was not a concerted one likely to impress politicians, and the animal welfarians were comparatively few in number. The Moslems however, were highly organised, concerted, unified and in an ugly mood. Not surprisingly, the City Council endorsed its earlier decision.

Since this cost me the support of many of my staff in supervising school dinners I pursued the matter further. On making enquiries through the RSPCA I learnt that halal meat did not have to involve ritual slaughter. A percussion gun that stuns without penetrating the brain has been developed especially for use in Jewish and Moslem slaughterhouses. Half the halal meat produced in Britain is obtained by this means. I approached an official. Why not, I asked, put the following argument to the Moslem leadership. Bradford public opinion, reflecting traditional British concern for dumb animals, was offended by the notion of publicly funded ritual slaughter, as were many teachers who helped to supervise Moslem children at lunch time. Why not therefore acknowledge this feeling, and agree to use the stunning gun and so avoid the cruelty to the animal? I got very short shrift. The official informed me that the Moslems were adamant and would not compromise. It was pointless to approach them.

This inflexibility was a major stumbling-block. The English gift for compromise and settlement by give and take is, in places like Bradford, confronted by an Islamic fundamentalism which perceives compromise as weakness. This can create bad feeling, which has nothing to do with bigotry but the violation of something deep in the English character—a sense of fair play. This rigidity and unwillingness to try to understand English attitudes operates at every level of the Islamic community. It was displayed, for instance, in a paper delivered to the Islamic Academy by the Bradford City Council's own adviser in 'multicultural education', Mr Akram Khan-Cheema. In referring to the protests about ritual slaughter in school dinners, he said: 'This protest goes on and in the local press particularly it has revealed the worst sort of prejudices and racist attitudes.'

Now for six years I had regularly read the local press to which Mr Khan-Cheema is here referring. I never once saw the publication of racist, offensive material, although I did see from time to time criticism of some aspect of the behaviour or attitude of the ethnic minorities. I also saw vigorous letters from blacks and Asians engaging in a similar process in the same journals. In truth, the two local newspapers—the *Bradford Telegraph and Argus* and *The Yorkshire Post*—are exceedingly circumspect about what they publish in this area; although, being the honourable papers they are, they seek to reflect all viewpoints. However, Mr Khan-Cheema, typically, could not grasp that there are genuine, deeply felt and sincere objections to a practice which he—as a Moslem—finds acceptable. This lack of empathy, this constant tendency to ascribe any disquiet felt by the majority population to 'racism' assumed almost manic proportions in a Bradford dominated by the Moslem presence. The imputing of ill-will, even malice, to the majority population became a more or less standard response of large numbers of City Council officials.

The sad thing about all this was that I always found the great majority of Moslem parents, as *individuals*, pretty reasonable. If I could have negotiated with the parents I still believe that I might have won them over to a compromise solution. However, *collectively*, and under the sway of communal and traditional emotions orchestrated by inflexible leaders, they closed ranks and relapsed into age-old responses.

I was defeated. I found myself deprived of teacher-support in school dinners and said goodbye to lunch hours. Much more important, the halal meat issue — or rather the contribution of Islamic rigidity and Bradford City Council's weakness it encapsulates — did little to improve race relations.

The Education of Girls

The primacy of man over woman is total and absolute. Woman is chronologically secondary. She finds her finality in man. She is made for his pleasure, his repose, his fulfilment . . . the Islamic family was to be essentially male-worshipping. For *noblesse oblige:* the right to beat one's wife also implies the duty to maintain and work for her . . . In the *Quran*, God always addressed himself to men and never to women.

It might be imagined that this is from a book produced in the Middle Ages, perhaps an injunction of St Paul in his first-century travels, or perhaps something culled by Sir Richard Burton during his exotic travels in the reign of Queen Victoria. In fact, it is from *Sexuality in Islam*, first published in 1975 and issued in translation in Britain in 1985. It is by Abdelwahab Bouhdiba, Professor of Islamic Sociology at the University of Tunis, and an adviser to UNESCO, the UN and to the Tunisian government on human rights. Although this quotation refers to the Islamic *view* of sexuality, the practice has been somewhat different, although by no means to women's benefit. In practice, for complex social and economic reasons the theory was distorted (in reality the *Koran* accords legal equality and confers many liberties unknown to women at the time of the Prophet) to create the more or less total subjection of women who existed for man's purpose only. Sexual licence for men became the norm. As a result, in many areas the irrational segregation of women led to their male control, a state of affairs that still continues in many parts of the Islamic world.*

This tradition is alive and well in the Moslem district of Bradford. I hasten to add that a large proportion of Moslem fathers in the city are anxious for their daughters to do well. The experience of living in a society which at least tries to respect the principle of sexual equality has undoubtedly had a broadening effect. Also, there are hopeful signs from some Moslem girls themselves that they are no longer prepared to accept the kind of sexual subjection that Professor Bouhdiba outlines. However, it remains true that some Moslem girls in Bradford never arrive in school, particularly adolescents. I was told by a responsible official there could be as many as 700 such girls. They effectively 'disappear'.

The reason for this is twofold. The Moslem father (the mother in such cases is irrelevant) believes that Western culture generally is morally decadent and degrades those exposed to it. The school is an agent of that culture. Second, he correctly perceives that the notion of male hegemony to which his whole outlook, experience and tradition are attached will be undermined in a school devoted to the principle of sexual equality. He realises, for instance, that the institution of the arranged marriage is unlikely to withstand forever the fact that his daughters have English friends for whom the notion of personal choice of marriage partner is second nature. He also knows that the relaxed relationship between boys and girls in mixed schools represents a threat to the mystique of the superior male, which is largely sustained by sexual segregation. The male hegemony principle is unlikely to survive the exposure to girls of the fragile male psyche. Secrecy and separation have been the necessary conditions for generating and sustaining the appropriate myths.

This tradition, conflicting with a culture alien to it, generates considerable tensions. Every teacher in Bradford with experience of traditional Islam has stories to tell that indicate the human consequences of this profound cultural collision. In 1985 a Bradford inquest found that a 22-year-old Pakistani nurse had taken her own life while depressed. According to press reports, her former boyfriend stated that a major factor in the girl's state of mind had been the insistence by her father on an arranged marriage to a middle-aged, mentally retarded man living in Pakistan. She was,

* I owe this insight to Dervla Murphy.

apparently, terrified of her father. There are, fortunately, few such tragic illustrations of the transformations involved for Moslem girls struggling to maintain the bi-cultural identity chosen for them by their father's decision to settle and raise a family in a society whose view of female sexuality offends him. However, my own lengthy experience, which includes regular contast with a close Asian friend, convinces me that the problem is a real one.

Let us contrast this with the norm regarding sexual equality now prevalent in British state schools. Not only are these schools required by law to demonstrate that girls are enjoying equal opportunities but co-education is now the norm for most boys and girls. Moreover, in recent years, thanks to radical feminism, the objectivity of the curriculum and the very vocabulary of academic discourse has been challenged as to its sexual neutrality. There has developed a marked tendency to prevent girls from perceiving certain subjects as being typically male or female. Alongside this we have seen the development of a society in which not only is the notion of the arranged marriage anathema but, increasingly, the institution of marriage itself is not thought indispensable to the creation of a family. Is it any wonder, therefore, that many Moslem girls trapped between two such diametrically opposed traditions are in despair?

What should the school's role be in this regard? What kind of choices should *it* make in the education of Moslem girls? Another way of putting this is to ask: to whom is the school chiefly responsible? In a sense these questions are already answered. The Equal Opportunities Commission, a statutory body with considerable powers, has repeatedly made it clear that girls are to receive equal treatment to boys. Girls must not, either through curriculum, organisation, ethos or teacher-attitude, be denied understanding and appreciation of their own human possibilities. Schools are bound by that principle, and could be, ultimately, prosecuted if they violate it. On the other hand, home–school co-operation is essential to the educational progress of the child. Respecting parental wishes has naturally to be an important part of that concordat, but what does a school do if legal requirements and parental wishes clash? That was the very difficult question which I, as head of a school with a large number of girls from Moslem homes, had to resolve.

Unfortunately, I was not helped in this matter by some of the current orthodoxies in 'multi-ethnic education', by the kind of material produced by the NUT, for instance. Here is part of the NUT's submission to the Swann Committee:

> The key to gaining the confidence of Moslem parents, that the school will provide satisfactorily for their children's faith . . . is to engage in dialogue with them, initiating contact through the Imam who holds their respect.

What if the imams are the source of the girl's oppression—the fountain heads, as it were, of the very doctrines of prescribed and narrow female roles that the school was bound to reject? Such empty, high-sounding platitudes completely evade the real issues, although no doubt they give their authors a nice feeling of occupying the moral high ground. The same kind of emptiness pervades large tracts of the Swann Report.

In the event, when I reached the school in 1980 I discovered that certain desirable things were happening naturally. At that time half the girls were white and British. There were many cross-racial friendships. Moreover, the staff had enlightened attitudes, and insisted on treating girls—all girls—as the equal of boys. While respecting parents' wishes to allow the wearing of trousers under the school skirt, we insisted that girls did woodwork, crafts, metalwork, technology and science. Classes were mixed. *All* pupils did PE and games and the great majority of Moslem girls dressed exactly as their English counterparts. We rarely received any parental complaints. The only real problem we had was in persuading the parents of Moslem girls to let them stay behind for after-school activities—particularly in the darkening late afternoons of the autumn and spring terms. Besides, they had to attend the mosque.

On the whole, though, I was optimistic at that time. The home was clearly transmitting the mother-culture effectively and the school was containing the influence of the Islamic fundamentalists on the education of the girls. The girls, influenced mainly by their English friends, were showing signs of confidence and ambition. This was, I felt, as it should be. After all, we were not an Islamic school. We were not, indeed, a religious foundation of any kind. We were an essentially secular state school, funded by the public. A natural process of integration was occurring, to the particular benefit of the Moslem girls.

However, several influences coalesced to threaten this. The CRE had Bradford very much in its sights since the city had a large ethnic-minority population. It had already intervened to stop bussing of Asian pupils and had alleged that there was discrimination in the city's arrangements regarding promotion in the bus services. Both bureaucrats and politicians went in fear of further visits from its officers. Politicians were increasingly aware of the importance of the ethnic vote and the need to placate the Asian leadership—and in the case of the Moslem majority this meant the Council of the Mosques, the source of traditional views about the education of girls. Because dispersal (bussing) had ended, the number of Moslem girls in school was rapidly increasing, and correspondingly fewer English girls were available, so that their influence was declining. The LEA was to appoint an advisor in 'multi-ethnic education', who was himself a Moslem activist and an obvious source of advice on matters affecting the education of Moslem girls. The notion of civil rights for minorities was providing a useful rationale for the creation of yet another educational bandwaggon—a phenomenon which the intelligensia of the state education service was always ready to seize on in order to justify its existence. (This statement will appear cynical only to those who have not had my lengthy experience in the state education service.)

As a result of all this, the LEA issued a mandatory memorandum for schools on 10 November 1982 and followed this up with a pamphlet for parents. This was an extraordinary document. It was called *School Arrangements for Moslem Children*, but its opening sentence ran thus: 'This booklet has been written to tell Moslem, Sikh and Hindu parents of the new instructions and guidelines the Council has recently sent to all Bradford schools'. Was this *faux pas* an indication of the Moslem hegemony in the city, or did the officials concerned actually believe that Sikhism and Hinduism were simply sub-sects of Islam? I wrote to the officer responsible and suggested that the LEA ought to have used the term British/Asian children, which would have signalled religious neutrality and acknowledged the children's actual bi-cultural identity.

Parts of these documents were unexceptionable and merely repeated what was happening in the schools anyway. However, there were aspects touching on the education of girls which, we felt, were ominous for our efforts to promote equality of opportunity. For instance, it said, 'Children may wear traditional dress at school', and this, everyone knew, applied only to girls. Parents had no qualms about how their Moslem sons dressed. We wanted girls proclaiming their equality with boys, and assenting to their British identity, by wearing a common school uniform. The LEA officers, no doubt responding to political pressure, were now undermining this aim by explicitly and in writing going over the heads of schools and governing bodies, and granting 'rights' to Islamic fundamentalists committed to an anti-Western concept of female education. Physical Education, too, caused us concern. The LEA bureaucrats informed Asian parents that their girls could be covered while taking a shower. How this purdah process could be combined with the real purpose of taking a shower after vigorous exercise was not explained. (In point of fact, our Asian girls had been taking showers for years, thanks to sensible and experienced PE teachers.) Moreover, parents were informed, girls could be required to wear pyjamas in swimming lessons if the parents so decreed, despite the fact that the (female) swimming instructor said that this was absurd and impractical. In PE girls could, effectively, dress themselves from top to toe. Worst of all, perhaps, parents were told that they had the right to withdraw their girls from swimming if single-sex lessons could not be arranged—and this for nine-year-olds. (There were no swimming lessons for children over the age of nine in Bradford schools at that time, unless the school had its own swimming pool—and *very* few had.) This meant that LEA officials were literally inventing parental 'rights', since there is no legal right of withdrawal from swimming lessons in English schools.

The general effect of these documents was to focus on girls, and to underline not their equality with boys but their difference. The emphasis on covering the girls to an extent which actually interfered with the activity in hand was not simply impractical, it carried with it strong symbolic connotations. The effect was to restrict and enclose, to wrap girls up in a purdah mentality, as it were. What, I asked myself, would be the effect on the girls' concept of themselves, their potential and ambitions? It might well be that upper-class Moslem girls in Egypt would, while enclosed in purdah, attend Cairo University and read physics. Could that apply to Moslem girls who attended school in a Bradford committed to female emancipation? How could Islamic reaction be combined with Western notions of sexual equality? Many Moslem parents had been developing enlightened ideas about their daughters' education. They were showing evidence of supporting the school. However, many remained cocooned in ideas entirely unsuited to a girl's life-chances in the Western world. I have observed attitudes in many Bradford Moslem paterfamiliases which would not have been out of place in Khomenei's Iran.

It was this latter, unenlightened view of girls which, I felt, the LEA was seeking, very unwisely, to impose upon the schools. The schools' informed and patient 'bridge-building' exercise, which was undoubtedly paying dividends as far as the education of girls was concerned, was to give way to an officially ordained and mandatory system of concession-making.

The White Minority

One of the ways we come to realise that what we call the 'multiracial society' is unique in British history is the presence of an increasing number of schools in which the ethnic minority consists of white, indigenous children. The educational anxieties that this can cause were acknowledged in the 1960s by the then Minister of Education, Sir Edward Boyle. In response to parental protests, he publicly stated that there would never be a time when a British state school would contain more than a third of children using English as a foreign language. Given local housing patterns, and the attitude of the CRE regarding bussing, this undertaking was bound to fail. Schools serving multiracial areas suffered the same fate as so many inner-city comprehensives. They became not representative of 'society' but of the immediate locality, i.e. neighbourhood schools. If comprehensives were genuinely so, then none would contain more than about 4 per cent of non-white children. Inevitably, since immigrants and their descendants have a strong tendency to congregate in the same district, we have seen the emergence of white ethnic minorities in inner-city schools. As I write, there are at least 20 such schools in Bradford, and the same is true of many other inner-city areas, and the phenomenon is growing.

Does this matter? As far as concerns the white child's sense of who he is, and his development of a sense of his own national loyalty and identity, it is very difficult to say. We have no empirical evidence to guide us. The children in this group appear to have little interest for politicians, bureaucrats or researchers. They do not, officially, exist. We have no word for them. There is no pressure group acting on their behalf and no government or local authority quango to plead their cause; but there is anxiety about the children, not least among parents.

This was reflected as early as 1963 in a statement to the House of Commons by the Minister, and was reflected in DES Circular 7/65, which printed the following in italics, presumably for emphasis: 'It will be helpful if the parents of non-immigrant children can see that practical measures have been taken to deal with the problems in the schools, and that the progress of their own children is not being restricted by the undue preoccupation of the teaching staff with the linguistic and other difficulties of immigrant children.' In 1981 there were indications that this had fallen on deaf ears. In that year the Schools Council published a survey, *Multiethnic Education: The Way Forward*, based on evidence from 70 LEAs. In a section headed 'White Children in Multiracial Schools' we find the following observations: 'Several authorities reported concern about the situation of white children in schools with high proportions of ethnic minorities.' One LEA said ' . . . In schools of very high proportions of ethnic minorities the situation of white children (usually of economically and socially depressed families) is greatly ignored and deserves further detailed research.' Fifty-four per cent of head teachers in schools with more than 30 per cent or more from ethnic minority groups drew attention to 'the special needs' of their white pupils, many stressing that the needs of this group tended to be ignored: 'We are not acting in a positive way on this need of which we have long been aware.' Seventy-eight per cent of schools said that in-service courses on multi-ethnic education should cover the needs of white children in these schools and 60 per cent considered the present in-service courses do not do so: 'This is a neglected aspect.'

Predictably, the attitude of those responsible for the Swann Report is dismissive of this issue. Very scant attention is paid to white English minorities in Swann, although its terms of reference do not preclude concern. Indeed, the authors specifically state: 'We have already made clear that we interpreted our task in far broader terms [than Asian and West Indian] and did not limit our work to looking at any one particular ethnic group but attempted to consider the needs of ethnic minority groups within the broader question of the education of *all* children for life in a pluralist society.' Attention is, indeed, cast wide, and there are sizeable sections in the Report on Chinese, Cypriot, Italian, Ukranian, Vietnamese and travellers' (gipsy) children, but none on those British children who constitute the ethnic minority in an increasing number of inner-city schools. Concern about the fortunes of these children is dismissed in Swann as being due to unenlightened attitudes to do with the despised notion of 'assimilation'. Swann shows no awareness that the concern many parents and others have expressed could possibly be genuine.

However, having said this, my own hunch (and it is no more than that) after sustained experience of white minority children is that we need have no fears about their identity, self-image or national loyalties. Like all children, they are very resilient and very adaptable. Their sense of identity depends not simply on school but on family, and on exposure to an out-of-school culture that is still recognisably British.

What, however, of specifically educational consequences for the children? Again, it is difficult to be certain in any scientific sense in the absence of valid and reliable research. However, given that there is now a consensus that the language and competence in using it are central to the whole learning and teaching process, it is reasonable to raise the question. If a school contains a majority of children who speak, read and write English as a second, foreign, language (and this would apply to West Indian as well as Asian children, if we are to believe the linguists who argue that Creole and Patois are distinctive languages in their own right), then is this likely to lead to a decline in academic standards? Are the children, not least the indigenous white ones whose parents might reasonably expect that attendance at an English school guarantees the primacy of the English language, likely to suffer educationally?

I suspect that the majority of teachers and almost all parents would give an emphatic affirmative response to this question. Such a response accords with common sense, but one has to be cautious. Education is a very complex process, and common sense is not always a good guide. It is *sometimes* the case that common sense is no more than a reflection of common ignorance. We have to bear in mind here the very different academic performances of West Indian and Asian pupils in British schools. If a significant proportion of the pupils in a particular school are West Indian, then it is not unlikely that the general academic tone and the average examination results will, at least at this stage, decline. There is consistent, unquestioned evidence that, at every age level, West Indian children do considerably less well, on average, than other white or Asian pupils. The reasons for this are not understood, but it is a fact—although not, we hope, an unchangeable one. Language difficulties have frequently been invoked as a significant factor, but Asian children are quite different. On the whole, they do about as well as white children, at least in public examinations at sixteen and eighteen.

However, this may simply reflect the performance of bright Asian children, i.e. the ones who do public examinations. Clever pupils have a habit of doing well, whatever the handicaps they face. Moreover, we have no means of relating these academic results to the kinds of schools, in terms of ethnic proportions, that the Asian children concerned have attended. It could be that encouraging Asian outcomes are influenced by the presence, in the majority of schools who submit pupils for public examinations, of a majority (on average) of indigenous, white children, with all that that implies for competence in the medium of instruction. Even if that were not so, it would not follow that good academic results at sixteen and eighteen were incompatible with relatively poor results in primary and middle schools. In short, the detailed comparative studies relating performance in school to different ethnic proportions amongst the pupils are not available with regard to Asian children.

A faint light—but no more—was cast on this question by research produced by the National Council for Educational Standards (NCES). After examining public examination results in a large number of LEAs in 1981 and 1982 the authors concluded:

> Correlations and regression analyses also suggest that examination results per pupil are *lower* in LEAs with:
> (a) Higher expenditure per pupil
> (b) Higher proportions of pupils who are non-white or born abroad.
> (c) Higher proportions of inexperienced teachers.

Again, we have to be cautious. Each of these factors is inter-correlated, so the *independent* effect of the ethnicity or foreign origin is difficult to assess. Moreover category (b) groups together Asian and West Indian children, and, as I have said, these perform very differently.

Given, then, that really detailed and convincing research evidence in this area is difficult to come by (and Swann failed even to consider the issue), we have to use our own professional judgement as a guide. On that basis, I became convinced that the general academic level was, indeed, declining as the proportion of

Asian pupils in the school grew and language problems became increasingly apparent. This intuition received some (perhaps, to be candid, dubious) support from a report issued by the Bradford Asian Youth Movement, which claimed that Asian pupils were 'underperforming' in public examinations, although the source of this report made no attempt to relate its finding to two obvious causative factors: language difficulties and the Asian parents' habit of absenting children from school in term time. As usual with radical groups of this kind, the whole issue is 'explained' as the outcome of 'racism'.

I began to feel concerned for the white children, not because I was unconcerned about the Asian ones but because they and their parents had no voice in the educational debate. They were, and remain, the forgotten minority, but even to suggest this anxiety is very difficult in a society where the whole multi-ethnic debate is dominated by aggressive and vociferous political groups and various kinds of professional and electoral vested interests. This is particularly so when one is working for an LEA which regards itself as being in the vanguard of the anti-racist movement, but I took the risk of voicing my concerns.

The result was the creation of a virulent campaign of abuse and harrassment, and shock–horror response from the LEA—which rather confirmed my suspicion that on this question free speech was in short supply. By misrepresenting my concern for the white ethnic minority as an attack on the Asian majority my adversaries on the streets and in the LEA offices and council chamber were able to make common cause. I became a target. The anti-racist agitators sought crudely to intimidate, physically and psychologically. The LEA officers and 'advisers' used the device of a draconian school inspection (at the height of the NUT's campaign of disruption) to convert questions about my beliefs into those about my competence which, in over 20 years' service, had never been in doubt.

Conclusions

These specific experiences permit me, perhaps, to draw certain conclusions. Assuming that children from the ethnic minorities need to develop a bi-cultural identity in order to be true to their ancestral origins on the one hand, and to deal successfully with their British experience on the other, then the policy of ethnic concession-making being pursued by LEAs such as Bradford seems unwise and not in the interests of either the children concerned or the process of harmonious integration that the great majority of people appear to think desirable. Provided that the schools do all they can to respect parents' religious sensibilities, then the community culture (often misleadingly called the 'mother culture') can be, and is being, very effectively maintained and transmitted in the home and neighbourhood. Attempts to impose Islamic or West Indian cultural values in the schools run the risk of creating resentment and confusion among both teachers and parents of white, British children. Perhaps as serious is the danger of creating a ghetto mentality, particularly among British Moslem girls, who may be the single most vulnerable group of children now in Britain's schools. The explicit rejection of the principle of 'bridge-building', with each school negotiating with parents so as to work out a *modus vivendi* based on experience, time and patience, and the substitution for this principle of that of cultural appeasement imposed via bureaucratic process is surely questionable. Far from assisting integration, this policy seems more likely to create a separation mentality, with different ethnic groups competing for special status and ever-growing council largesse. One wonders how long it will be before we start to hear demands from Jewish and East European as well as Chinese, Vietnamese and Italian parents who have children in British schools to have *their* ancestral cultures selfconsciously imposed in the schools at public expense. How long, also, must we wait for acknowledgement of the situation of the white minority pupils and *their* parents' anxieties?

Moreover, I believe that the attempt at a Moslem takeover of five local authority schools indicates that the voluntary-school principle should be renegotiated. Times have changed. The context in which the original voluntary-school principle was established has undergone unprecedented and considerable alterations. The presuppositions behind voluntary-aided schools no longer exist. If the state is to subsidise Islam as it subsidises Judaism and Christianity, then it needs to be assured that its own rights in the schools concerned can be maintained. The present legal and administrative framework is manifestly inadequate for this purpose. Public opinion via Parliament should determine how the voluntary-school principle should be applied in Britain's unprecedented multi-ethnic society. It should not be assumed that this is a settled question.

Further Reflections on The Situation in Bradford, following the Tragic Murder of an Asian Pupil in Burnage

'Burnage High School presents a paradox. Its governors and senior management are committed to anti-racist policies in perhaps a more wholehearted way than any other Manchester School. Yet at the same time the school has been the scene of greater racial conflict and polarisation of its students along racial lines than any other school we have heard of.'

These words are taken from the report of a committee of enquiry headed by Ian McDonald, Q.C. Why, one wonders, did the committee find the co-existence of anti-racist policies with racial conflict and polarisation paradoxical? No-one who has studied the origin, provernance, tactics and ideology of the anti-racist movement in this country would be surprised at the situation at Burnage High School. Anti-racist ideology is, by its very nature, likely to create resentment and conflict. As I tried to show in chapter   anti-racism is sustained only through sociological and historical distortion, ideological opportunism and self-interest. It is morally bogus and inherently damaging to human relationships. An anecdote will bring out its predictable consequences. A colleague who worked in a management position for Bradford Council had been required to attend one of that Council's Racism Awareness Training (R.A.T.) Courses. These courses seek to transmit the beliefs, attitudes and values of anti-racism. The people who run them are paid, professional anti-racists. In Bradford a group of seven officials known as "Race Trainers" were specifically responsible for R.A.T., but there were many more involved in anti-racist policy-making. Their basic technique is a form of brain washing. I bumped into my colleague shortly after she had undergone this process. It is important to bear in mind that my colleague was an extremely reasonable person, who had worked and lived amongst people from the ethnic minorities for many years. She had great goodwill, a quiet, unaggressive temperament and a fund of common sense. I asked how she had got on. Her reply was delivered with a wholly untypical vehemence: "I wasn't a racist before I went, but I'm a bloody racist now". Her dramatic transformation was not surprising. She and her fellows on the course had been systematically made to feel guilty for being white and ashamed of their own history and culture; they had also been instructed to change their ways. A more effective way of creating the sort of conflict and polarisation discovered at Burnage High could scarcely be imagined.

However, I found myself confronted by a local education authority that was totally committed to the doctrines and techniques of anti-racism. This commitment was expressed in a series of mandatory policy documents distributed to the schools. Perhaps the best way of conveying the essence of this policy is to present and discuss the documents.

Anti-Racist/Multicultural Education in Bradford.

The first of these documents had appeared in 1977, three years before my arrival. My first taste of the L.E.A.'s policy came in a Local Administrative Memorandum (L.A.M.) No. 2/82 issued in November 1982, "Education for a Multicultural Society: Provision for Pupils of Ethnic Minority Communities". Much of this was unexceptionable, and merely repeated what had been common practice for many years. Although there is reference to the rights and duties of ethnic minority parents and headteachers, the document contained no reference whatsoever to the duties of parents; it was essentially a series of concessions to the Moslem leadership regarding the education of Moslem girls – though there is reference to parents' rights regarding morning worship and religious education, rights which all schools have known about and implemented for forty years or so. Schools were instructed that if Moslem parents objected to the school's arrangements regarding swimming and P.E. for girls then they had the "right" to withdraw them. In fact no such "right" exists in English Law; and Moslem girls had, in fact, been participating in swimming and P.E. for over twenty years before this document appeared, and no-one seemed upset or offended. Heads were also told that Moslem parents, ". . . may have strong reservations about the kind of relationships between boys and girls especially at the age of 10 and over, that are customary in our schools". How this implication of something vaguely improper connected in any way with the sort of completely relaxed, unselfconscious relationships between the sexes we observed every day was not immediately obvious. Nor was there any attempt to explain how, in a mixed state school committed to the principles of sexual equality, we could begin to reconcile Western notions with the sort of purdah mentality which was here being supported. The absurdity of this was underlined by the order to all heads that if the parents wanted their daughters to go swimming in pyjamas they must be allowed to do so. Rarely can the refusal to face facts have been so clearly illustrated – age old Islamic fundamentalism and the Western notion of the freedom of the individual simply do not, and cannot, go together. Sadly, this document contravened the common sense principle of bridge-building between parent and teacher which the school had been successfully pursuing for many years. We had been quietly, and without conflict, integrating all our children, including girls, into the school's values and principles. How this desirable process was to be enhanced by a mandatory edict which owed far more to the growing power of Islam than to properly thought out educational aims was not apparent to us. I sent a brief note of protest to the responsible official, but this was, predictably, ignored.

But the most ominous part of the document was its reference to "racism". We in the schools were informed that, *inter alia*, the aims of education in Bradford were, "to counter racism and racist attitudes, and the inequalities and discrimination which result from them." Whether "racism" was a problem in Bradford schools was, at best, an open question. It certainly was not in my school, and I never met a head or teacher from other schools who considered it so. The reference to "inequalities" was even more puzzling in a city in which significantly more money was being devoted to the education of ethnic minority than to ethnic majority children – at that time Bradford employed no fewer than 200 *additional* teachers to teach English to minority children. But from this time the L.E.A. was clearly committed to the notion that Britain is a society rotted with endemic, institutional racism, whose people are consciously or unconsciously hostile to Asians and blacks. And the schools must become centres of that anti-racist ideology which was the only means of ensuring the necessary transformations.

This process was not confined to the children. Bradford L.E.A. felt that the creation of the correct, officially sponsored anti-racist attitudes in pupils needed to be complemented by the suitable treatment of their teachers.

The headteachers had been catered for by the compulsory R.A.T. courses mentioned above. The classroom teachers were now invited to a "Racism Awareness Workshop" at a local in-service training centre. All schools were informed that this was "to further the Authority's Equal Opportunity Policy (Race Relations)". The "workshop" aimed not only "to study racism firstly in personal attitudes and beliefs" but also to study it "as perpetuated in the structures of our educational institutions". The picture these aims created, of schools disfigured by personal hostility to black and Asian children, and of an officially sponsored colour bar, bore no relation whatsoever to what was actually happening in Bradford's multiethnic schools. But the ideological fantasies, liberal self-flagellation and professional self-interest which sustain committed anti-racism effectively prevent pre-supposition from running the risk of exposure to the truth.

Those who faithfully attended this workshop might perhaps have been sustained by its creators' commitment to the latest techniques of "work in small groups, through experimental methods". The thinking teacher, though, might be less than impressed by the tortuous, conspiratorial language the course announcement employed. Headteachers are enjoined to check that only a teacher charged with the proper anti-racist zeal is allowed to go on the course: "it may be important for you to send a colleague whom you will be able to support to initiate and develop change towards appropriate education for a multi-cultural society in your school". Thus do certain L.E.A.'s get their way. Cadres of anti-racists in the classroom and moles in the staff room may sound a far-fetched proposition – more to do, surely, with doings behind the iron curtain than the implementing of official thinking in schools here. But that is precisely how things can work in our state education service. Remember, the people who put on these courses are the self same "advisers" who play a crucial role in the development of teachers' careers, and in many areas it is the "advisers" who have taken a *leading* role in creating and furthering anti-racist education.

In order to ensure that the L.E.A.'s edict "Education for a Multi-cultural Society" was being faithfully implemented, an education official sent out a questionnaire to all relevant schools. This ran to sixteen pages. I will not bore the reader by giving chapter and verse. A few appropriate quotations will suffice to show the gulf between official thinking and my own position.

Q. Have you made any changes in those arrangements since Jan. 1983 (i.e. information to parents) such as special meetings for ethnic minority parents?

A. No. I should find it as invidious to arrange meetings especially for "ethnic minority parents" as to arrange meetings only for white parents. I deal with parents as individuals, and make them welcome whenever they come to school. If they cannot cope with English I enlist the help of our Asian teacher, Mr —, even to the extent of calling him out of lessons.

Q. Give details (regarding Parental Rights) of any additional steps you have taken since January 1st or intend to take in the coming months.

A. I simply intend to continue the good practice we have established over the past quarter of a century in handling Asian parents.

Q. Give details of your arrangements to cover religious festivals prior to January 1983 and how those affected attendances.

A. Parents (i.e. Moslem parents) simply keep their children off – some for two days, some for three. There seems to be no real awareness that Eid is for one day only – and the L.E.A. do nothing to enforce school attendance regulations in this respect. (Parents are legally allowed to keep children off school for one day for religious festivals.)

Q. Special provision for Muslim prayers. Give details of any requests you have had from parents for facilities to be made available for Muslim prayers to be said during the lunchtime period either before January 1st or since.

A. None – ever – from parents. I had a small group of boys asking for lunchtime prayers about 18 months ago. After taking advice from our Mr — (a Muslim) I provided a classroom at lunchtime. As Mr — had predicted, the practice lasted about three or four days, then simply died out. None from anyone since January 1st.

There was much more of this kind of stuff. Underlying the whole exercise was the obvious supposition that schools like mine were hotbeds of racial animosity, and staffed by ignorant and insensitive teachers; and, further, that this deplorable (though entirely fictional) state of affairs could be put right by some sort of bureaucratic exercise. The reader, I hope, will forgive me for the somewhat testy conclusion. I appended to this questionnaire: "the approach of the Council to relationships in schools like this is, in my view, profoundly misguided. The assumption that such schools are the focus of prejudice and insensitivity is as insulting as it is fallacious – the staff here display astonishing tolerance and goodwill in far from favourable circumstances. They should be given due credit for this, not constantly badgered by bureaucratic interference – edicts, "experts" and racial head counts do not produce better human relationships; they are far more likely to create resentment, anger, and, ultimately, a backlash effect."

Needless to say this *"cri de coeur"* got me precisely nowhere.

Mention of racial headcounts brings me to the next piece of anti-racist bumph the school had to cope with. This informed us that the council had decided all its employees had to be counted according to skin colour. There were four categories: Afro-Caribbean, e.g. African, West Indian; Asian, e.g. Pakistan, Bangladeshi; U.K./European, e.g. British, Irish, Polish; Others, e.g. Australian, Chinese, American. Though this appears to be based on Country of origin, it was, in reality, exclusively to do with skin colour – an appended note made it clear that place of birth was irrelevant. People with black and brown skins born in the U.K. were to be recorded as Afro-Caribbean or Asian. This was puzzling, since there might well be significant differences, from the point of view of the job market, between those born here and immigrants. There is good evidence to show a firm connection between time spent in this country and socio-economic progress. Moreover, it was interesting to note that the Council had no interest in European minority groups – of which there are significant numbers in Bradford: Poles were lumped with British and Irish; Hungarians, Ukrainians and Yugoslavians were ignored altogether. It was also interesting to note that people of Chinese background were lumped with white people from Australia or America. This presumably implied that the council believed black or brown skin evoke prejudice, while yellow skin do not. This might well be true, but to raise the question why would be firmly ruled out of order; such a question would have challenged some of the anti-racist orthodoxies to which the Council was committed.

None of those complexities counted. The council simply wanted to know how black, brown and other people were doing in the labour market, created by the Council's activities. The basis for this was the Council's "Equal Opportunity policy". The underlying assumption was that ethnic disparities would prove "racism", i.e. if a proportionate number of black or brown people were not employed by the Council this would prove the Council was operating some sort of colour bar. This equating of the concepts of opportunity and outcome is the great, mindless egalitarian fallacy on which the anti-racist mentality rests. If X proportion of the population is black then X proportion of doctors, teachers, town planners and candle-stick makers must be black. Such a belief totally ignores how the labour market actually works in a free society. It ignores the fact that, presented with the same *opportunities*, individuals, and possibly the groups to which they belong, make systematically different *choices*. (For instance, we know that Asian parents with bright children prefer them not to go into teaching, but into other professions.) There is also here an assumption that all groups have precisely the same desire to work for the Council; and all are equally qualified to do so. Not surprisingly, fallacious thinking produces erroneous policy. If the Council really wanted to investigate the question: Is colour prejudice a factor in our employment procedures? then its enquiries should have focussed, not on crude outcomes, but on the question of how far *equally qualified* people from the different population groups were faring in the Council's selection procedures. Failing a complex enquiry of this sort, the whole exercise was meaningless. It was difficult to avoid the conclusion that the ill-conceived exercise was a concession to the anti-racist activists now employed by the Council. They were determined to impose on the Council the entirely false notion that if the Council employed proportionately fewer blacks or Asians than existed in the general population, this "proved" the Council to be "racist". It would also, of course, "prove" that the Council needed to employ more anti-racist activists. However, my attempts to voice these issues were ignored.

The next missive in the war of attrition against "racism" was L.A.M. 6/83, "Racialist Behaviour in Schools". This informed all headteachers that racism had to become a high profile, significant issue in the classroom ". . .the issue of racialist behaviour should become a regular feature of staff and school meetings"; racialist literature, badges or insignia (which no-one in my school had ever seen) had to be confiscated and "publicly emphasised"; and reports had to be made, one copy of which was to be sent to the offices. No doubt the L.E.A. was motivated in part by a desire to shield itself against any future accusation of failing to condemn racial bullying. But to impose mandatory documents of this kind seemed to us very unwise. Will bad behaviour tend to decrease if it is publicly emphasised, if the school makes a constant fuss, and constantly seeks to focus the attention of the whole school community upon it? I have never met any experienced teacher who does not, in fact, believe the very opposite. The general secretary of the National Association of Head Teachers described this document as an "insult" to his members. My fear was that any school which faithfully attempted to implement its instructions would very likely create the very thing to which we all took the gravest exception. By pointing up, and virtually glamourising, racial bullying in the eyes of attention-seeking, bolshy adolesants – rather than dealing with actual incidents on the basis of discretion and professional judgment – the school could well *create* racial animosity.

In March, 1984 we received another questionnaire checking up on our adherence to L.A.M. – 2/82 "Education for a Multi-Cultural Society". Any difficulties we might have had with this document could be answered by contacting a Sikh gentleman now employed by the Council, and previously a leading member of the militant Asian Youth Movement. Essentially we were asked how far we were treating Asian children and their parents as a special case – namely, as people who were having their rights, but never their responsibilities, constantly pointed out to them. Needless to say, the high-minded talk about the importance of respecting religious festivals made reference only to Eid-ul-Fiter, Gurpurb and Diwali, i.e. Moslem, Hindu and Sikh festivals. There was no reference to Christian or Jewish festivals. Needless to say, too, when I used this document to repeat my concern that many Moslem parents were violating school attendance regulations by taking not the statutory one, but two or even three days holiday to cover religious festivals – my protest was ignored. Parental duties were not part of the exercise.

In April 1985 "Towards Education for All", a discussion document was issued to the schools. The title and the contents made it clear that this was the L.E.A.'s response to the Swann Committee's report on the education of ethnic minority children. Essentially it re-gurgitates some of the Swann allegations about multi-ethnic Britain (See Chapter 6), draws on the Inner London Education Authority brochure "Race, Sex and Class", No. 2 and repeats aspects of Berkshire County Council's "Education for Racial Equality: Policy Paper 1". This latter document's allegations are endorsed vigorously, "Britain is a racist society . . . Further, racism in the wider society is reflected in and reinforced by racism in the education system." The authors of this document show no awareness of the cogent criticisms to which their sources had already been subjected, nor were they to know that in 1988 Berkshire County Council was to begin dismantling its anti-racist policy, a process likely to be accelerated in the light of the Burnage High School report.

Schools are enjoined to dismiss previous ways of looking at multi-ethnic matters. The "Assimilation Perspective" of the 60's, and the "Cultural Diversity Perspective" of the 70's are dismissed as out-dasted and irrelevant. We are now, the authors assert, committed to "The Equality Perspective". This appears to consist of four elements or beliefs: Black (i.e. all non-white people) in our society are victims of rampant individual and institutional prejudice and discrimination (". . . the central pervasive influence of racism"); all black people are suffering from social and economic disadvantage and exploitation; schools must perceive ethnic diversity as an in-evitable and obvious blessing; and the whole of the school's curriculum and ethos must be permeated with "anti-racist" strategies. There is the predictable commitment to cultural rela-tivism; competition and objective assessment are condemned; and there is talk of the importance of considering colonialism, the Third World, resistance struggles and the historical inevitability of im-migration. The notion that there is a distinctive British cultural heritage is, by implication and omission, contemptuously dismissed – the term "standard English" is placed in inverted commas so as to stress its questionable status.

The transformation of this consultative document into a full-blown mandatory edict appeared in July 1987, after I had left Bradford. The edict is expensively produced with glossy multi-coloured cover and reproduces the original document almost word for word, despite the fact that the first issue was presented as a "document for discussion" – the "discussions" clearly having functioned as a rubber-stamping exercise: However, there are two interesting additions. First, we are told about the procedures which have created this mandatory document, and secondly, the advisers have added comments about how their bit of the curriculum can function as a vehicle for anti-racism.

The mechanics of production are interesting since they throw light on how the most radical changes can occur in the state education service. We are told that "the original draft was the result of the work of a group of headteachers, officers and advisers produced in 1982 which was added to by the Advisers. Further consultation and discussion involving all headteachers, Teacher Associations, Advisers with special responsibilities took place in 1984, before going to the Schools (Education) Sub-Committee, the Race Relations Advisory Group and the Multicultural Education Support Group during 1985 and 1986." It would be difficult to parody this picture of political and bureaucratic interference in the life of the school. The one vital partner in the educational enterprise which was, of course, totally ignored in this massive exercise was the parent of the child who is the target of this whole top-heavy edict. Despite the fact that the L.E.A. was now committed to imposing monumental changes on the schools of Bradford, the Council never attempted to discover the state of public opinion in general, or parents' views in particular. And yet the mandatory implementing of the doctrines enshrined in this policy would effectively mean the abolition of that British cultural tradition to which at least 80% of Bradford citizens still belonged and, presumably, hoped would be transmitted to their children. There could scarcely be a more effective argument for allowing parents to opt out of L.E.A. control and run schools which respect their wishes and aspirations. (It is worth noting that the central criticism of the McDonald report on Burnage High School was that the School's multicultural/anti-racist policy was imposed from the top, and effectively excluded white parents.)

The second point of interest is the curriculum section. Here each "adviser" seeks to demonstrate his or her commitment to the document's anti-racist stance, and to show how each subject must now be primarily concerned with transmitting anti-racist ideology to the pupils. We are assured that the division of this section into traditional, established subjects is merely for the sake of convenience and not of "policy". "Cross-curricular approaches" are, we are enjoined, to be "developed wherever possible". We are also informed that each adviser's statement is only "a starting point for fully developed guidelines which will be drawn up by working parties". The anti-racist bandwaggon it seems will never stop; schools are forever to have these mandatory documents imposed upon them. The self-generating and self-serving imperatives of educational bureaucracy, together with the demands of political necessity, are vital, motivating features of the system. Remember, the first steps towards a multi ethnic/anti-racism curriculum began in 1977 and now in 1988, eleven years later, the movement is still in full swing.

The necessity to "permeate all curriculum areas" with an anti-racist/multicultural perspective is asserted, and we are informed that "similar guidelines" will be drawn up to cover every age range from pre-school and nursery to further education. The anti-racist doctrine is, then, to be total and mandatory: "The first response towards the implementation of those guidelines within the context of each school/institution and the community that it tries to serve will be required by September 1988." And all involved in the education service are informed, perhaps somewhat ominously, that "the Multicultural Education Support Group and the Education Committee will consider further action in the light of developments". What, one wonders, happens to those schools which remain unconvinced of the ideology of anti-racism? What happens to those heads and teachers who do not feel able to abdicate their professional consciences and be dictated to by an L.E.A. which claims such total powers?

The statements by the advisers cover the whole of the curriculum – thirteen subjects in all. Though they appear to vary in their commitment to multicultural/anti-racist education – some are decidedly tentative, others decidedly zealous – all accept the necessity to display the appropriate professional credentials. None avoids the necessity to regard the curriculum as a vehicle for promoting multiculturalism, though not all mention anti-racism. Often the required injunction is tagged onto unexceptionable curriculum statements as if to pass muster. Art and Design, Craft Design and Technology, and Environmental Education are of this nature. But other advisers have clearly swallowed the official doctrines whole. Thus the English adviser uses all four of her discussion points regarding the teaching of English to promote the idea that English functions, not as a distinct and credible subject in its own right, but as a medium for establishing the required attitudes towards multicultural and anti-racist orthodoxies. "Are the staff knowledgable about the range of languages their pupils speak . . .?" "Does the school acknowledge and support pupils' bilingualism . . .?" "Do the resources for English in classroom, departmental and school libraries present the multicultural nature of our society and nurture positive attitudes towards difference?" "How can teachers work to deepen their pupils' understanding of the issue raised by living in a multicultural and multiracial society? Is there a policy giving advice and help to teachers on how to handle expressions of racism or stereotyped representations which might arise?"

Home Economics is somewhat tentative, taking refuge in a vague, barely articulated liberalism and a more or less mindless support for cultural relativism. "Are all patterns of household life valued equally?" (*All* patterns?) "Are learners encouraged to share and discuss experiences within a non-evaluative non-threatening environment?" (How do you establish that some meals are better prepared and served than others within this sort of moral vacuum? Has this "expert" ever tasted British Rail tea or coffee?) There is a long-winded, tortuous statement about physical education which amounts to saying schools must now seek to accommodate Islamic views about the physical body, human relationship and nudity – though, to be fair, there is also some attempt to assert the rights of Western notions to be respected. Modern language advice includes the totally vacuous statement "Do we respect the right of students to speak a language different from our own?" (How could schools *prevent* this in social situations, and how could they fail to insist upon English as the medium of instruction?) Music, inter alia, is to function as a means of "challenging racist attitudes", mathematics must henceforth use examples and illustrations which "reflect the multicultural nature of our society" and employ "strategies . . . to build on and develop the strengths of cultural and linguistic diversity," whilst the science adviser raises the question "Can scientific facts, principles and laws be free of cultural bias?" The purpose of this rhetorical question is to evoke a negative response, whilst the thinking teacher is bound to point towards the inevitability of a positive response. (How can a fact or law be anything but free from bias of all kinds?)

But the most unashamed and total bowing of the knee to the new, obligatory orthodoxies can be seen in the statements made about

Humanities and R.E. – both written by the same person (history and geography as distinct subjects do not appear). The R.E. statement reduces religion to a sort of tour round supermarket shelves with the pupil taking a bit of this and a bit of that to fill his theological basket. It is asserted that Hinduism, Islam, and Sikhism, are to have equality of status with Judaism and Christianity. We are told that "Bradford, rich in diversity of faiths and cultures, needs to assert that the major religions, Hinduism, Islam, Judaism, Sikhism, as well as Christianity, have an equal right to the maintenance of their distinctive identities and loyalties of culture, language, religion and custom; furthermore their rich diversity should be seen as contributing to the life of the whole community". This contribution, it is implied, is bound to be beneficial. This may be so, but it is a point of view difficult to sustain from the history of multi-faith societies. The presence of distinct religious communities within the same society has far more often led to conflict than to harmony. The notion that profoundly different world views can be readily reconciled and the result used to sustain a multicultural conensus is taken as read. One can only hope that such optimism is justified. That a child might well come to understand the essence of the religious life and beliefs through prior immersion in one consistent faith is implicitly rejected. Nor is there any awareness of the intellectual difficulties children may have in coping with the very complex concepts presented by the major world religions. The status of the subject is questioned by the insistence that much of the required work will be done in "Integrated Humanities", in "Personal Social Education" (whatever that is) and, in the early years, in "topic work". In short R.E. is to be perceived not as a grounding in religious realities but as a justification for, and celebration of, a distinctive kind of society i.e. a "multicultural society". "Is the curriculum designed towards developing an understanding and appreciation of the various faith communities that are part of Bradford today?"

But the most blatant illustration of how *ideological* presupposition can influence *educational* proposals is seen in the humanities section. The Humanities proposals, too, are interesting as an illustration of the sort of woolly, impenetrable language multiculturalists are so fond of. We are told, for instance, "The diversity amongst peoples should be portrayed with respect for integrity of the individual and the community. This will be supportive for children growing into citizenship in a contemporary society where there is a need for sensitivity towards a variety of cultural perspectives and an awareness of the need for developing an inter-cultural appreciation.

Children and young people need this perspective consciousness if they are to pursue their own interests wisely and without harming the legitimate interests of others".

This actually sounds sympathetic, even high-minded. But what precisely, or even approximately, does it mean? What, for instance, do the terms "supportive for", "sensitivity towards a variety of cultural perspectives", "developing an inter-cultural appreciation" and "perspective consciousness" actually *mean*? My own feeling is that the person who writes like this is saying to the teacher, "Please do all you can to persuade your pupils to suspend their critical faculties in considering other cultures". A more or less uncritical acceptance of any belief, value or practice should be encouraged – at least if it is embodied in some non-British culture. The essence of this adviser's aspirations for children in the classroom is contained in one key paragraph:

"In History care should be taken to avoid a Eurocentric bias that, in effect, may deny any pre-colonial history in countries that were formerly part of the British Empire, for instance, or describes white figures of importance but not black, that sees modern Western society as intrinsically superior to any earlier civilisation. In Geography, life in a country should be shown in both rural community and city to avoid stereotyping. The image of a 'poor' Third World needs balancing with a careful account of the factors involved in that poverty and the link with the economic advance of the 'developed' world. It is important not to avoid a discussion of controversy around issues of racism, prejudice and dis-crimination in Sociology or of multi-national monopolies in Economics. The background to immigration needs to be set in its global context of the movement of peoples, so that the black immigration to Britain is not seen as a special case, but part of normality."

No-one who is aware of the world view of the political left can be in any doubts about the origins of this sort of rhetoric. All the code words are there "Eurocentric", "British Empire", "stereotyping", "developed world", "Third World", "racism", "multi-national monopolies" "global context". The notion that the Western world is to be held responsible for the difficulties of the "Third World", and that the villain of the piece is the multi-national monopoly is here scarcely concealed. Nor is the idea that Britain's present multi-ethnic population is historically inevitable conveyed as a highly questionable assertion, but as a self-evident part of "normality". Perhaps the most ironic part of this statement lies in the fact that whilst the writer waxes lyrical about the importance of recognising ethnic differences, she effectively cancels all cultural variations amongst Britain's ethnic minorities by employing the anti-racist code word "black" to describe all our non-white communities.

This document, the most recent document in the eleven year long process of Bradford's conversion of the educational process into a vehicle for conveying the imperatives of multiculturalism and anti-racism, will surely rank as the last word on the subject. Or will it? We are, remember, promised more bumph of a similar nature.

EPILOGUE

Reflections on Britain's Multi-ethnic Society

Britain has seen significant changes in the character of its population over the past 30 years or so. The white, Christian and Anglo-Saxon stereotype is no longer valid as an image of British identity. Although the country has a long history of immigrant settlement, there are no precedents for the mass influxes from the Indian subcontinent and the Caribbean that occurred in the 1950s and 1960s. Britain is now a multi-ethnic society in a sense unique in its history. Although a mixture of peoples living in the country may be validly understood as a legacy of Empire, the size of Britain's ethnic minority populations and the developments in the social and political order they have created were by no means inevitable or prefigured.

A multi-ethnic society, with its admixture of languages, religions, ways of thought and creative energies, carries with it possibilities of cultural enrichment. It also holds potential for social and ideological conflict. Which of these possibilties comes to predominate in Britain will depend crucially upon how we, as a nation, manage the inevitable tensions and transformations involved. The most striking thing about our response so far has been the absence of informed public debate about the issues at stake. There is little public awareness of the nature of a multi-ethnic society. We have not even settled on an agreed vocabulary with which to create dialogue: words such as race, culture, nationality, prejudice, discrimination and ethnic are daily misused. The extent of ethnic variation throughout the world is little understood, and the concept of ethnic revival is buried within the covers of obscure textbooks read only by specialists. There is much ignorance about the notion of race, and the debate about the fortunes of Britain's ethnic minorities is marred by ill- informed allegations and countercharges. There is no convincing definition of the term 'a racist society' and no objective attempt to verify how far it applies to contemporary Britain. It is to illuminate these issues that I have written these reflections.

The absence of public debate has been paralleled by the growth of a race relations movement. This has impeccable, humanitarian origins based on well-meaning liberal impulses. Many worthy people have been associated with this development. Parliament has sought to articulate concern in the Race Relations Act 1976 and the creation of a statutory body, the CRE. However, the whole area of race relations has become tainted with ideological opportunism. What began as a concern for the ethnic underdog and his rightful place in an integrated, harmonious society has become a largely political movement. An illustration of this can be found in the history of the Institute for Race Relations. This began as an eminently worthy and politically impartial organisation based on the kind of concern for peoples of the former Empire which enlightened imperialists had always displayed. It is now a neo-Marxist propaganda outfit run by a committed ideologue. The race relations movement is now overshadowed by an 'anti-racist' lobby which has great influence and whose political provenance is clear to anyone who cares to consider the rhetoric and policies it produces. The distinction between the basically liberal race relations impulse and the hard-left 'anti-racist' thrust is now impossible to draw.

The politicising of race relations has had two unfortunate consequences: it has intensified the emotional climate surrounding the subject of race and it has propagated the questionable and negative notion that Britain is riddled with endemic racism. It has also distracted attention from the central issue: What kind of multi-ethnic society ought Britain to be? The options of separatism, assimilation and integration have never been the subject of public debate. Instead, the necessity for ridding the social and political order of alleged 'racism' has seen the creation of the intellectually dubious and entirely undemocratic notion of cultural pluralism or multiculturalism. This concept is not a product of society—of people living and working together, expressing their multifarious and legitimate interests—but rather of the state and its agencies under pressure from those with an axe to grind.

An unfortunate result of making the ethnic minorities the subject of special measures and a new, politically inspired cultural mosaic is the playing down of that determined self-help which has been the key to success of Britain's established minorities, such as the central Europeans and the Jews. Multiculturalism systematically undermines the role of cultural values in the progress of minority groups. It tends to create welfare dependency and to generate intercommunal rivalries; and there is no evidence that the 95 per cent of the public who do not belong to any ethnic minority group find officially sponsored multiculturalism acceptable. Moreover, this kind of multiculturalism tends to obscure that essential distinction between the public and private domains in matters of culture which is crucial to civil liberties. Worst of all, there is good evidence that unscrupulous political agitators are using the notions of anti-racism and multiculturalism to foster inner-city tensions.

Perhaps the most important area in which the anti-racists and multiculturalists are operating is the state education service. There the concept of what is variously called 'multi-racial/cultural/ethnic education' has been fashioned. This is much more than a simple curriculum development: the management, discipline and ethos of the school are all involved. It is no exaggeration to say that 'multi-ethnic education' carries with it profound implications for the whole character and future of Britain's schools. Despite this, there is no evidence of support from parents of children in school—least of all, perhaps, from ethnic-minority parents. Moreover, some of the advocates of 'multi-ethnic education' are claiming separate language rights for minorities, such as exist in the USA. If this demand is granted, the status of English as Britain's national language will be undermined, as will its role in supporting our social and political coherence.

My conclusion is that there is an urgent need for an informed public debate about the issues surrounding Britain's multi-ethnic character. Our future in this respect should not be determined by those unrepresentative groups who inhabit the race relations/anti-racist lobbies. Unless we base our ethnic policies on public opinion, they cannot succeed in our representative system.

I believe that we must commit ourselves to the principle of harmonious integration. We need a multi-ethnic society in which everyone's first political loyalty is to Britain, and in which the maintenance and transmission of ethnic cultures is the responsibility of the communities concerned. There should be minimal state intervention in race relations. The Race Relations Act 1976 should be replaced by much simpler and more logical legislation guaranteeing racial equality for the ethnic minorities. The continued existence of the CRE should be questioned. The notions of reverse discrimination, special needs and positive action should be firmly rejected. The role of cultural and group values should occupy a central place in the debate about the fortunes of minority groups.

The schools have a crucial role in determining Britain's multi-ethnic future. The notion of multi-ethnic education as a curriculum concept should be rejected. Minorities will best make their way in Britain's complex, meritocratic society by sending their children to schools in which the pursuit of excellence in all things is the central value. Moral education, rather than the intellectually dubious and politically tainted notion of anti-racism, will play an important part in producing a population free of racial prejudice. Schools in Britain's inner cities have a particularly important part to play in building an ethnically harmonious society.

Given this fundamental shift in our approach to its multi-ethnic character, we may all be enriched by Britain's cultural diversity. If we persist on our present misguided path, the consequences could be grave.

INDEX

aborigines 83
advisers 2, 63, 117, 118, 243, 244, 246, 255, 269, 280, 292–297
Africans 6, 33 ("The Africans")
Afro-Caribbean Teachers' Assc. 112
Akinpeya Greta 202
ALTARF 112
Anglo-Saxon 76, 84
anti-racism 2, 3, 22, 25, 33, 48, 60, 61, 76, 107, 116, 119, 124, 149, 241, 280, 283, 289, 300
  ideology 3, 108–121
  structure 3, 107–108
anti-racist strategies team (ILEA) 113, 122
apartheid 11, 28, 36, 66, 82
Aryans 130, 131
Asian children/pupils 1, 8, 9, 156, 157, 159, 234, 235, 278, 279
Asian school attendance 247–253
Asians 6, 8, 22, 60, 69, 140, 142, 148, 149, 205
assimilation 27–29, 40–41
attitudes 22, 125
Australia 29, 38, 41, 44, 83
Avon Council 122

Bakke case 59
Bangladesh(ies) 16, 26, 138, 205
Bantu Education Act 36
Barley Nigel 64
B.B.C. 120
Berkshire 122

Bernstein Basil 233, 238
bi-cultural 87
bigotry 48
Black (British-Caribbean) children/ pupils 1, 65, 98, 100, 102, 122, 156, 157, 171, 173, 199, 205, 228, 230, 232, 233, 234, 278
Black community 146
"Black Britain" 110
Black Power 10
Black Sections 9, 35, 69
Black Studies 31, 83, 101
Black underclass 146–150
Blacks 6, 8, 22, 54, 58, 59, 60, 98, 99, 100, 115, 131, 142, 146
Black Vernacular English 234, 237
Bouhdiba Abdelwahab 270
Bradford 1, 63, 114, 116, 122, 135, 143, 203, 212, *241–281*, 283, 288, 291
Bradford Telegraph & Argus 244, 268, 269
Bradford University Int. Centre for Inter-Cultural Studies 203
Brent Council 109, 114, 116, 122, 143
Britain 1, 2, 13, 25, 48, 123, 212
British 2, 7, 8, 9, 61, 64
British Nationality Act 1948 26
Broadwater Farm 26
Brotz Howard 38
Burchfield Robert 85
bureaucracy 30, 31
bureaucrats 2, 3
Burnage High School 283, 284

Censorship 2
Chamberlain H.S. 130
Chinese 6, 17, 27, 28, 35, 54, 59,
    145
Choice school of thought 15
Christian(ity) 19, 61
Church of England 18
civil liberties 39, 128
Civil Rights 35, 128, 129
class 14
cohesion national 88
colour 11
colonialism 58
Commission for Racial Equality
    (C.R.E.) 14, 21, 29, 31, 42,
    48, 57, 59, 61, 66, 73, 77, 78,
    90, 107, 108, 113, 114, 116,
    139, 152, 153, 155, 217, 273,
    302
Commonwealth 11
community culture 281
Community Relations Councils
    (C.R.C.'s) 14, 21, 29, 91,
    107, 116
comprehensive school 87, 117
Coard Bernard 166–169, 207
conflict 13
Conservatives 35, 41, 50, 79, 117,
    123
Constraint school of thought 15
Council for National Academic
    Awards 77
Council of Mosques
    (Bradford) 241
Cox Baroness 111
Craft Alma 77, 205
Creole 230, 232, 234, 237
cirteria for multi-ethnic
    curriculum 81
cross-racial friendships 87
culture 1, 2, 5, 16, 17, 43, 47, 54,
    60, 63, 66, 74, 88
cultural cringe 62, 64, 65
cultural genocide 83
cultural pluralism 89
cultural relativism 31, 81, 82, 165,
    233, 294

curriculum 2, 76, 292
Cypriots 16

Dale David 110, 141
Davidson Basil 33, 61
Department of Education and
    Science (D.E.S.) 250, 251
Derbyshire Council 122
determinism 164, 165
Deva Nirji 50
discrimination 11, 12, 21, 37
"District Trends" (Bradford) 243
Duncan Carlton 201, 202
Dworkin Road 57

East Europeans 8, 12, 65
educational achievement 155
"Education for All" (Swann
    Comm.) 76, 186–197, 203,
    208
"Education for a Multi-Cultural
    Society" 284
"Education and Leisure"
    (Bradford) 242, 243
Educational Support Grants
    (E.S.G.'s) 135
education system 49
egalitarianism 10, 58, 96, 165, 231,
    232, 234, 229
Empire British 7, 11, 32, 33, 49, 61,
    62, 118, 146
employment 153–155
Enlightenment The 264
English as a second language 193–
    194
enrichment thesis 2, 13
entryism 115
equality 57
Equal Opportunity
    Commission 272
ethnic conflict 11
ethnic group 31, 32
ethnic minorities 3, 6, 9, 11, 29, 54
ethnic variation 6
ethnic vote 9
ethnicity 5, 10, 11, 13
ethnicity and the law 132

ethnocentricity 84, 85
European Economic Community
(E.E.C.) 11, 58

"Faith in the City" 18
Fanon Franz 33, 108, 109
foreign aid 68
French Revolution 8
"From Doom to Hope" 19

General Certificate of Secondary
Education (G.C.S.E.) 89
genetics 21, 57
Germans 17
Ghana 34
ghettoes 48, 87
Glazer Nathan 10
Greater London Council
(G.L.C.) 112, 116, 127
Green Dr P.A. 172–176, 207
group differences 16
group entitlements 55, 65

Halal meat 267–270
Handsworth 26
Harringey 114, 122, 212
Harringey Black Parents' Pressure
Group 142
Harris Ernie 200
Hastie Tom 124
Hindus 9
"History in the Primary and
Secondary School"
(H.M.I.) 93
Holocaust 12, 30
Home Affairs Committee of the
House of Commons 142
Home Affairs Committee on Racial
Disadvantage 48
Honey John 229, 231, 233, 234, 237
housing 150–153
housing patterns 86
"How Racism Came to
Britain" 111
Huguenots 8
human capital thesis 53, 54, 66, 69,
70

Humanistic psychology 96

identity 2, 27
ideology 14, 58
Inner London Education Authority
(I.L.E.A.) 43, 56, 77, 94,
101, 141, 143, 291
immigrants 1, 6, 7, 8, 10, 63, 65,
86, 137, 140, 143, 288
immigration (influx) 7, 13, 42, 48,
89, 136, 137
Imperial Guilt 60, 62, 65
Imperial reparation 32
India(ns) 11, 69, 140
Indonesia 27
inner-city riots 228
inequality 59
integration 1, 2, 11, 27, 37–40,
47–50, 65, 236, 281
interventionism 37, 49
I.Q. 228
Institute for Race Relations
(I.R.R.) 15, 30, 73, 108, 300
Irish 39, 40, 65
Islam 13, 46, 47, 140, 196–197, 241,
242
Islam and the Voluntary Schools
principle 196–197
Island Question 6, 147

Jacobovits Lord 19
Japanese 17
Jeffcoate R. 80
Jews 1, 8, 11, 12, 19, 27, 40, 54, 59,
65, 75, 130, 131, 143
Jewish-Christian tradition 46
jingoism 61

Khan-Cheema Akram
Muhammed 269
Klein Gillian 79, 190
King Martin Luther 35

Labour Party 30, 37, 115
Labov William 233, 234, 237
Lane Sir David 159
languages 9, 13, 43, 44, 85, 86

language controverses 211
"Language Trap The" 233
Law Lords 53
Leach Rev. Kenneth 18, 19
Lebanon 41
Left (political) 14, 33, 34, 117, 228
legislation 54
Leicestershire County Council 122
Liberalism 34, 49, 62, 108, 228, 294
Liberal Alliance 30
Liberia 35
Linguistic Minorities Project 194
linguistic relativism 232–235
Liverpool Blacks 25
Local Education Authority
    (L.E.A.) 2, 3, 63, 74, 120
local government 30
loony left 115

Mabey Dr. C. 102
Manchester City Council 116, 122,
    134
marriage statistics 148
Marxism 14, 15, 30, 32, 49, 64, 79,
    114, 115, 116, 118, 121, 126,
    140
Mazrui Ali 33, 61
McDonald Report 283, 292
melting pot 65
Metropolitan Police 127
Middle Ages 8
Milner David 87, 96, 98, 99, 100,
    101
minorities 14, 15
Morrell Frances 199
Mortimer Dr. Peter 180–185, 207
Moslems 9, 12, 44, 47, 89, 241
Moslem girls education of 270–276,
    284
Moslem takeover (Bradford) 260–
    267
mother culture 281
mother tongue 194, 195, 212,
    213–216 (and learning),
    220–221 (EEC Directive),
    226–228 (West Indian issue),
    237, 278, 279

multi-culturalism 29–34, 42–47, 50
multicultural education 2, 3, 13,
    76, 77, 208, 234, 241–281 (A
    case study), 301
multiethnic education 73, 76, 77,
    78, 79, 83, 84–95 (objections
    to), 103, 119, 241, 301
"Multiethnic Education: The Way
    Forward" 277
multiethnic experts 84
multiethnic history 94
multiethnic society 1, 9, 22, 26, 34,
    39, 54, 236, 299–302
multilingual classroom and
    achievement 222–226
Mullard Professor Chris 109, 204
Murray & Dawson ("5,000
    Adolescents") 101, 158,
    176–178, 207

nation 75
nationality 10
National Assc. of Head Teachers
    (N.A.H.T.) 199, 290
National Assc. of Schoolmasters
    and U.W.T. 199
National Foundation for
    Educational Research
    (N.F.E.R.) 77, 98
National Front 49
National Socialist Party 130
National Union of Students
    (N.U.S.) 80
National Union of Teachers
    (N.U.T.) 120, 199, 273, 280
Nazi Germany 130
negritude 108
New Zealand 38, 41
noble savage 43
non-racial variables 59, 67
Norman Conquest 7
Northern Ireland 41
numbers of immigrants 9, 137
Nuremberg Laws 130

Office of Population Censuses and
    Surveys 138, 148

O'Keeffe Dr. D. J. 165
Open University 61

Pakistan(ies) 11, 13, 15, 63, 64, 89,
    138, 139, 140, 241, 271
Parekh Bhikhu 78, 207
parents 3, 89, 91, 92, 119, 173, 292
Parkins Geoffrey 123, 152
Parkinson's Law 30
Partington Geoffrey 36, 44, 83
Patois 235
Pax Britannica 61
Peach Ceri 15, 18, 147
permeation (of curriculum) 76
Piaget 231
Pidgin 235
Plowden Report 217
police 22
Police Review 116
"Policing London" 127
Policy Studies Institute (P.S.I.) 22,
    127
prejudice 12, 21, 22, 46, 48, 125,
    126, 128, 131
pressure groups 78, 120
proletariat 115
public opinion 3, 48, 54, 58
Punjabi 85
purdah 270, 271, 285
"Pygmalion in the Classroom" 167

Quebec 35, 38
Quota System 56, 69, 70

race 5, 74, 76, 164, 228
Race Advisers 116
"Race Community and
    Conflict" 152
Race Officers 116
race relations 3, 7, 29, 49, 54
    (bureaucrats)
Race Relations Act 1976 53, 57,
    66, 75, 133, 134, 136, 155, 301
"Race Sex and Class" (ILEA) 77
"Race Today" 108
Race Trainers 116, 243, 283
racial bureaucracy 243

racial headcounts 288
"Racialist Behaviour in Schools",
    LAM 6/83 (Bradford) 289
racism 2, 3, 20, 22, 69, 79, 122–140,
    127, 131, 188–189, 280, 285
Racism Awareness Training
    (R.A.T.) 169, 283, 286
radicals 41
Radice Giles 199
rainbow coalition 49
Rampton Committee 77, 122, 170,
    199, 205, 230, 231, 236
Rastafarianism 44
Reformation 264
religion 9, 10, 13
Renaissance 264
Renan 130
repatriation 50, 58
representation in labour
    market 69, 70
responsibility for ethnic
    outcomes 15
reverse discrimination 58, 65, 66, 69
"Review of Race Relations Act
    1976" (C.R.E.) 66
Rex John 77
Right (political) 14, 117, 228
rights 55, 59
ritual slaughter 44, 64, 65
Roach Colin 116
Rose & Deakins 123
Rosenthal & Jacobson 167, 168
Rousseau 43, 63
R.S.P.C.A. 44
Runnymede Trust 14, 29, 108, 139,
    150, 153
Rushdie Salman 60, 62
Russia 35
Rutter Professor Michael 157

Sachs Rabbi Jonathan 19
Sandall Roger 63
Sarup Madan 74, 112, 113
Savery Jonathan 22
Scarman Lord 22
Schools Council 76, 77, 82, 98, 119,
    204, 235, 236, 277

Schools Curriculum Dev. Council (S.C.D.C.) 77, 119, 204
school uniform 253–259
Scotch-Irish 17
Section 11 (1966 Local Govt. Act) 66, 118, 135, 136, 198
segregation 129, 132
self concept and multiethnic education 32, 95–103
selfulfilling prophecy 96
separatism 34–37
separate schools 195–197
separation of church and state 47
"Sexuality in Islam" 270
Shah Samir 148
Sheffield Council 122
Shipman Professor Marten 123, 124, 168
Sikhs 9, 53, 54
Sivanandan Ambalvaner 15, 110, 112
skinheads 125
slavery 21, 58
South Africa 12, 28, 41, 66, 130–132
Sowell Thomas 4, 15, 16, 17, 18, 19, 20, 34, 53, 54, 67, 69, 143
special needs 53, 54, 57, 63, 64, 65, 69, 70, 133
squatters 55–56
Sri Lanka 11, 41
Standard English 230, 232, 235, 291
State The 4, 68
State Education Service 32, 116–117
stereotyping 16, 48, 178–180
Stone Maureen 77, 91, 98, 99, 101, 119, 169, 176, 232
Streaming 96
Swann Committee and Report ("Education for All" Report into Education of Ethnic Minority Children, Lord Swann, H.M.S.O. 1985) 25, 26, 30, 42, 73, 75, 77, 82, 89, 90, 99, 109, 122, 141, 156, 163–209, 212, 234, 273, 277, 278, 290
Swann and public opinion 197–205
Swann conclusions 205–209
Swann recommendations 185–186
Swift Profesor D.F. 165

Tanzania 68
Tamils 35
teacher-training 119
"their culture" 93
Third World 32, 34, 64
Thompson E.P.
Tomlinson Professor Sally 78, 90, 91, 101, 102, 170, 173, 227, 235, 236
tossed salad 65
"Towards Education for All" (Bradford), 1985 290
Toxteth 26
tribalism 36

"unconscious racism" 189–193
United Nations (U.N.) 11, 58
United States 17, 18, 29, 35, 37, 55, 56, 69, 129, 211
U.S. Supreme Court 129, 211

Verma Gajendra 203
Verwoerd Dr H.R. 36
Vietnamese 6, 281
voluntary aided schools 261, 263, 264, 265, 266
voluntary schools principle and Islam 196, 197

Walkling P.H. 81, 85
"Wealth and Poverty" 19
Welfare State 41, 47, 55, 132
Welsh 217
Western influences 64
West Indians (British Caribbeans) 6, 8, 11, 12, 13, 15, 17, 54, 58, 91, 98, 138, 171, 208, 229, 230
Westminster 49
White minority pupils 276–280

Williams J. 80

Yorkshire Post 269

Zec P. 82, 84